Additional Praise For
America's Health Care Crisis Solved

"Rooney and Perrin have accurately predicted every major trend in health care over the last several decades. In *America's Health Care Crisis Solved* they do it again by attacking the health care problem with innovative solutions. It should be on the desk of every policymaker, and is a must-read for anyone interested in addressing the problems in America's health care system."

—*Ed Corrigan executive director, United States Senate Steering Committee*

"*America's Health Care Crisis Solved* is far and away the smartest solution yet offered to America's number one domestic policy problem, the runaway cost of health care. The book's genius is that it offers ideas so sensible and fair. It's mandatory reading for those who believe that every American should have the health care they need, when they need it, at a price they can afford. Where others whine about problems, Rooney and Perrin offer a real solution."

—*Dean Clancy, former White House OMB official, who oversaw nearly $1 trillion in annual government health care expenditures*

"It has been an open secret inside the Washington, D.C., beltway that Rooney and Perrin have been working hand and glove to change health care policy for the last 20 years. They succeeded where some very smart and powerful people have failed. Whether you are a GOP or Democratic or independent voter, this book will help you to understand, in detail, the coming health care debate."

—*Scott W. Reed, Republican strategist and former presidential campaign manager for Bob Dole*

"Pat Rooney and Dan Perrin have already significantly changed the course of health care in the United States through Health Savings Accounts that put consumers and their physicians back in charge of their health care. *America's Health Care Crisis Solved* is a must-read book, regardless of whether you are a Republican, Democrat, or Independent. This important book explains health care policy problems and reform in language that everyone can understand. It will provide insight into the coming health care debate leading up to the next Presidential election, and more importantly, in Congress after the election."

—*Roy Ramthun, former senior health policy adviser to President George W. Bush regarding health care issues, and senior adviser to the Secretary of the U.S. Treasury for health initiatives*

"Rooney and Perrin have written a first-rate, easily readable book on the current health care crisis and provide a rational solution that does not bust the Treasury (or increase current spending!)—but they have even topped their own policy prescriptions with a commonsense set of tips to survive the crisis during the time it will take for our timid politicians to screw up the courage to adopt their conclusions."

—*Dr. Donald J. Devine, former director of the Office of Personnel Management (the U.S. civil service), 1981–1985*

"Pat Rooney is the man who came up with the concept of Health Savings Accounts as a way to cut medical costs, give power to medical consumers, and provide health coverage to rich and poor alike without either bankrupting the nation, ruining the best health care available anywhere in the world, or forcing providers and patients alike to dance to the tune of bureaucrats with little empathy for either. This book analyzes the health care 'crisis' so much on the lips of politicians these days and provides a solution that reasonable people should ponder as they work their way through the overheated and often wrong-headed solutions advanced by leading politicians of both parties."

—*David A. Keene, chairman of the American Conservative Union*

"Imagination can conquer mountains and Pat Rooney is the master of imagination. The seemingly insurmountable problem of no sick American left behind finds a solution in Pat Rooney's new book *America's Health Care Crisis Solved,* co-authored by Dan Perrin. Pat Rooney's brilliant and legendary Medical Savings Accounts went outside the box to employ human nature in saving billions in the purchase of human health care costs. Now, he and Dan Perrin have done it again on a much broader scale."

—*Andy Jacobs, Jr. (D-IN), former chairman of U.S. House Ways and Means Health Sub-Committee*

"Another major effort to reform the U.S. health care system is in the political wind, and we can only hope that those who want to make educated decisions about the ways to change the system will read this book. Rooney and Perrin reccomend changes with an eye towards reinvigorating personal initiative instead of constantly watering the entitlement tree. They just may save the system for our grandchildren before the baby boomers spend it all on themselves."

—*J. Kevin A. McKechnie, staff director, HSA Council, part of the American Bankers Association*

America's Health Care
Crisis Solved

America's Health Care Crisis Solved

MONEY-SAVING SOLUTIONS, COVERAGE FOR EVERYONE

J. Patrick Rooney and Dan Perrin

WILEY

John Wiley & Sons, Inc.

For general information on our other products and services or for technical support, please contact our Customer Care Department within the United States at (800) 762–2974, outside the United States at (317) 572–3993, or fax (317) 572–4002.

Wiley also publishes its books in a variety of electronic formats. Some content that appears in print may not be available in electronic books. For more information about Wiley products, visit our web site at www.wiley.com.

Library of Congress Cataloging-in-Publication Data

Rooney, J. Patrick, 1927-
    America's health care crisis solved : money-saving solutions, coverage for everyone / J. Patrick Rooney & Dan Perrin.
        p.   cm.
    Includes bibliographical references and index.
    ISBN 978-0-470-27572-6 (cloth)
        1. Medical care, Cost of—United States.   2. Insurance, Health—United States.   3. Health care reform—United States.   I. Perrin, Dan, 1963-   II. Title.
        [DNLM: 1. Health Care Costs–United States.   2. Health Care Reform—economics—United States.   3. Insurance Coverage—United States.
    WA 540 AA1 R777a 2008]
    RA410.53.R63 2008
    338.4'33621—dc22
                                                                        2007047646

Printed in the United States of America
10 9 8 7 6 5 4 3 2 1

Contents

Preface

America is headed for a giant financial disaster in the cost of health care. The only solution that makes any sense is to bring the self-interest of the American consumers into the purchase of health care.

The United States is headed for another national debate about providing health coverage for everyone, how to pay for it, and what other reforms need to occur to make the system more just and more affordable.

For nearly two decades, we have worked to inject key market-based solutions into the American health care system, a system that is increasingly dominated by government-financed health care. J. Patrick Rooney built an individual insurance company from $25,000 in reserves to one that had revenues of more than $600 million when he turned it over to his daughters to manage. At Golden Rule, Pat pioneered the first medical savings accounts (now called health savings accounts [HSAs]) in the U.S. insurance marketplace. He is known as a man who gets the job done. In fact, HSAs are one of the few health care reforms that have actually become law in the past two decades, and Pat is the one unelected person most responsible for the law's passage.

Pat was chief executive of Golden Rule Insurance Company for 20 years, until his retirement in 1996. He built the company into the largest provider of individual health insurance in the nation.

But this tells you only a small part of the Pat Rooney story. For decades, he has been a crusader for minority and low-income Americans.

In 1976, Pat initiated a civil rights lawsuit against the Illinois Department of Insurance and the Educational Testing Service (creators of the SAT college entrance exams), accusing the two organizations of discriminating against minorities in the design and implementation of a new exam used by the state to license insurance agents. "I never found a single minority person who had passed their new exam," said Pat.

Eight years and more than $1 million later, Rooney and Golden Rule achieved a landmark settlement to safeguard minorities from discrimination in employment testing.

In 1991, Pat and Golden Rule started the first *privately* funded educational scholarship program in America to assist low-income children to attend a nongovernment school of the parents' choice. That program has since been replicated around the country, with over 60 similar programs following the Rooney model.

It was in 1992 that Pat first recommended and began lobbying for what are today called health savings accounts. The medical savings accounts, now HSAs, combine a tax-exempt savings program for small medical bills with major medical insurance for big medical bills. This approach to funding health insurance reduces the combined cost of coverage by about 30 percent and is today making a lot of headway in the health insurance marketplace: HSAs covered 438,000 Americans in 2004, 3.2 million in 2005, and, according to projections by the United States Treasury, will cover 14 million people.

More recently, Rooney has been crusading for the uninsured, who are charged by hospitals *three or four times* what many insurance plans are charged for the same care. "Simply immoral," Pat says succinctly of these enormous prices. A Catholic himself, Pat has attacked many Catholic hospitals for the "non-Christian" prices they charge low-income Americans. Pat reminds these hospitals that America's Catholic leadership advocates a "preferential option for the poor" and that overcharging the poor for basic health care is *not* a preferential option.

Dan Perrin is widely credited with influencing health care legislation in the U.S. Congress, including being instrumental the passage of both the pilot medical savings account legislation and the expanded health savings account legislation.

Most solutions to resolving the health care crisis in the United States involve the government's paying—either through one of the government-run systems like Medicaid or via tax breaks that subsidize the cost of health insurance.

When the government is involved in paying, so is Congress.

What is politically possible in the coming years, or, specifically, what will or will not pass Congress and be signed into law by the president, will be the key deciding factor in how the American health care system is reformed under the next president and the next Congress. This book contains politically possible solutions and practical advice for everyone who is a health care consumer.

We believe the American health care crisis can be solved.

This book contains our proposed solutions.

J. Patrick Rooney
Dan Perrin
Washington, D.C.
April 2008

Introduction

This book defines and will solve America's health care crisis. Here are some of the ideas this book contains:

1. First of all, health care is about money. It's about how much money we will spend for health care, where the money comes from, and who controls it. It is no secret that the U.S. health care system is so expensive that traditional insurance coverage is out of reach for many members of the middle class. The problem is causing the political system to react. After the 2008 elections, health care will be front and center of the legislative agenda for Congress and the new president.
2. The charitable, nonprofit component of the industry does not want to give care to those who are unable to pay and who have no one else (such as the government) to pay for them.
3. Hospitals are the trendsetters for the health care industry.
4. Hospitals represent that they lose money on the uninsured, who only pay 10 percent of the time. That's good propaganda, but it's not true. In fact, for many hospitals, the uninsured are their most profitable clientele.
5. Most of the uninsured are not very poor. With aggressive collection efforts, money can be gotten out of the uninsured. People with very low incomes can qualify for Medicaid (called MediCal in California).
6. Greed plays a major part in the cost problem. Many hospitals charge the uninsured three to five times what they accept as payment in full from insurance. (Pay attention to the markup on ancillary services like lab work and anesthesia.) And they are successful in collecting from the uninsured. Go to the web site www.hospitalvictims.org.

7. A national health plan is not the preferred solution, though American public opinion is moving in that direction.

8. The "make sense" alternative to national health care is to give the uninsured money, as employers do for their employees, to apply to the cost of purchasing health insurance. The IRS could deliver the money. That would avoid another giant bureaucracy and could enable consumers' self-interest to control costs.

9. Where do we get the money for the government to subsidize the cost of health insurance for the uninsured?

   a. By stopping the current tax exemption of employer-provided health insurance; and

   b. By permitting seniors to have the option to choose health savings accounts (HSAs), which would create enormous savings for the U.S. Treasury.

10. In the 1950s, Americans began to rely on insurance to cover their routine medical costs. There is a direct link between the reliance on more and more insurance benefits to cover routine health needs and the health care cost explosion in the United States. (See Figure I.1.)

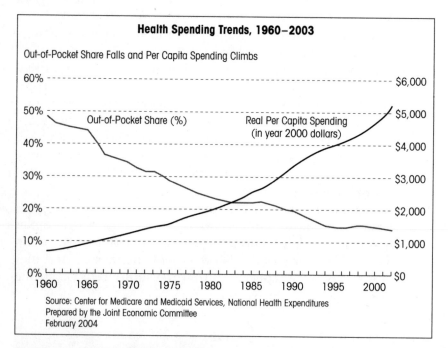

Figure I.1   Health Spending Trends

11. Health savings accounts are the most effective device that has been developed for controlling health care spending. These accounts cut payments to insurance companies by lowering the monthly insurance premium, and then put those savings, tax free, in people's pockets. With a family deductible of $2,200 to $2,500, health spending is reduced significantly. It's a cost-neutral exchange, but with an HSA, insured people have money out of which to self-pay the first couple of thousand in medical expenses. The money belongs to the insured family. (See Figure I.2.)

12. Health savings accounts were not a Republican idea. The first U.S. Senate "Dear Colleague" letter (a letter senators send each other about legislation they are introducing and want support for) about these accounts was signed by six U.S. senators, and four were Democratic U.S. senators. This 1992 letter is reprinted as Figure 7.2.

13. Hospitals will rip off money simply by overcharging on outpatient procedures that don't cost more than the insurance deductible.

14. This book proceeds to tell the uninsured how to defend themselves when they are charged excessively.

15. Medical prices must be made transparent. The public should be able to learn what they are being charged compared to what insurance companies are charged. The Centers for Medicare and Medicaid Services (CMS) has published the average hospital charges along with the average Medicare payments for 31 most common procedures.

16. For those high-risk individuals whom the insurance companies don't want to accept for individual insurance, use state risk pools as the insurer of last resort. State risk pools currently are subsidized by the federal government, and many states require health insurance companies operating in their state to kick in part of the cost (which is good).

17. Create a national marketplace for health insurance, permitting people to buy health insurance across state lines.

18. There is a new phenomenon: health care in the drugstore or the mall, called quick care clinics or mini-clinics. This is a good thing, very much in the public interest, enabling people to get medical care now without the high price of the emergency room.

Comparing Current Health Insurance Costs to Current Health Savings Accounts

$1,008.83   Average monthly premium of average 2007 family health insurance

$12,106.00   Annual 2007 cost of family health insurance in the U.S. according to the Kaiser Foundation

Family Health Savings Account Offered by an HSA Insurer

$583.00   Average monthly premium for a $3,500 deductible individual family health insurance policy, head of household age 49.

$6,996.00   Annual premium for a $3,500 deductible family health insurance policy

$3,500.00   Tax-free cash deposited in the HSA to cover the family deductible each year

$10,496.00   Total cost of premium and 100% funded HSA

This plan has no other out-of-pocket cost for the insured family, an important additional saving for the family.

Compare Costs

$12,106.00   Annual 2007 cost of family health insurance in the U.S. according to the Kaiser Foundation

$10,496.00   Total cost of premium and 100% funded HSA

$1,610.00   Savings a year with a fully funded HSA

"MSAs allow people to put money into tax-deductible IRA-like accounts. Tax-free MSA funds would be used to pay for routine checkups, vaccinations, and so forth, while costly medical procedures would be covered by high-deductible insurance policies. **Such plans typically cost 20 percent to 60 percent less than conventional health insurance policies.**"
MSAs = HSAs

"Health Insurance Crisis Again," October 1, 2003, *Reason* Magazine

Figure I.2   Current Health Insurance Costs versus Health Savings Accounts

19. "Get it right the first time." As discussed in Chapter 13, going to the more knowledgeable physician (the specialist) the first time is better than going to a gatekeeper physician. We'll get well sooner, and getting the right answer the first time will cost less.
20. The Medicare prescription benefit is not very good, and it's very costly to the U.S. Treasury, which is paying $3 for every $1 of premium paid by seniors. Estimated cost to the Treasury is more than $700 billion over 10 years.
21. Medicare is spending a bundle for the current Medicare benefit, Parts A and B: $10,221 per person.
22. If Centers for Medicare and Medicaid Services would allow her to allocate the money being spent for her herself, she could take part of it to buy major medical insurance and would have money left over to go into a personal medical savings account.
23. Add on to her savings the money she is now spending on a Medicare supplement and the money she will spend for the Part D Premium, she would have combined cash of $5,375.64 yearly with only a $3,000 deductible on her major medical.
24. With that savings Medicare could take 10 percent off the top of the annual $10,221 expenditure. She'd still have plenty of money and a much better benefit.

America's Health Care Crisis Solved

PART

I

REALITIES

CHAPTER 1

No Money, No Health Care

Scott Ferguson was admitted to St. Anthony Central Hospital in Denver with what was first thought to be a case of severe pneumonia. Over the course of a six-day stay, doctors discovered the underlying cause of his problem: The 51-year-old musician had a serious heart ailment. Though he didn't have insurance, he did have need for immediate treatment.

Once that treatment was successfully completed, the hospital expected payment in full.

Scott did some research into the actual costs involved and offered to pay St. Anthony $8,000—which is more than what Medicare would have paid for the treatment he received. The hospital declined, saying that wasn't enough. Scott then offered to pay $10,000—which is more than a private insurer would have paid for the same treatment. The hospital declined, saying it still wasn't enough.

Just how much did it want?

St. Anthony Central Hospital, a nonprofit, Catholic institution—a charity whose goal, according to its mission statement, is to "extend the healing ministry of Christ"—wanted Scott to pay not a dollar less than $67,000.[1] It wanted an uninsured patient to pay out of his own pocket an amount of money *ten times* greater than what the federal government believed was a fair price.

Who Can Afford to Get Sick?

A recent *Reader's Digest* poll revealed that two-thirds of American adults feel they "can't afford to be sick."[2]

That shouldn't surprise us.

Since 1970, health care costs have risen at twice the rate of inflation. Today America spends almost $600 billion a year on hospital care, about $400 billion on doctors' services, and almost $200 billion on prescription drugs. Add the money spent on long-term care, home health care, dental care, and private insurance and, all told, we're spending $2 trillion a year on health care.[3]

Unfortunately, Americans can't afford to pay $2 trillion a year for health care. We read about what Scott Ferguson went through, and we readily see that health care *can* be unaffordable. But the 66 percent of America responding to the *Reader's Digest* poll didn't all have a Scott Ferguson experience. Two-thirds of Americans are saying they can no longer afford *basic* health care, much less a catastrophic hospitalization.

Scott Ferguson is just the tip of a very large and menacing iceberg that lies directly in our path. Unless we come about quickly, our country is on a collision course with disaster.

A Helicopter View of Health Care Financing

How did we get to this precarious point?

Our nation's health system evolved largely from happenstance.

During World War II, the federal government imposed wage and price controls on the economy, which was generally seen as a good thing. Otherwise, the large increase in government spending for the war would have caused wages and prices to spiral. The wage controls caused businesses to come up with creative ways to attract and retain workers. Some companies seeking a competitive advantage came up with the idea of paying employees' health insurance costs.[4]

As Americans became wealthier, health insurance benefits became richer, and deductibles began to fall and then disappear. With no deductible and with the insurance premium being paid by the employer, as far as the employee was concerned, health care was "free." (You cannot imagine what a radical idea it was when Golden Rule Insurance Company introduced the first $25 deductible.)

As a result of a no-deductible world, where Americans relied on health insurance to cover routine medical costs, out-of-pocket spending on health care dropped, and health care costs began their upward march.

Because insurance shielded consumers from the actual cost of care, hospitals could charge high prices. Insurance companies would just raise premiums to pay the hospitals, and consumers were completely out of the loop. The result: Health care costs have increased far more rapidly than the rate of inflation. (See Figure I.1.)

Over time, employer-based health insurance became the norm in the United States. Now 174 million Americans get their insurance through their employer.

Another 79 million—the elderly, the poor, and members of the military—are insured by the government.

And 27 million people, many of them self-employed or working for small businesses, are buying insurance on their own.

Sadly, 47 million Americans have no health insurance at all.[5]

Under this system, the two groups that buy their health care in bulk—the 253 million insured through work and government assistance—pay wholesale prices, while the two groups that don't— the 74 million individually insured and the uninsured—pay retail. (The individually insured pay retail prices for their insurance, the uninsured pay retail prices for their hospital costs.)

Today, according to the Kaiser Family Foundation, the average monthly premium for family health insurance in the United States is $1,008.83, or an annual cost of $12,106. That is an average of all plans, group and individual, from all parts of the United States, since a health plan bought in Boise, Idaho, will cost less than one bought in New York City. Between 2000 and 2006, insurance premiums rose 87 percent.[6]

In 2005, the United States spent $2 trillion on health care, about 16 percent of the gross domestic product, or nearly $6,700 per person.[7]

The Good Bad News

If there is any good news for those forced to pay retail, it is that health care costs have risen so high that the status quo is no longer sustainable even for those getting group discounts. There is now widespread support throughout the country to "do something about it."

Do something.

But do what? No one seems to know what to do but talk.

Meanwhile, health care costs continue to overwhelm the national economy. Today, these costs consume 16 percent of the nation's economic output—the highest proportion ever. By 2015, the government projects that one in every five dollars spent in the United States will go toward medical costs. And this at a time when median incomes are *falling* for homeowners under the age of 45.[8]

A recent study by the Harvard Business School shows that medical problems account for about half of all personal bankruptcies in the country.[9]

We now spend so much on health care—we buy so many new drugs and use so many new technologies—that many of the companies we work for can no longer afford to cover our costs.

The percentage of people who have health insurance through their employers is dropping. While an overwhelming majority of large businesses still offer some level of coverage, many have reduced their benefits, shifting more of the cost on to employees.

Currently, 40 percent of small businesses offer no health insurance at all to their employees. As Todd McCracken of the National Small Business Association has said, "For many small companies, the price of their health insurance premium per employee is soon going to equal the average wage. And it's unsustainable."[10]

No More Business as Usual

Starbucks, the national coffee chain, isn't exactly a small business. But Starbucks chairman Howard Schultz has come to the same conclusion as McCracken.

Schultz says that his company's health care costs have spiraled so high, it now spends more money on health care than it does on coffee beans.[11] Similarly, Rick Wagoner, the chief executive of General Motors, says GM spends more money for insurance than it does for steel. "Based on the current data, it would be $1,525 per vehicle that we produce," he told ABC News. "That's the total health care cost per vehicle. And interestingly, it's a lot more than we pay for steel per vehicle."[12] The outrageous costs of insuring its workforce is the primary reason why GM must lay off 30,000 workers and close nine North America plants. As *USA Today* has reported it:

> In one of the largest buyout plans in U.S. corporate history, General Motors will offer money to about 126,000 hourly employees. . . .
>
> Workers will be offered $35,000 payment if they agree to retire early. Workers who promise to sever all ties with GM—leaving with no retirement benefits—will get $70,000 to $140,000, depending on time with the automaker.

> GM's unionized workers earn an average of $27 an hour,
> $56,000 a year without overtime. Benefits increase the hourly
> average to $73.[13]

Americans should take heart on hearing such news, for a corporation the size of GM has a lot of clout. It's the nation's largest private provider of health insurance, insuring more than 1.1 million people. The company buys more health services and drugs than any other in the nation.

If GM can't make a go of the current system, who can?

The answer: No one can.

Small employers are no longer providing health care for their employees simply because they can't afford the health insurance premiums.

Any way you look at it, our system is in crisis, and it's crying out for a cure. To tens of millions of people without insurance, tens of millions of people paying too much for individual policies, and tens of thousands of American companies that can no longer cover their employees' basic health care costs, the question is no longer *Should we change?* The question now is *How do we change?*

If American health care truly is not sustainable, what then do we *do* about it? And perhaps a better question is, how do we *pay* for it?

For we must remember this: If we can't afford $2 trillion a year in health care costs today, there's not a chance in hell we'll be able to afford the projected $4 trillion a year within the next decade.

2

Why the Money's Running Out

In early 2004, Rodney Vega's mother took him to Florida Hospital, a nonprofit medical center in Orlando, Florida. The Vega family had recently relocated to Florida from Venezuela, where little Rodney had previously undergone two surgeries for a brain tumor, apparently brought on by a head injury suffered in a car accident.

Concerned that the tumor had come back, the family scraped together enough money to pay for an MRI. The test confirmed their fears: The tumor was back. Rodney needed a third surgery, and soon.

Rodney's father happened to be a pastor in the Seventh-Day Adventist Church. Unfortunately, the family had no health insurance. They could not afford the amount Florida Hospital wanted for the surgery.

No Room at the Inn

Florida Hospital told the Vega family that if they couldn't pay, then they needed to take Rodney elsewhere for his care. So that's what the family did.

What's ironic is that Florida Hospital was started by the Seventh-Day Adventist Church—the very church for which Rodney's father pastors!

Though the hospital's mission statement claims it delivers care "in harmony with Christ's healing mission," its usual and customary practice is to charge the uninsured far more than it charges those with insurance.

But that's only half the story.

As a nonprofit "charitable" hospital, Florida Hospital applied for and receives full tax relief. It doesn't pay a dime in local, state, or federal income taxes. Yet this self-proclaimed extension of "Christ's healing mission" made more than $81 million in profit (retained earnings) in 2005. At the same time it refused to care for Rodney Vega, it was sitting on $2.52 *billion* in cash assets!

Not counting its physicians, the hospital pays 13 executives more than $400,000 each per year. Two executives are paid more than $1.5 million each. One other executive earned more than $2.2 million[1] in 2005.

And yet even with that abundance of worldly wealth (or perhaps *because* of it?), the hospital could show no mercy to young Rodney Vega. There was no room at the Florida Hospital for this young child in need.

Standard Operating Procedure

It would be a terrible thing if Florida Hospital's callous disregard for Rodney Vega were an isolated incident, but it's not. Florida Hospital simply operated according to standard operating procedure followed by nonprofit hospitals all across the nation. The unwritten rule is to avoid the uninsured when possible, and when not, gouge them with prices three to five times higher than what others pay. Almost all of our hospitals are doing this.

No religious denomination seems to have clean hands in the matter. The Catholic Church is making more money off of this than anyone, because it happens to operate more nonprofit hospitals than anyone. As Catholics who will someday stand for account before Christ, this bothers us. Our hope is to hear him say "Well done, thou good and faithful servant," not "Depart from me, I never knew you."

Jesus would not tolerate "Christian" hospitals that plead for mercy from the government to get generous tax relief and then turn around and seize the Rodney Vegas of this world by the throat, demanding payment in full when the money isn't there.

And if Jesus wouldn't tolerate this practice, neither should we.

It is not the same in other countries. The rest of the Western world has socialized medicine that is government run. The way they ration care and spending is to create waiting lines so if you need a procedure you have to wait months or years for care. Many patients die waiting for their care.

The Motive Is Profit

Why are they doing it? *Because they can.*

The California Public Employees' Retirement System (CalPERS) and the Pacific Business Group, which buys $10 billion in health care services among the employers who are its members, jointly commissioned a study in California of hospital prices, which was published in January 2008. Their public statement summarizing the results of the study begins: "A new study designed to uncover the key to understanding hospital prices confirms what large purchasers have long suspected: A disturbing number of hospitals appear to be grossly overcharging and not being held accountable."

Peter V. Lee, Chief Executive Officer of the Pacific Business Group, said, "This report underscores what we have long suspected: that some hospitals are basing their prices to private insurers and patients on what they can get away with."

In particular, the CalPERS media release is courageous. It explicitly states that this study exposes only the "tip of the iceberg," and that a closer look at hospital costs as compared to service levels "could help expose the wrongdoing." (The use of word "wrongdoing" is reflective of the moral certainty of the study's sponsors. CalPERS did not say there *might* be wrong doing.)

Of course there is wrongdoing by hospitals in their prices, with some hospital markups about "five times that of others"(and those markups cannot be explained "by charity and indigent care or by teaching status"). Then, the only explanation can be that these hospitals are using their system of hiding prices through incomprehensible bills, overcharges, and their antitrust exemption to price-gouge and profiteer from people and employers whose health and lives as they now know them are at stake.

Politically, taking on the hospitals is no small trick. Hospitals are one of the largest employers in every congressional district. Leading local citizens are involved in raising money for hospitals as tax-exempt charities. Their status as places of healing and caring has allowed hospitals to be given the benefit of the doubt when it comes to questions of integrity and what they charge and their profits.

Experience shows that nonprofits, whether they're insurance companies or other organizations, act just like for-profit enterprises. There is often little difference in how business is conducted in nonprofit insurance companies (mutual companies with no shareholders) and in for-profit enterprises. The goal is the same: to make a profit.

And for what? To put the money in a bank.

Nonprofit insurance companies (or hospitals) have no share-holders to give the profits to. They make money to build bigger buildings and to pay top executives more, and that is it. For those who want to make a lot of money, health care is a great place, because very few people are willing to say no when it comes to their health, regardless of the cost involved. Today, the market has never been better for making money. Health care companies keep coming up with new procedures, products, and pills—and they keep persuading us we have to have them. So we keep buying them.

Frankly, since someone else has always been picking up the tab, few of us have had reason to care until recently. But now the bill is falling back onto our own plate.

The Problem Is Greed

There's a very good reason why U.S. health care hasn't altered its own course: The ship has lost its moral rudder. It is awash in greed. We can't expect the industry to fix itself. There's just too much self-interest at stake. We can exhort our health care providers to charge less, but we doubt that it will work. The money is too easy, and the greed too strong.

Religious hospitals, such as St. Anthony's Central Hospital in Denver and Florida Hospital, used to be the "good guys" of American health care, established out of love for God, but now they serve mammon. Today religious hospitals are as bad as the rest: They're filled with greed, and their greed is being rewarded. If they've been consumed by such greed, then no one is immune—not even nonprofit hospitals.

In March 2005, Mark Everson, Commissioner of the Internal Revenue Service, wrote in a letter to the United States Senate Finance Committee: "Some tax-exempt health care providers may not differ markedly from for-profit providers in their operations, their attention to the benefit of the community or their levels of charity care."[2]

Two months later, David W. Walker, Comptroller General of the United States, in testimony before the U.S. House Committee on Ways and Means, said:

> [C]urrent tax policy lacks specific criteria with respect to tax exemptions for charitable entities and detail on how that tax exemption is conferred. If these criteria are articulated in accordance with

desired goals, standards could be established that would allow nonprofit hospitals to be held accountable for providing services and benefits to the public commensurate with their favored tax status.[3]

The fact that some nonprofit hospitals have billing policies and levels of charity care nearly the same as for-profit hospitals is not a new problem. In July 1991, for example, Mark Nadel, the associate director of National and Public Health Issues of the General Accounting Office, told Congress:

> For many nonprofit hospitals, we found the link between tax-exempt status and the provision of charitable activities for the poor or underserved is weak. Currently, the Internal Revenue Service . . . has no requirements relating hospitals' charitable activities for the poor to their tax-exempt status. If the Congress wishes to encourage nonprofit hospitals to provide charity care and other community services that benefit the poor, it should consider revising the criteria for tax exemption.[4]

On the Front Lines with Nora Johnson

Nora Johnson is on the front lines of the battle against unreasonable hospital charges.

Every day, Nora helps people to make sense of and to reduce their hospital bills. She has years of experience, and her clients are Jane Q. and John Q. public. Nora started out in the business of helping people with excessive hospital bills, because the hospital bill for her husband's hip replacement had a suspicious $1,900 charge. When Nora challenged the charge, the hospital removed it within a couple of hours. Nora decided then and there that there was a future in being a hospital bill watchdog and patient advocate.

In a presentation about hospital billings that she gave to Texas Medicaid and the Texas Office of the Inspector General, Nora explained that the phrase "hospitals' total billed charges" is synonymous with "total billed fantasies."

There isn't another business in America that wouldn't be envious of the way hospitals bill and get away with it!

"As the health care business morphs into hospital billings, one discovers that there is no relationship between a hospital's cost and total billed charges. There is also no relationship between 'total billed charges' and the reimbursement expected for the same bill from different payers," Nora said.

"What is consistent is that only the smallest percentage of a hospital's patient population (mostly uninsured patients) is expected to pay full billed charges. How can it happen that a hospital's cost for providing the setting and all the services for an appendectomy is about $4,000, but Medicare will pay about $4,700 to the hospital.

"The total billed charges to the patient are $30,000. The travesty here is that when an uninsured patient can't cough up $30,000 to pay the hospital, the hospital will drag the uninsured patient to court and petition the judge to grant a lien or garnish wages or tax returns for the full $30,000."

As Nora explained: "That $30,000 number is on every bill that every payer gets—Medicare, BlueCross, it doesn't matter. That's going to be the total billed charges. So hospitals are able to say: 'Well, we charged everybody the same,' but what is not said is the reimbursement that they accept as payment in full differs according to payer.

"Hospitals almost always win in court because they don't charge discriminatorily. Reportedly, the charges are the same. It is the amount that the hospital elects to accept as payment in full that is discriminatory."

Nora continued, "For some unfathomable reason, judges and juries assume the bill, as presented by the hospital, is correct. What judges don't know is that every hospital bill is laden with incorrect charges and duplicate charges. Try telling a judge he is complicit with the hospital in perpetuating fraud on an unsuspecting but still outraged uninsured patient."

So, Nora said, It is imperative to educate the court and to distinguish in court between hospital billed charges and demanded reimbursements. Lawyers for the opposition do not make that distinction enough times and should do so at every opportunity.

"Hospitals are the only business that draws upon and prevails through exploiting the misconception that these terms [billed charges and accepted payments] are synonymous."

As Nora said, "When approaching a hospital to rectify a billing error, one quickly realizes that hospitals shroud themselves in a cloak of papal infallibility."

But some hospitals, especially state-sponsored ones like the University of Virginia hospital chain, have an added advantage.

As Nora explained, "The Office of the Virginia Attorney General is the acting collection agency for the University of Virginia hospitals, and are very aggressive about instituting liens on patients. So, the Attorney General's office is forcing its voters to pay for fraudulent errors on University of Virginia hospital bills, and the courts blindly grant the motions for judgments."

Nora Johnson has advised congressional investigators for the U.S. House Committee on Energy and Commerce during their investigation into the overbilling of the uninsured. Nora wants to force hospitals to sign a pledge to extend to the uninsured the lowest price they give to large insurers; she intends that the pledges will be enforced by shaming hospitals into signing through the media.

To get a glimpse into the life of one person who has lived through the trauma of being overcharged, below is a letter sent to the Fairness Foundation in late February 2007.

Mr. Ferguson's bill was reduced to zero. The letter he received from Centura Health reads, in part, "[i]n regards to the balance on

Dear Mr. Rooney:

I just wanted to personally express my heartfelt thanks to you for all that you have been doing to help the uninsured that have been so unmercifully gouged by not-for-profit hospitals. I have signed the Mandates for Michael Ritty of Canon Law Professionals, to pursue remedies through Canon law with the Catholic Church and Hospitals. I will assist him in every way possible to stop these egregious practices. I cannot thank you enough for making his services available. I was charged $67,000 by St. Anthony Central Hospital in Denver. Insurance would only have paid them $8,200. I offered to pay what insurance would have plus 30 percent profit in cash, but they want the full amount.

For three years I have been meeting with legislators, the Attorney General, health groups, and everyone else concerned to stop these unjust practices and try to prevent others from going through what I have. Most of the victims I run across are simply too overwhelmed with trying to deal with such powerful institutions. Most are not well off, and suffer from deep depression, knowing that they will never recover financially from even their one visit to the hospital. Many like me feel their lives have been taken away by a place where they went to be healed. I am doing my very best to help them.

(Continued)

> I was released from the hospital after being told that my heart was too damaged for any remedy but transplant. That was depressing enough; to have to wage a long battle to protect my home and those of others from effect of unjust gouging is a huge burden. I am trying to get bills passed, similar to those in California and New York, that prohibit hospitals from charging the uninsured more than insurance or Medicare would pay them, and the Colorado Attorney General to follow the lead of states like Wisconsin and Minnesota.
>
> You have renewed my faith in humanity. The church leaders refused to meet or speak to me about this matter. The head of the Adventist Church in Denver, which co-owns the hospital I went to, also refused to speak to me. It is only from men like you that care for others and act that I draw my faith. If there is anything I can do to be of more help, please contact me.
>
> God bless you.
>
> Scott Ferguson

the account in question . . . the account is now at $0.00. Nothing further is owed on it."[5]

Figures 2.1 and 2.2 present a partial list of other patients helped by the Fairness Foundation from the fall of 2006 to the fall of 2007. While some amounts may seem small in size, these amounts are large to the patients, given their income and uninsured status.

The California Office of Statewide Health Planning and Development (OSHPD) is one of the very few third-party resources that exist to determine, on a hospital-by-hospital basis, how much the uninsured are being overcharged.

In 2003, Loma Linda University Medical Center in California had a total profit of $19,158,227. Eighty-six percent of that profit ($16,551,566) came from billing the uninsured three times the cost of their care.[6] In 2005, the date of the most recent available OSHPD report, Loma Linda University Medical Center earned a profit of $53,133,974, of which 50 percent ($26,710,085) came from charging the uninsured almost four times the cost of their care.[7]

Here are four other stories of what other patients in other states are forced to put up with.

James in Alabama had a hospital bill of $21,903 for 12 hours in the emergency room (ER) for surgery. By sending the letters in this chapter, he was able to hold off any adverse legal or credit action

Name	Original Bill	Negotiated Settlement	Amount Saved
Doretta M.	$224.50	$0.00	$224.50
Susan N.	$486.00	$150.00	$336.00
Judith W.	$994.00	$497.00	$497.00
David C.	$87,000.00	$17,106.00	$69,894.00
Joan R.	$19,662.75	$6,000.00	$13,662.75
Joyce B.	$30,792.36	$3,079.00	$27,713.36
Dawna L.	$15,296.00	$5,900.00	$9,396.00
Valerie J.	$780.00	$501.00	$279.00
Steven W.	$125,954.30	$34,157.38	$91,796.92
James F.	$21,903.00	$5,733.00	$16,170.00
Kevin O.	$52,049.00	$6,000.00	$46,049.00
Anita H.	$4,178.00	$960.00	$3,218.00
Ina M.	$1,269.90	$952.43	$317.47
Alton G.	$52,573.00	$28,000.00	$24,573.00
Jean R.	$772.75	$695.47	$77.28
Joel B.	$3,000.21	$755.00	$2,245.21
Thomas K.	$5,730.80	$2,000.00	$3,730.80
Carol P.	$2,097.55	$1,153.65	$943.90
Carol M.	$8,890.08	$4,445.04	$4,445.04
Kevin G.	$137,541.82	$36,000.00	$101,541.82
Leonardo L.	$11,940.00	$5,000.00	$6,940.00
David S.	$7,300.00	$0.00	$7,300.00
Janet R.	$15,889.00	$11,000.00	$4,889.00
Paul D.	$6,677.00	$3,338.50	$3,338.50
Aaron G.	$8,950.40	$2,500.00	$6,450.40
Ronald F.	$1,481.77	$200.00	$1,281.77
Alan S.	$39,000.00	$23,333.00	$15,667.00
Marcel W.	$31,000.00	$15,500.00	$15,500.00
Dianne M.	$17,106.00	$4,273.00	$12,833.00
Totals	**$710,540.19**	**$219,229.47**	**$491,310.72**

Figure 2.1   Patients Who Received a Negotiated Settlement, Fall 2006 to Fall 2007

while he requested the UB-04 from the hospital (a UB-92 and a UB-04 are standard forms for showing hospital bills). After several months, he was able to get the form. We determined that Medicare plus 25 percent would be $5,412. Faced with this information, the hospital agreed to settle for $5,733.

Name	Original Bill	After Charity Care	Amount Saved
Charlotte B.	$29,313.15	$0.00	$29,313.15
Chris R.	$1,100.00	$0.00	$1,100.00
Matthew B.	$1,500.00	$0.00	$1,500.00
Roman T.	$70,976.00	$16,675.00	$54,301.00
Judy N.	$10,234.25	$0.00	$10,234.25
Milo P.	$15,500.22	$0.00	$15,500.22
Judy M.	$16,694.00	$0.00	$16,694.00
Kathy C.	$10,840.00	$0.00	$10,840.00
Melvin L.	$78,330.67	$0.00	$78,330.67
Linda A.	$31,342.30	$4,000.00	$27,342.30
William S.	$16,736.70	$0.00	$16,736.70
Natalya L.	$16,487.58	$2,600.00	$13,887.58
Roy T.	$25,302.27	$0.00	$25,302.27
Judith D.	$20,049.60	$6,014.88	$14,034.72
Tyler F.	$507.60	$0.00	$507.60
Brandon B.	$12,225.21	$0.00	$12,225.21
Leann E.	$8,877.07	$2,600.00	$6,277.07
Karen B.	$21,000.00	$0.00	$21,000.00
Shawna H.	$18,000.00	$11,500.00	$6,500.00
Rhonda G.	$25,676.92	$0.00	$25,676.92
Linda M.	$72,453.00	$0.00	$72,453.00
Virgina C.	$16,090.21	$0.00	$16,090.21
Barbara W.	$1,797.00	$0.00	$1,797.00
Robert B.	$60,199.00	$0.00	$60,199.00
Debra R.	$2,200.78	$0.00	$2,200.78
Melissa C.	$1,562.00	$0.00	$1,562.00
Malino K.	$23,022.00	$0.00	$23,022.00
Totals	**$608,017.53**	**$43,389.88**	**$564,627.65**

Figure 2.2   Patients Who Qualified for Charity Care, Fall 2006 to
Fall 2007

Linda of New York, who became uninsured following a 2006 divorce, is unable to buy affordable insurance coverage because of a preexisting heart condition. She faced a $72,453 hospital bill following angioplasty surgery. The hospital social worker told her the only help might be through Medicaid but that she couldn't qualify because she makes $25 per month too much. After several phone calls, Linda was finally sent a charity care application, which she completed and returned. Within 30 days, she received a letter from the hospital informing her that her entire balance had been written off.

Carl of Texas was dealing with his wife's $30,792.36 inpatient hospital bill. The hospital offered a "prompt pay discount" of 25 percent, if they could pay the entire bill within 30 days, which was impossible. Carl requested and received the UB-92 form, and we determined that Medicare would have paid $6,861.53. He negotiated a settlement of $3,079—even less than the Medicare allowance.

Kevin in Florida needed help with his $137,541.82 hospital bill for bypass surgery. Prior to the procedure, he was quoted an estimate of $30,000, which he planned to pay. When he received the total bill he tried to negotiate, based on his $30,000 preoperative estimate. The hospital offered to settle for *double* what Medicare would have paid, $55,753.20. Kevin sent the letters in Chapter 8 disputing the charges and requesting the UB-92 form. Within three days he got a call from the hospital's chief financial officer offering to settle for $40,000. He was able to negotiate a settlement of $37,000.

If you are uninsured and are presented with a huge hospital bill, just keep in mind Nora Johnson's words: "hospitals' 'total billed charges' is synonymous with 'total billed fantasies.'"

CHAPTER

A New Scarlet Letter

Not long ago, the *Washington Post* published a commentary by George Askew, an assistant clinical professor of pediatrics at George Washington University in Washington, D.C., and a senior fellow at the Center for American Progress about a study his medical students conducted by posing as either low-income uninsured adults or parents of low-income uninsured children who needed a wellness exam.

In short, if you are uninsured, "You might as well have a scarlet letter sewn on your shirt, because you will be identified as someone who can be ignored, discarded, and shamed with impunity."[1] Half of the medical students could not get an appointment; those who were able to had to wait two and a half weeks to see the doctor. One in five reported either rude or very rude behavior from those with whom they were trying to make an appointment.

A Lady in Red

In May 2002, Orenta Toombs was stricken with a severe back pain which turned out to be a gallbladder attack. A single mother of three, Orenta was unemployed at the time and had no health insurance. In severe pain, she had to be admitted to St. Joseph's Regional Medical Center in Milwaukee for emergency surgery. Using a laparoscopic procedure, doctors were able to remove her gallbladder successfully and without complications. But Orenta's trouble was far from over. Had her surgery been covered by Medicare, the hospital would have accepted $5,000 as payment in full for the services provided her. As it was, St. Joseph's charged her $31,614. According to the hospital itself, if a private insurer had paid for her care, it likely would have been charged less than $20,000.

Like the hospitals already mentioned, St. Joseph's is a charitable Catholic institution. Its parent company is Wheaton Franciscan Healthcare, whose mission statement says that it is "committed to living out the healing ministry of Jesus by providing exceptional and compassionate health care service that promotes the dignity and well-being" of the patients it serves.[2]

Was the hospital living out the healing ministry of Jesus when it charged Orenta six times more than it charges Medicare for the same surgery? Was it promoting her dignity and well-being when it turned her account over to a collection agency that sued her to get the full amount of the inflated bill?

Apparently, Wisconsin's attorney general didn't think so: The state filed federal complaints against St. Joseph's on Orenta's behalf, alleging that the hospital engaged in unfair trade practices by overcharging uninsured patients.

An isolated incident? No, it's just another example of the standard operating procedure firmly in place within America's health care system today.

Thankfully, Orenta's story has a happy ending. St. Joseph's parent company, Wheaton Franciscan Healthcare, recently agreed to give uninsured patients a discount consistent with that charged to patients with insurance. In the Milwaukee area, that amounts to a discount of about *45 percent*! As part of the settlement, the company forgave Orenta's bill altogether.[3]

Who Are the Uninsured?

Today, 47 million Americans have no health insurance. That means that nearly one in every six U.S. residents is walking around with a scarlet letter on his or her chest, "suffering the indignity and physical harm" that goes with it.

Just who are these people?

Most are not poor, for the poor have access to Medicaid, the government assistance program. Surprisingly, nearly one in three live in households that earn more than $50,000 a year.[4] Most are self-employed or work for a small business. And most do not go without insurance as a lifestyle choice—they simply cannot afford the monthly insurance premiums.

Because most of the uninsured are young (41 percent are under the age of 25), as a group they have very little political muscle to help turn the wheels of justice on their own behalf.[5]

The Danger of Secondhand Smoke

Perhaps you have health insurance and think, "Well, that's unfortunate for them." But even those of us *with* insurance must inhale the damaging secondhand smoke of uninsurance. Whether it is for a concussion or a cold, when the uninsured need to see a doctor, more often than not they go to the hospital emergency room (ER), which by law must treat all the patients it can handle, without regard to their ability to pay. In 2004, more than $25 billion worth of health care bills went unpaid, and the bulk of these were for ER services. This is one reason why many hospitals no longer offer emergency care, and it's also why the remaining ERs are so dangerously overcrowded.

ABC News has highlighted the plight of ER patients in Houston, Texas, where, incredibly, one out of every three residents is uninsured. ER patients in that city often must wait five to six hours to see a doctor. Many are left to wait in the ambulances that hours earlier rushed through traffic lights to get them there.[6]

Deficiencies in emergency care constitute only one side effect of the problem of uninsurance, but it's one we can all relate to, whether we have insurance or not.

Injustice for All

What if *you* had to wear the scarlet "U"? (That's "U" for *uninsured*.)

In addition to the indignities described by Dr. Askew, you would be charged greatly increased prices by hospitals seeking to make extra dollars off those who are uninformed and generally helpless. That's standard operating procedure in American health care.

Speaking of the "uninformed and generally helpless," do *you* have any idea how to defend yourself from a hospital charging you three times what it would charge an insurance company?

Hospitals commonly argue that they are not able to collect from the uninsured. That's generally not true. The situation varies, of course, but in the only state in which the data on hospital collections are reported—California—the collection rate is high.

Here are a couple of examples from California OSHPD:

- One hospital with an operating cost of $2,036 per day charged uninsured patients $10,130 per day, 497 percent times cost. The hospital has collected an average of $7,815 per day, or *77 percent* of its high charges.
- Another hospital with an operating cost of $2,172 per day charged the uninsured $11,098 per day, and it is successful in collecting $8,535 per day. (This same hospital collects $2,563 per day as payment in full from managed-care California OSHPD report insurers.)[7]

Of course, patients facing these prices will avoid them if possible.

After looking at the numbers hospitals are trying to charge, one individual said, "If the hospital is going to charge me a million dollars, there is no point in my paying anything. If I'm not able to pay the hospital and get them off my back, then what's the point of making partial payment?"

For the patient who is charged $10,000 a day on a hospital cost of $2,000 a day, the sensible thing for the patient is to escape the bill entirely—if he or she can. For them, the system is both unaffordable and unjust.

Just ask Carlos Ferlini.

Carlos was repairing a rain gutter when he fell off his ladder. Though he fell just eight feet, he fell awkwardly and fractured his skull, an arm, and several ribs. The 42-year-old construction worker was rushed to Providence St. Joseph's Hospital in Burbank, California.

Eighteen days later he was released from the hospital. At the time Carlos entered the charitable hospital, the Ferlini family did not have health insurance. The family earned about $40,000 a year.

But Carlos's hospital bill totaled $253,035.

Ironically, had Carlos had health insurance, the insurance company would never have paid such a large amount. Nor would the hospital have demanded the same high payment from an insurance company. The insurance company would have settled the claim at a previously established discount, a fraction of the full sticker price Carlos was charged.

Had Carlos been of age to receive Medicare, Providence St. Joseph's would have accepted just *$43,000* as payment in full from the U.S. government.

But according to standard operating procedure within the health care industry, this "charitable" hospital charged Carlos Ferlini, an uninsured construction worker, six times the price the U.S. government felt to be fair compensation from Medicare.[8]

Why Nationalized Health Care Is No Cure-All

Do you remember HillaryCare from the early 1990s?

The Clinton administration's attempt to nationalize American health care in 1993, an effort spearheaded by First Lady Hillary Clinton, offered "managed competition" for all.

Now, what exactly was that?

The HMO Idea

The term "managed competition" was coined by Paul Ellwood, MD, the father of the health maintenance organization (HMO). Basically, an HMO is a health plan in which a bureaucrat or somebody in the sky oversees what your doctor can do for you and what tests or prescriptions your doctor may order for you. HMOs operate on the assumption that there is too much medical care and that a little corporate supervision will eliminate a lot of unnecessary procedures and costs. Under an HMO plan, your care is overseen by a bureaucrat at the other end of a telephone line or by a "gatekeeper" physician you must always visit first.

You may go to a general practitioner for an antibiotic or a few stitches, but if your ailment is too serious or your wound too severe, your general practitioner will send you to a specialist. At one time or another, most of us have gone to a family doctor who has told us that we need to see a specialist.

Ellwood believed that we should regularize that process in medical care, and the gatekeeper physician should get a financial incentive (a bonus) for keeping us away from high-priced specialists.

An Idea Rejected

Hillary Clinton and Ira Magaziner, her health care designer, worked with Dr. Ellwood and Alain Enthoven, a professor at Stanford University, to come up with health maintenance care for all Americans.

That's where the word "managed" in managed competition came from. If we were to make this kind of managed health care compulsory for all Americans, the "competition" would arise when the HMOs compete with one another for an employer's business. "Managed competition" was the health care plan that Hillary Clinton tried to sell for the American people.

We should remember that in those days, the Democrats held a majority in both the House and the Senate. This plan was not successful in either house even though it came from a Democratic administration and Democrats held the majority in both houses.

In the 1994 election, the Republicans gained control of the House of Representatives. Suspicion of the Clinton health plan for America played a significant role in causing voters to give control of the House, and a few years later, of the Senate, to the Republicans.

Phoenix Rising?

Just like the fabled phoenix of classical mythology, after HillaryCare went down in defeat in Congress, it now seems ready to rise from the ashes of its own destruction with renewed youth and vigor.

When Senator John Kerry ran for president in 2004, he told the Associated Press that his first act as president would be to "send to Congress a health care plan that stops spiraling costs, covers every child in America, and makes it possible for every American to get the same health care as any member of Congress."[1]

He lost his bid for the White House.

In the same year, Senator Clinton herself, when preparing her rhetoric to run for the presidency, renewed her call for a "new social contract" on health care, a contract based on government management and standardization.[2]

Senators Clinton and Kerry are simply giving voice to what many Americans seem to believe: The only cure for our health care crisis is centralized management.

Today, Americans are divided on the subject. Fifty percent of American voters favor government-guaranteed universal health care coverage.

Here is what the press release by the pollster said: "For example, while the current survey finds 50 percent in favor of government-guaranteed health insurance, an earlier survey found that just 33 percent favor a national health insurance program. Additionally, while half of all voters favor government-guaranteed insurance coverage, only 36 percent believe that such a program would be better run by the government. Forty-three percent believe it would be better run by 'private companies under something like current private insurance' programs."[3]

Government-run health care cannot be dismissed out of hand. Many countries—Sweden, Japan, Australia, England, France, and Canada among them—now provide some form of government-managed medical care.

But looking at the evidence, is a nationalized health system really the answer?

Former Senator Dan Coats of Indiana recalled the following about Hillary Clinton's testimony for her health care plan before his committee back in those days: "I said to Mrs. Clinton when she testified before our committee, 'Do you know any government program that has operated as efficiently as the private sector is able to perform?' She was unable to name even one. After a short hesitation, she added, 'But this program will.'"[4]

An interesting interchange.

On June 8, 2006, the Citizens' Health Care Working Group, a 14-member committee established by Congress, reported that the majority of Americans now favor the federal government guaranteeing that all Americans have basic health insurance coverage.[5] The committee reported the public desire but did not estimate the cost—nor did members have a plan to pay for such a program.

HillaryCare II

Today, Senator Hillary Clinton is much more shrewd about her health care proposal. There are no secret documents, plans, or meetings. Chris Jennings, former White House Senior Health Care Adviser, was the main health care policy adviser to President Clinton during their effort to pass Hillary Clinton's health care reform plan in the 1990s. Jennings, visiting family in Ohio, met with the *Athens*

(Ohio) *News* for an interview about his years in the Clinton White House, and what went wrong with their reform effort. The Health Security Act (HSA) was the bill's title, and Jennings said that they made some mis-steps.

One was that the closed (secret) task force meetings were resented by everyone who had not been included, or as Jennings put it: "There were many mistakes made by us that we're culpable for. One was setting up a task force to study the issue interminably behind closed doors—a move that alienated press, public, and all the people who didn't get appointed to the task force and thought they should have been. That was a process mistake."[6] In fact, the Clinton White House was sued in federal court to release the task force documents. The lawsuit was dismissed because the Clinton White House "voluntarily" released its secret health care task force files. [7]

In other words, the Clinton White House was forced to do what it had earlier refused to do, which was release the task force documents—mostly. We say mostly because according to the *Chicago Tribune,* "virtually all of the 3 million pages of documents that detail the internal workings of the health-care task force . . . remain stored away in boxes" at the Clinton presidential library in Little Rock.[8] Naturally, the Clinton Presidential Library has been sued to release the 3 million unreleased documents, that the Clinton White House said they would release voluntarily, in order to have the original lawsuit dropped.[9]

Senator Clinton pledges no tax increase to pay for her plan to allow Americans universal coverage. You can keep the plan you have now, if you like it, or you can choose from the list of plans members of Congress get to choose from. And if you don't like any of those plans, you can choose a new Medicare-like plan that will be created for those under 65 years old. Or, you can add some of your own post-tax dollars to the mix and get a really expensive private plan.[10]

Pledging an end to discrimination, Senator Clinton will force all individual insurers to accept all applicants; no one can be refused due to a preexisting condition. As Senator Clinton said recently, "We're going to change the way insurance companies do business in America. Right now, [they] spend $50 billion a year trying to figure out how not to cover people. Well, I'm going to save them a fortune and a whole lot of time because the new policy is, no discrimination, period."[11]

By forcing everyone to pay the same premium, regardless of age or health—a process that is known as community rating—Clinton will drive the prices of private health insurance plans through the roof.[12] This is exactly the effect that guaranteed issue and community rating has had in states that have tried it, like New Jersey (see Figures 10.1 and 10.2). It has had the exact effect that Senator Clinton wants. In New Jersey everyone pays the same premium, regardless of their health. It is just that no one can afford the rates of this fair insurance, or insurance that is "nondiscriminatory."

In New Jersey today, there are only four insurance companies that offer health insurance for a single individual (whose employer does not provide health insurance). Premiums range from $923.30 to $1,528.00—*per month.* The average monthly premium of all insurers offering singles a $1,000 deductible is $1,204.61 *a month,* or $14,455.29 a year. Two other plans for single individuals in New Jersey are even more expensive, with one insurer charging a premium of *$6,009.00 a month*—that's $72,108 a year—for its $1,000 deductible. (People who need to buy these individual health plans are those whose employers do not provide health insurance.)[13] These Standard Plan rates for monthly premiums for individual health insurance in New Jersey are as of January 2008, and can be found at the official New Jersey State Department of Banking and Insurance's web site.

Who can afford these New Jersey community rating and guaranteed-issue monthly health insurance premiums?

These are the health insurance rates that will result nationwide from HillaryCare II. Her plan will do to the entire private individual insurance market what guaranteed issue and community rating has done to the health insurance prices in New Jersey. Perhaps if guaranteed issue and community rating were mandated in another state, the result would be different.

New York State also has guaranteed issue and community rating. Senator Clinton's home is in Westchester County, New York. There are eight POS plans to choose from in Westchester, with the least expensive costing $1,073.20 a month for any individual. See Figure 4.1 for the average *monthly* premium rate for an HMO plan for a family in Westchester County: $2,839.41, or $34,072.92 a year.[14]

The idea is to drive the cost of private insurance through the roof to the point most cannot afford it, making government-run health care the only logical option. In other words, force, through high premium prices, the American public to pick government-run

Rates may vary depending upon the month in which you enroll.
To verify the rates listed below, please call applicable HMO directly.

Westchester County

HMO		What You Pay Per Month	
		HMO	POS
Aetna Health, Inc.	Individual	$945.60	$1,188.54
800/435-8742	Husband/Wife	$1,891.44	$2,377.34
	Parent & Child(ren)	$1,673.62	$2,103.76
	Family	$2,810.97	$3,532.85
		HMO	**POS**
CIGNA HealthCare of	Individual	$920.46	$1,225.51
New York, Inc.	Husband/Wife	$1,840.92	$2,450.98
800/345-9458	Parent & Child(ren)	$1,564.79	$2,083.31
	Family	$2,761.35	$3,676.47
		HMO	**POS**
ConnectiCare of	Individual	$820.52	$1,073.21
New York, Inc.	Husband/Wife	$1,641.04	$2,146.42
800/846-8578	Parent & Child(ren)	$1,398.17	$1,828.75
	Family	$2,550.18	$3,335.54
		HMO	**POS**
Empire HealthChoice	Individual	$836.88	$1,398.41
HMO, Inc.	Husband/Wife	$1,673.76	$2,796.82
d/b/a Empire BlueCross	Parent & Child(ren)	$1,506.38	$2,517.14
BlueShield HMO	Family	$2,510.64	$4,195.23
800/662-5193			
		HMO	**POS**
GHI HMO Select, Inc.	Individual	$1,603.40	$1,924.10
d/b/a GHI HMO	Family	$4,088.65	$4,906.45
914/340-2300			
877/244-4466			

Health Insurance Plan of	**HMO**		**POS**
Greater New York, Inc.	Adult	$602.10	Individual	$1,263.51
800/447-8255	Per Child*	$280.07	Husband/Wife	$2,527.02
		Parent & child(ren)	$2,211.06
		Family	$3,641.33

		HMO	**POS**
Health Net of New York, Inc.	Individual	$1,004.79	$1,204.25
914/682-9192	Husband/Wife	$2,009.68	$2,408.55
800/762-3511	Parent & Child(ren)	$1,819.56	$2,180.74
	Family	$2,824.35	$3,384.98
		HMO	**POS**
Oxford Health Plans	Individual	$776.58	$1,298.30
(NY), Inc.	Husband/Wife	$1,553.15	$2,596.60
800/216-0778	Parent & Child	$1,514.32	$2,531.69
	Family	$2,329.73	$3,894.90

*Maximum of $1,120.28 for 4 or more children.

Figure 4.1   Premium Rates for Standard Individual Health Plans, January 2008

health care. By driving the price of private health insurance policies to these unaffordable levels, the only plan that will make economic sense for people to choose is the new, government-run Medicare-like plan Senator Clinton will create.

It is a simple plan. It has all the proper buzzwords, such as "choice" and "guaranteed coverage," and it will result in whole-sale enrollment in government-run health care by everyone who is without employer-provided health insurance. By making it impossible for the private plans to compete with Senator Clinton's new Medicare-like health plan because of community rating and guaranteed issue, and because this new government-run plan is subsidized and does not have to make a profit, the private individual insurance companies will be forced out of the market.

HillaryCare II will destroy the individual health insurance marketplace, in the name of reform.

Most polls show that American voters trust Democrats more on health care than they trust Republicans. The only time this was not true was after the failure of the first HillaryCare plan. Today, polls show that Democrats have a 16-point advantage over the Republicans on the question of, "Who do you trust more on the issue of health care, the Republicans or the Democrats?" Further, two-thirds of the public believes health care is a very important issue.[15]

It is worth noting that all of the Democratic presidential candidates rank health care reform as their number one issue for their domestic campaign platform, but only one, Congressman Dennis Kucinich (D-OH), has endorsed a Canadian-style health care system. None of the Democratic front-runners—Senator Clinton, Senator Obama, and Senator Edwards—has endorsed such a system. There are both political and policy reasons that a Canadian-style health care system is not being considered seriously as a way to reform the U.S. health care system.

O Canada

Many in the United States have expressed admiration for the Canadian health system, which was nationalized long ago. Canada's early results appeared good, and everyday services—visits to the doctor for common colds, sprains, and the like—continue to satisfy the needs of many.

But the *New York Times* in February 2006 reported that Canada's state health system is "gradually breaking down."[16] In its place, one private clinic is opening each week, and private insurance is gaining clout. Although it's *illegal* for doctors to take money for operations or care in Canada, the law is flouted with impunity because patients' needs are so great.

When doctors bet their careers on acts of civil disobedience, the decline of the fabled Canadian health system must be grave.

"We've taken the position that the law is illegal," says Dr. Brian Day, who runs a private hospital in Canada, "This is a country in which dogs can get a hip replacement in under a week and in which humans can wait two to three years."[17]

Murray Perrin lived in Alberta, Canada, and waited well over a year in the mid-1990s for his hip to be replaced. By the time he was operated on, the hip bone had degenerated so much that the top end of his femur was gone, he had to sleep sitting up in a chair, and he was on pain killers the entire time he waited his turn for surgery. For a man in his late 80s, it was a traumatic experience.

In a study done a couple of years ago and reported in *Health Affairs,* 81 percent of hospital administrators in the Canadian province of British Columbia said that a 65-year-old male had to wait six months or more for a hip replacement.[18]

Canada is the only industrialized nation that outlaws privately financed purchase of medical services. Change is coming, however, and not just by renegade doctors; the Supreme Court of Canada recently ruled that Quebec's ban on private health insurance is unconstitutional because patients were suffering and dying due to the long wait for care.[19]

Even Canadian politicians are beginning to speak up. "Why are we so afraid to look at mixed health care delivery models when other states in Europe and around the world have used them to produce better results for patients at a lower cost to taxpayers?" asked the premier of British Columbia, Gordon Campbell.

Meanwhile, the Canadian hospital system has been relying on Dr. Day's private hospital to help shorten their waiting list; it "has been under contract by overburdened local hospitals to perform knee, spine, and gynecological operations on more than 1,000 patients."[20]

Even members of the Canadian parliament leave the country to avoid the long waits. Consider Liberal Member of Parliament Belinda Stronach. According to the Harrisonburg, Virginia *Daily News-Record,* Ms. Stronach "is a strong supporter of the national health care service," notwithstanding the fact that "the Canada Health Act mandates that no one should pay for a health service if others get it free; no matter how bad they need surgery, they must wait in line."[21]

"Anything different," said Ms. Stronach, would be "a two-tiered health system and . . . I'm not in favor of a two-tiered health system." Except when she has breast cancer, then "she is not in favor of waiting either, and long medical waits are common in Canada." Instead of waiting, Ms. Stronach traveled to California for her operation, but, in keeping with her support of Canada's health care system, she denied that the speed of medical care in the United States was the reason for her trip.[22]

The dangers of the Canadian health system are well known to anyone who seriously examines it. People die in Canada waiting for their care, and those waiting often suffer terribly.

Americans would not put up with HMOs that ration care, and if any politician tries to institute Canadian-style health care, with waiting lists and delays that cause patient suffering and death, they will be run out of Washington, D.C. We still have HMOs but they do not exercise the amount of control they did in the past. Public reaction against the strict controls and rationing of care has caused their reins to be loosened.

The Cost of Inefficiency

A 2006 study by the Fraser Institute, a Canadian think-tank, showed that among industrialized countries with nationalized care, Canada's system ranks among the lowest in several key areas, although it spends more money per person than the rest.[23] The evidence indicates a great frustration among Canadians with the timeliness and quality of care for needs such as bypass surgeries, bone fractures, magnetic resonance imaging (MRIs), cancer treatments, and hip replacements. Half of Canada's hospitals report that a 65-year-old man in need of a routine hip replacement must wait an average of six months. In nine out of ten American hospitals, in contrast, the average wait time is less than three weeks.[24]

Ninety percent of Canadian heart specialists say they have given preferential treatment to patients for nonmedical reasons. Translated, this means doctors are routinely bumping people with connections up to the front of the waiting list, which lengthens the waiting time for all other patients.[25]

So much for equal access.

When nationalized health care was first introduced in Canada in July 1958, the federal government paid for half of its total cost, with each province paying for the other half. Today, the federal government pays for less than 25 percent, forcing the provinces to pick up 75 percent of the cost.

In the province of Saskatchewan, health care costs now eat up 40 percent of the budget. On average, Canadian provinces spend one out of every three dollars on health care. Furthermore, Canadians have a special provincial payroll tax that is used to finance each province's health care costs. This tax is taken directly from Canadians' paychecks.

Dr. David Gratzer of the Manhattan Institute estimates that Canada's health system costs each Canadian worker 21 cents out of every dollar he or she earns. "This means," he said, "that Canadians earning $35,000 a year pay $7,350 for Medicare [Canada's health system]."[26]

God Save the Queen

The problems beginning to plague the Canadian health care system have long been observed in Britain.

Over the course of the first eight years of Britain's National Health Service, hospital staffing in England increased by 28 percent while administrative and clerical help increased by 51 percent. At the same time, medical care production—as measured by the number of hospital beds occupied daily—actually *decreased* by 11 percent. Did the health of the nation improve by 11 percent over the course of those eight years? Apparently not. During this time, 600,000 Britons who needed a hospital bed couldn't get one.[27]

Speaking of waits, one English patient recently made headlines as she waited for a serious surgery. Having been prepped for surgery and having bidden farewell to family members (just in case), Margaret Dixon got bumped by a more urgent case. This happened to her not once or twice, she claimed, but *seven* times. British health officials said Ms. Dixon is exaggerating. They maintain she was bumped from surgery just *four* times.[28]

Even when you do get in, Britain's public hospitals are notorious for being stocked with old and sometimes damaged equipment. The hospitals are overcrowded. And they are unclean: The country has the worst rate of hospital-acquired infections in Europe, and a study by Britain's Health Protection Agency showed such infections play a role in the death of 32,000 patients every year.[29]

England's problem isn't a lack of knowledge, it's a lack of money.

Look No Further

In presenting evidence of the downsides to nationalized health care, we're not suggesting there are no positive aspects from such systems. But there are trade-offs.

Real life teaches us two important lessons:

1. You get what you pay for.
2. The bigger the bureaucracy, the greater the waste.

As economists Milton and Rose Friedman have said: "Two major arguments are offered for introducing socialized medicine in the United States: first, that medical costs are beyond the means of most Americans; second, that socialization will somehow reduce costs. The second can be dismissed out of hand—at least until someone can find some example of an activity that is conducted more economically by government than by private enterprise."[30]

One would think that here in America our less-than-satisfying experience with HMOs and managed-care gatekeepers would be enough to scare us away from ceding health decisions to any sort of centralized bureaucracy, private or public. But the pull of a possible panacea is strong.

However, we don't have to cross any border to see the inefficiencies of nationalized health care: We have Medicaid and Medicare right here in our own backyard.

New York, New York

Medicaid is America's health insurance program for the poor. It is state administered and federally subsidized. In 2006, the United States spent about $330 billion on Medicaid.[31] Not coincidentally, the country's largest Medicaid program, in New York, is the one most plagued by problems. The state of New York spends $10,600 on each of its Medicaid enrollees.[32]

Why so much?

Among other reasons, as the *New York Times* reported in 2005, a single New York dentist once billed Medicaid for 991 procedures in one day. One New York school referred 4,434 students to speech therapy in a single day. And one New York physician alone billed $11.5 million worth of prescriptions for a synthetic muscle-building hormone. The drug was designed to help AIDS patients from wasting away, but prosecutors charged the drug was, instead, diverted to body builders.

The former chief state investigator for Medicaid fraud and abuse in New York City, James Mehmet, told the *Times* that he believed *40 percent* of all Medicaid claims in the state are questionable—10 percent are outright fraudulent, another 30 percent medically unnecessary. He estimated that New York's Medicaid program spends $18 billion a year on fraudulent or medically unnecessary services.[33]

That's one window into government-run health care.

Florida, Here We Come

Another window can be found at the opposite end of the economic spectrum, in the upscale community of Boca Raton, Florida. There, according to yet another article in the *New York Times,* doctor visits have become a "social activity" among the area's seniors.[34]

"Many patients have 8, 10, or 12 specialists and visit one or more of them most days of the week," the newspaper said. "They bring their spouses and plan their days around their appointments, going out to eat or shopping while they are in the area. They know what they want; they choose specialists for every body part. And every visit is covered by Medicare."

Medicare is America's health insurance program for people over age 65. It's entirely a federal program, one that uses no state money. In 2005, the United States spent *$335 billion* on Medicare. The most recent per-senior figure for the cost of Medicare is from 2006. At that time, Medicare spent $10,221 per senior.

Researchers point to South Florida as "a case study of what happens when people are given free rein to have all the medical care they could imagine." The fact is Medicare spends more money per person in South Florida than just about anywhere else in the country. Research conducted by Dartmouth Medical School has shown *no medical benefit* for all of that excess medical attention.

"In our research," said Dartmouth's Dr. Elliott Fisher, "Medicare enrollees in high-intensity regions have *2 to 5 percent higher* mortality rates than similar patients in the more conservative regions of the country."[35]

Ouch.

Regardless, Medicare consumption will likely increase dramatically in the next few years as millions of health-conscious baby boomers flood into the system.

The Evidence Speaks

Looking at the experiences of other countries and at our own experiences, can we say that nationalized health care as an approach has proven to be *pro bono publico,* for the public good?

Think about this: If health care consumption has rocketed under America's current system, where we're paying out of our own pocket just 14 cents out of every health care dollar spent, can we really expect a system of "free" health care to remedy the situation?

Nationalized health care is good in theory, but it isn't a cure-all. Thankfully, we do have other options.

PART

II

STRATEGIES

Fair Care

The theme of this book is money. Earlier we discussed the impact health care spending will have on the economy. Perhaps the correct verb to use is "having," for it's doing a lot of damage right now. In order for this nation to compete globally, we must constrain health care spending. Health care is all about money, who controls it and who has access to it. The government can impose health care budgets and price controls, but it has only limited what Medicare will pay.

Here is a new approach to financing our health care, called Fair Care. This is the most important chapter in the book because it will fix this terrible problem of the uninsured in America.

This financing mechanism would give a refundable tax credit to every American who is not on a government-run or government-sponsored health care program. The Fair Care refundable tax credit is tax-free money, just as the employer's payment for health benefits is tax free. The amount is:

- $2,000 for each adult.
- $4,000 for husband and wife with no children.
- $1,000 extra for one or more children.
- $5,000 for husband and wife with children. (The plan could be changed to $1,500 for children, $5,500 for a family, at a small additional cost.)

Fair Care is for everyone as long as they don't get their health care from a government plan (which is already tax free), such as Medicaid, Medicare, or VA for veterans.

Among those who would benefit from Fair Care would include:

- **People who work for an employer that provides health insurance.** These people can use their Fair Care dollars to pay for their employer's plan, or they can opt out and buy their own if they don't like their employer's choice.
- **Self-employed workers.** They will use their Fair Care money to buy their own policies.
- **Americans who work for employers where health insurance is not offered.** These people could use their Fair Care dollars to buy their own insurance.

Money not spent for health insurance can be deposited into a health savings account (HSA), where it is tax free. Today, employees of big corporations have employer-provided health insurance where the employer pays most of the cost; typically the employee pays part through payroll deduction.

Fair Care calls for the federal government to act as if it were the employer that provides health insurance to its employees. For example, for a family, the government would pay $5,000 a year for the family's health insurance; the employee would pay the balance by payroll deduction, typically an additional $2,000 or $3,000 a year.

The result is *everyone would have employer-provided health insurance* with the federal government acting in the role of the employer.

But the federal government would, at the same time, stop the tax givebacks it currently provides for employer-provided health care.

As mentioned, many Americans today are fortunate that their employers are buying health benefits for them. And those employees are getting the employers' contribution tax free. Employers get a tax deduction for their cost. Employees get the benefit of the employers' payments and don't pay taxes on the money their employers have paid for them.

Under Fair Care, the government would do for everyone what rich employers are now doing for their employees. The government would pay:

- $5,000 a year for a family.
- $2,000 a year for a single employee.

Cost: $376 billion a year (or $389 billion, if you make it $1,500 a year for children).

The Fair Care program can be paid for if the government stops giving tax givebacks. The tax giveback system now in place has a cost of $260.1 billion in 2008. Over the years that cost is projected by Fiscal Associates, Inc. to rise to:

$292.6 billion in 2009
$326.4 billion in 2010
$348.8 billion in 2011
$383.1 billion in 2012

The money is there. Let's just distribute it differently—more fairly.

Three Keys to Make Fair Care Work

The Fair Care refundable tax credit is money. To make it work, the money must be:

1. **Refundable.** This means that the recipient gets the money even if he or she doesn't owe income taxes.
2. **Advanceable.** The recipient doesn't have to wait until he or she files an annual income tax return before the money is paid out, so the money is there when the person buys insurance.
3. **Assignable.** The government actually pays the money directly to the insurance plan, guaranteeing that the funds will be used as intended. (In this way, health insurers will be more willing to cover applicants immediately.)

Why is Fair Care more fair than the current system?

1. It provides health insurance to everyone.
2. It empowers people to choose a health plan that's right for them.
3. It provides a step toward tax equity for all Americans.
4. It gives everyone the same tax break on health insurance.

Since this is a refundable tax credit that is equal for all Americans, the cost will grow only to cover population growth, which amounts to about 8/10th of 1 percent per year (0.008%). Americans will pay for Fair Care by using money that is currently available in the health care system.

As you can see, the current tax break is growing at a compound rate of 8 to 10 percent per year. We can give refundable Fair Care tax credits that will treat everyone equally at a cost that will be about the same as the current tax giveback system by 2011.

The only people who do not get a tax break today are those who buy their own health insurance, such as early retirees, the self-employed, restaurant employees, and temporary workers.

Today, 47 million people don't have health insurance. The pool of uninsured Americans is growing each year because small employers are dropping out of providing health insurance. In 2000, for example, 69 percent of employers provided health insurance to their employees; today 60 percent of employers provide health benefits.

We need to understand that the money American employers use to buy health care for their employees is *high-powered* money, because it buys these services for their employees with *pretax* dollars. If this same money went first to each employee, taxes would be taken out before the funds could be used to buy any insurance or medical services.

Today, the more highly paid Americans avoid paying out as much as 35 percent of their health care money in income tax. In addition, there's the additional 6.2 percent in Social Security tax that's paid by *both* the employer and the employee on the first $102,000 of income (in 2008). After earning $102,000, Americans pay a 1.45 percent Medicare tax, which also is paid by both employer and employee on all income.

The Social Security and Medicare taxes are called payroll taxes; combined, these taxes amount to 15.3 percent of the employee's salary, paid by both the employer and the employee.

Who do you believe benefits more from the current health insurance tax break? The highly paid and their employers, who escape paying income taxes and payroll taxes. Our government is already paying more than 35 percent of the cost of health insurance for our highest-paid workers. Isn't it only fair for the government to help pay part of the cost for our lower-income workers?

Under current law, Bill Gates and Peyton Manning and everyone else with access to employer-provided insurance are getting a tax break to help them pay for their health care—even if they don't need the money. If we're all helping to fund health benefits for multimillionaires and the wealthy, then we should help everyone get health care!

The current government-run system for assisting with the purchase of health insurance is highly discriminatory. "Discriminatory" is a nasty word, for America has done so much in attempting to end discrimination. Discrimination is immoral, but in most venues it is illegal as well. Not in the financing of health insurance, however. The discrimination that exists is legal, for it is brought about by the government. The government has created and maintains this discrimination.

If we stand back and look from a distance, we would conclude that the discrimination is biased for the upper-income taxpayers, whose employers provide them with health insurance.

It's time we helped those who have to purchase health insurance on their own: the self-employed, the unemployed, and those who work for companies that don't provide health benefits.

In a private conversation, one member of Congress, a prominent Republican member of the House Ways and Means Committee, was so vigorous in his words he was almost yelling: "Neither one of us needs a tax exemption for health insurance. We can afford to pay our own. We could take all that money that would be saved, put it in a large pile, then give a worthwhile benefit to the low-income workers who can't afford to pay their own."

Note that when we propose to give a refundable tax credit to every American, this means that those in the upper tax brackets will have a tax increase. Under Fair Care, Americans in the highest tax brackets would be treated equally. Today they are not treated equally; they're treated better, since the tax forgiveness they receive on the employer's contribution toward health benefits is generally greater than what they will receive from the refundable tax credit that would go to every American.

What we are proposing is exactly what the congressman was recommending, except that Fair Care is not proposing a new form of discrimination by denying the upper-income taxpayers the same refundable tax credit. Under Fair Care, everyone will be treated equally.

Congressional Action

For members of Congress, who would have to vote for this, they are voting on fairness.

It's a fairly simple issue for a vote in Congress. Does the member favor fairness for every American in health care coverage, yes or no?

For us, it's a fairly simple issue: Do we support an equal tax break for health insurance? Fair Care gives equal treatment for all.

Two Crucial Points on Fair Care

First, the program is doable because the money is there now. We're already spending money on the tax exemption for employer-paid health benefits. You could have a simple, not costly, exchange: no tax exemption on employer-provided benefits and instead a dollar grant to everyone.

Second, the program should appeal to the Democrats because it helps low-income voters while not being overly generous to those with higher incomes.

Fair Care Effect on Employers

Short answer: There is none.

Employers are now expensing (and deducting) what they pay for employees' health insurance. When employers give the employees the money instead, the expenditure is still tax exempt for employers.

Fair Care Effect on Employees

Giving employees money that they can spend on health insurance will doubtless have a major impact on employee behavior: It will impact their self-interest. Today employees don't have any choices except to take what is given—or not—by the employer. With Fair Care, employees can purchase the health insurance they choose.

It's reasonable to expect that insurance companies will object to the Fair Care alternative because they will not be able to make one sale to cover all of a company's employees.

We should end this debate on health care coverage by giving Fair Care to all Americans now ($5,500 for a family) and not wait until 2012.

The State of the Union Proposal

In his 2007 State of the Union speech, President George W. Bush proposed "a standard tax deduction for health insurance that will be like the standard tax deduction for dependents. Families with health insurance will pay no income or payroll taxes on $15,000 of their income.

Single Americans with health insurance will pay no income or payroll taxes on $7,500 of their income."

The principal deficiency in Bush's proposal is that it's not *money*. The tax giveback is attractive, but if your income is low and you don't have up-front money to buy health insurance, you still may not be able to get coverage. It might be a good deal for some workers but no help for another family because it doesn't have the money to make the purchase.

The president's proposal offers a nice tax reduction, but it fails to help the low-income people who do not have money to purchase health insurance up front.

We should give them money they can use to purchase health insurance. If a family receives $5,500 cash to purchase health insurance, most of its costs would be covered. In the typical employer-provided plan, employees pay a portion of the cost through payroll deductions. The same would be true under Fair Care if employees got a cash grant of $5,500 for the purchase of health insurance.

Two classes of people don't have health insurance:

1. Those who can't afford health insurance.
2. Those who choose to use their money on something else.

As far as the second group is concerned, it's a reality that people want to get what is theirs. Some will buy just to get their government benefit. Under Bush's proposal, the better-off would buy health insurance just to get the government deduction.

The president's proposal probably won't do a lot to help the uninsured who can't afford health coverage. If we see the government's role as to help those who are financially unable to purchase insurance, the president's proposal doesn't do enough.

You could buy a $7,000-a-year family health plan and get a $15,000 tax exemption. A lot of people will think that's pretty nice. It's giving money away—giving to the upper class. Is that what we think the government should be doing?

The president has signaled that he would alternatively support "a flat tax credit," which Fair Care would be (a refundable tax credit).

CHAPTER

Give Seniors What They Want (and Save Money Doing It)

AN INNOVATIVE APPROACH TO MEDICARE

Before looking at Medicare and alternatives that will make the program better and less costly, we need to know what the overall cost per person currently is.

The average per capita cost for the 43.2 million people covered by Medicare in 2006 was $10,221. That's the average amount the government pays with our tax dollars and the Part B premiums (the benefit that pays for doctor visits and laboratory tests) it collects from seniors.

But that's not all.

In 2007, under Part A of Medicare (the hospitalization benefit), there was a hospital deductible of $992 for seniors entering the hospital, which rose to $1,024 in 2008. Under Part B of Medicare, seniors pay the first $135 in 2008 of doctor and outpatient charges, then 20 percent of charges after that with no limit. Part B is voluntary. If you're not enrolled in Part B, you pay all the doctor charges. Seniors are so intimidated by the potential costs of doctors that virtually all pay the extra premium of $96.40 a month in 2008 to obtain Part B coverage. Because of their fear of deductibles and copayments, almost 90 percent of seniors also voluntarily buy Medicare supplement insurance, commonly called Medigap.

To illustrate the cost for you, let's look at the situation in Champaign, Illinois, the middle of America and home to a major state university, the University of Illinois. Using the AARP (American Association of Retired Persons) Medicare supplemental insurance Plan F (the most popular plan) for a person age 74, the median age for seniors, the cost was $2,442 per year in 2008, with a monthly premium of $203.50.

Let's return to the cost. If the senior bought Plan F, the supplement will pay all of the deductibles and copayments—meaning the senior pays nothing for hospital or doctor care. (See Figure 6.1.) This increases the senior's propensity to consume.

Part D of Medicare: Prescription Drugs for Seniors

The Medicare prescription drug coverage is called Part D. The average premium seniors will pay in 2008 is $25 a month. In spite of this giant $10,221 expenditure for every person on Medicare, the senior might still be out of pocket a considerable amount for prescription cost, as Part D by no means provides full coverage. Also remember that the costs just described are not for a husband and wife but *per person*—for every person on Medicare, all 43 million.

When you look at that cost of almost $13,000 (including the Medicare Supplemental policy) each year per person for health care, it's hard to remain calm. It is difficult to imagine that we are paying that much for Medicare. Worse, the cost per person will grow every year as the cost of medical care continues to grow.

Now let's look at alternatives.

$10,221	Treasury per capita cost, which includes the government expenditure of the senior's $96.40 premium in 2008
+ $2,442	Senior pays for supplemental coverage
$12,663	**Total money paid out by the Treasury and the senior for Part A and B coverage**

Figure 6.1   Supplement F Summary So Far

The Future of Medicare

The number enrolled in Medicare will start to skyrocket within the next five years, as baby boomers begin to hit age 65. Today Medicare costs America more than a third of a trillion dollars (about a billion dollars a day) every year. Medicare will cost far more tomorrow, as the program faces far more than just a population shift.

- The people now knocking on Medicare's door aren't your grandparents' Medicare recipients. This incoming group is in tune with its health, insatiable in its consumption, discriminating in its taste, and demanding of its doctors. Just as Medicare consumption has spiked in parts of Florida (as we saw in Chapter 4), so it will rise all over the nation.
- Newer medical technologies are helping people live longer lives. That's good. But this results in seniors needing coverage for longer periods of time. That's costly.
- Newer medical technologies come with added cost.
- For the first time in the program's history, in 2005, Medicare Part A payroll taxes brought in less money than the program paid out in benefits. This shortfall is expected to continue.
- The new prescription drug benefit (Medicare Part D) alone is projected to cost the program above $700 billion over the first 10 years.[1]

With the passage of the Medicare Part D prescription drug legislation at the end of 2003, Congress enabled tax-free health savings accounts (HSAs) for all Americans for the first time. An HSA is simply a savings account used in conjunction with a moderate- to high-deductible health insurance policy that allows people to save money tax-free against current and future medical expenses.

We'll explore the advantages of HSAs for everyone in Chapter 7, but first we'll look at what HSAs can do for America's seniors.

Defining the Terms

For the purposes of this chapter, we will refer to HSAs for seniors as MSAs (medical savings accounts). Here's why: These accounts were called medical savings accounts when they were introduced in 1993, but in the process of creating accounts for everyone in 2003,

Congress used the term "health savings accounts" in reference to all users who are not under Medicare; it retained the name "medical savings accounts" in regard to all users who are under Medicare. So for the purpose of this chapter, we will follow the government's lead and refer to HSAs for seniors as medical savings accounts, or MSAs.

Before we discuss MSAs any further, let's briefly examine Medicare's prescription drug benefit, Medicare Part D.

Drug Money

Why did Congress approve a new Medicare prescription drug benefit?

America's seniors needed help.

Ed McClain, a senior advocate who has worked with seniors for 30 years, said that as he traveled extensively talking to seniors prior to the establishment of this benefit, the seniors' number one concern was how to pay for their prescription drugs.

Why?

Medicare has a number of gaps in its coverage for seniors who don't have supplemental coverage; and one major gap before Medicare Part D was instituted was its lack of coverage for prescription drugs. Seniors who didn't have drug coverage through an employer, through Medicaid, or through a supplemental private insurance policy (Medigap policies) were liable for thousands of dollars in out-of-pocket expenses. Congress had to do something—it couldn't just tell 14 percent of voters to bug off.

Unfortunately, the benefit they came up with is not a very good one. Some insurance companies looked at it and decided they couldn't sell it. Here's why: For the Medicare Part D standard benefit, in 2008, a person would have to pay:

- A $275 deductible.
- An average Part D premium of $25 per month.
- 25 percent of drug costs from $275 to $2,510.
- 100 percent of drug costs from $2,510 to $5,726.25 (called the doughnut hole).
- 5 percent of drug costs above $5,726.25.

Here's how those numbers break down in the real world: Let's assume the person spends $2,000 for prescriptions for the year, which is a typical per year expenditure by seniors on prescription drugs. How much would she have to pay out of her own pocket?

She pays the first $275. Then she pays 25 percent of the next $1,725, or $431.25. So with $2,000 in drug costs for the year, the woman picks up $706.25 of the total and Medicare picks up $1,293.75.

But we haven't yet added the cost of the monthly premiums, which she must also pay out of pocket. At an estimated $25 per month in 2008, the total would be $300 for the year, so we'll need to add that to the $706.25 she's paying.

The result?

For $2,000 in annual drug costs, she will pay out $1,006.25.

In other words, she's paying about half of the cost of her drugs out of her own pocket! That's not a very good benefit.

An Unfunded Mandate

While Congress's new drug benefit was a compassionate response to low income seniors with high prescription drug costs, it doesn't fully solve the problem for many seniors. And it leaves a huge question unanswered: Where is the government going to get all the money it needs to pay its share for these drugs?

Most people love the idea of helping millions of seniors get affordable drug coverage. But, in fact, the government has another tool at its disposal that can do the job better. And it's a tool the taxpayers can afford: the MSAs that Congress created along *with* the prescription drug benefit.

A Bureaucratic Snafu

A number of members of Congress have said that they voted for the new prescription drug benefit only because of the HSAs the legislation enabled for people under age 65.

The Centers for Medicare and Medicaid Services (CMS), the government agency that runs Medicare, decided that Medicare reimbursements for MSAs should be "risk adjusted" according to the health of the senior. The result of such risk adjustment is that healthy seniors would get a lot less money from Medicare and seniors with heart trouble and diabetes would get a lot more money.

The risk adjustment imposed by Medicare on MSAs for seniors has proved to be a deal-breaker for many insurance companies that would like to offer MSAs to seniors. Only a very small handful of insurance companies have been willing to offer MSAs to seniors.

It's not that the companies don't want to. Rather, they just cannot risk their companies' solvency on the risk adjustment that CMS insists on imposing. Even though this practice is *forbidden* within the private sector of the health insurance industry, CMS—an executive agency of the U.S. government—has insisted on it. Interestingly, when a private insurance company attempted this same tactic, regulators declared it illegal.

Thus, even though Congress has directed CMS to give seniors MSAs, this government agency has, for whatever reason, unilaterally opted to thwart the will of the people by imposing unrealistic conditions on the congressional directive. These unrealistic directives were not in the law passed by Congress. This bureaucratic obstructionism is costing America many billions of dollars every year.

Cost Comparison

You cannot help but get angry when you consider how much this obstinacy is costing each Medicare recipient.

Understand that CMS budgets a fixed amount of Medicare funding for every county in the United States. That amount is then adjusted for the age and sex of each senior (or disabled person) who receives Medicare benefits, for the person's institutional status (such as nursing home residency, if applicable), and for any Medicaid benefits received.

Let's consider a typical example.

Medicare pays benefits based on what county a senior lives in. For example, if a senior lives in New York City, the benefit dollars available are much higher than if the senior lives in Boise, Idaho.

We could choose an example from any area of the country, but for this purpose, we'll look at Champaign, Illinois, due to its location (and because it's consistent with our prior cost example). Let's use the age bracket of 70 to 74, because the median age for seniors is about 74. The age bracket applies to all in that age group, whether 71 or 74. For a woman in the age group not on Medicaid, Medicare budgets $6,473.64 annually.

Let's use her as an example.

According to Congress, the woman should be able to choose a moderate- to high-deductible insurance plan that she wants for her MSA, and Medicare would pay for that plan for her. Let's assume that she chooses a major medical plan that will pay 100 percent of any hospital, doctor, and drug costs over $3,000. Her estimated cost would be $3,688.56, leaving $2,785.08 in Medicare's coffers that has not been spent for this woman. That remaining money would be retained in her MSA, which is her account in a bank of her choice. She has access to those tax-free funds for her health care needs and to meet her $3,000 deductible. Medicare would deposit these funds at the beginning of the year in a bank account of her choice.

Thus, starting with her Medicare allotment of $6,473.64, she buys the $3,000 deductible major medical policy and has $2,785.08 that can go into her MSA.

As mentioned, most seniors also have a Medigap supplemental insurance plan. The most popular plan with seniors is AARP Plan F, which costs $2,442 in 2008 in Champaign County. Since the woman's MSA has no gaps in coverage, she no longer needs supplemental insurance. So on top of Medicare's contribution of $2,785.08 to her savings account, she could add the $2,442 she no longer needs to pay out to a private insurer.

On average, the Medicare Part D prescription drug coverage is costing seniors about $25 a month in 2008. This woman will not need to pay this monthly premium because her drugs will be paid for out of the funds in her MSA. That's another $300 for the year that she won't have to pay out.

Figure 6.2 shows how much money this woman would have available in her MSA each year.

$2,785.08	Provided by Medicare after purchase of a $3,000 deductible policy
+ $2,442.00	No longer spent on supplemental insurance
+ $300.00	Not spent for Medicare Part D drug coverage
$5,527.08	**Money she could put in her MSA each year**

Figure 6.2 $5,527 Available Each Year in a Senior's MSA

Medicare Payment	$6,473.64	($539.47 monthly)
Cost of $3,000 deductible insurance	− $3,688.56	($307.38 monthly)
Medicare Savings Account (MSA)	= $2,785.08	(A) remainder after insurance cost
Medigap Premium Saving	+ $2,442.00	(B) in 2008
Saving on Prescription Coverage Part D Premium Savings	+ $300.00	(C)
Money in Senior's Hands	= **$5,527.08**	**(A) + (B) + (C)**

Full coverage for prescriptions—brand or generic

Figure 6.3   Medicare Savings Accounts (Women)

Medicare Payment	$7,531.00	($627.58 monthly)
Cost of $3,000 deductible insurance	− $5,269.11	($439.09 monthly)
Medicare Savings Account (MSA)	= $2,261.89	(A) remainder after insurance cost
Medigap Premium Saving	+ $2,442.00	(B) in 2008
Saving on Prescription Coverage Part D Premium Savings	+ $300.00	(C)
Money in Senior's Hands	= **$5,003.89**	**(A) + (B) + (C)**

Full coverage for prescriptions—brand or generic

Figure 6.4   Medicare Savings Accounts (Men)

Remember, this woman has bought major medical insurance that provides full coverage beyond her $3,000 deductible, so once she spends $3,000 in medical expenses, she doesn't have to spend *any more* out of pocket. She can roll that excess money into the next year, growing her savings that much more. And, remember, the amount the government deposits into her savings account is *tax free*. The money she's currently spending for supplemental insurance and for prescriptions under Medicare Part D is *after-tax* money.

The numbers for men are somewhat different, but the bottom line is pretty close to the same. Where the woman 70 to 74 would have $5,527.08 in cash to fund savings, a man of the same age in the same county would have $5,003.89. (See Figures 6.3 and 6.4.)

Saving the U.S. Treasury Money

Another aspect to this savings is vastly important to the U.S. Treasury.

When a senior pays $25 a month for the prescription drug coverage under Medicare Part D, the estimated expenditure by the Treasury is $75 per month, or $900 annually. That's because the senior's premium only covers about 25 percent of the benefit's cost.

The many members of Congress who had misgivings about the cost of the prescription benefit plan should recognize the immense savings opportunity for the Treasury once seniors are finally able to get MSAs. In our illustration, the money used to fund the major medical insurance and the money contributed to the MSA come from Medicare Part A and Part B. *Not one dollar* had to be spent from the Medicare Part D prescription benefit.

The bottom line?

If CMS would let each senior allocate his or her Medicare funds to the senior's best advantage using an MSA (as Congress intended for them to be able to do), seniors could have:

- Full major medical coverage.
- Full funding of their MSA.
- No extra prescription drug costs.
- More than $2,000 a year left over!

Remember, these are *yearly* numbers. They will repeat next year and again *every* year after.

There are immense demands on Congress to fund very expensive programs. One such demand was the billions of dollars spent for victims of Hurricane Katrina. But there was no money built into the budget for that, so the cost is added to the deficit.

A lot of members of Congress are very concerned about this ongoing deficit. If CMS would modify its rules so that the seniors could have an MSA alternative, there would be great savings for the Treasury—and a lot of highly satisfied seniors.

There is widespread concern about the "doughnut hole" under Medicare Part D; the term refers to the fact that once seniors' drug costs reach $2,510 in 2008, they must pay all drug costs up to $5,726.25, after which the government takes over. (The gap between $2,510 and $5,726.25 is referred to as the doughnut hole). There would be *no doughnut hole* with the MSA option. Our premium price estimate for a $3,000 deductible MSA covers all prescription drugs above the $3,000 deductible.

Remember that what we've just delineated allows *full coverage* for prescriptions: The first $3,000 would be paid out of the savings account, and after that, the major medical insurance would pay 100 percent.

How Much Could Our Country Save?

The MSA alternative would be so rich in funding that it would be possible for the government to cut back the total funding for Medicare by, say, 5 percent per senior per year. It wouldn't hurt anybody, and it would be a giant additional saving for the Treasury. Five percent of the female allowance of $6,473.63 in this county is an additional $323.68 per person per year that would be saved.

Here's one more savings to consider: the senior's annual health care costs to Medicare. (See Figure 6.5.)

This is the amount of money our country could save *every year* by allowing MSAs under Medicare, assuming half of the seniors enroll for MSAs instead of plain old Medicare.

21,000,000 people	(If half the people currently enrolled in Medicare opted for an MSA)
x $511	(5% of the Treasury's per capita cost, $10,221— see first page of this chapter)
$10.7 Billion	**Annual Savings for the Treasury**

Figure 6.5   Example: Treasury Savings

Give Seniors What They Want

We've done focus group studies with seniors and have found that they would love to have the option of MSAs. This is not surprising, given the amount of money seniors are spending per person under Medicare.

Do you realize how much of a deductible Medicare recipients have to pay out of pocket when they go into the hospital? Apparently many seniors do, because 89 percent of them carry a supplemental insurance policy. In other words, most seniors are paying another $2,000 a year to supplement the $6,000 per year the government is spending. Plus they're paying an additional $300 a year to get prescription coverage.

Which would you prefer: insurance in which you had deductibles and copayments, or money in a savings account that fully covers your deductible until the insurance clicks in to pay the rest?

Too Good to Be True?

Does this look too good to be true? Perhaps, but the numbers are compelling. The reality is that Medicare could take *10 percent* off the money it allocates to seniors rather than 5 percent—and it would *still* be a wonderfully advantaged choice for seniors. So what's the problem?

In addition to CMS's obstinacy, giant financial interests want to protect the money that's coming to them now. The companies (including AARP) that are selling Medigap insurance have a big stake in the way it is being done today. We believe, however, that the best interests of the people and the financial welfare of the country should prevail.

The Bush administration has been in love with a competitive market. Here's how a competitive market would work well for seniors and also work very well for the U.S. Treasury: It would save enough money to pay for a lot of other things that the federal government would like to fund. U.S. Senator James Inhofe (R-OK) and U.S. Senator Jim DeMint (R-SC) introduced the Medicare Health Savings Accounts Act of 2007 as legislation. Its bill number is S.173. (S.173 is reproduced in this book as Appendix E.)

Medical savings accounts for seniors would reduce the total cost of Medicare to the U.S. government of Parts A and B by 5 or 10 percent, eliminate the Treasury's Part D costs, and make seniors happier. (See Figure 6.6.)

How Much Money in Each Senior's Hands?

With Medicare MSAs, money would go into seniors' hands every year from these sources:

- Medicare money going as a deposit to the senior's MSA that can be spent on any dental, vision, or health care needs (prescription

About:	$25.00 Premium per Month $275.00 Annual Deductible
	$275.00–$2,510.00 — Senior pays 25% $2,510.00–$5,726.25 — Senior pays 100% Above $5,726.25 — Senior pays 5%

Example: $2,000 in Prescriptions in 2008	
$275.00	You pay the first $275.00
$431.25	You pay 25% of remaining $1,725.00 (Medicare pays remaining 75%)

Totals:	
$1,293.75	Medicare Pays
$706.25	You pay out of pocket
+$300.00	You pay Part D premium
$1,006.25	Your combined cost

If you spend $3,000 for prescriptions instead of $2,000, you will pay more out of your pocket, because you are in the doughnut hole.

You will be spending $1,623.75 (including your $300 premium) to get coverage of $3,000 of medicines.

Figure 6.6   2008 Standard Medicare Prescription Benefit—Part D

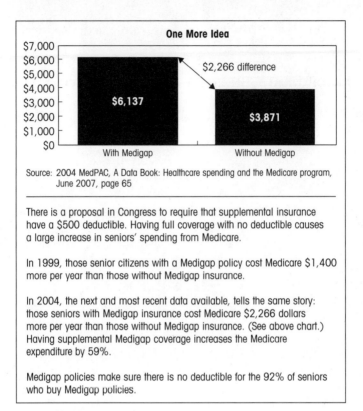

One More Idea

$2,266 difference

$6,137

$3,871

With Medigap   Without Medigap

Source: 2004 MedPAC, A Data Book: Healthcare spending and the Medicare program, June 2007, page 65

There is a proposal in Congress to require that supplemental insurance have a $500 deductible. Having full coverage with no deductible causes a large increase in seniors' spending from Medicare.

In 1999, those senior citizens with a Medigap policy cost Medicare $1,400 more per year than those without Medigap insurance.

In 2004, the next and most recent data available, tells the same story: those seniors with Medigap insurance cost Medicare $2,266 dollars more per year than those without Medigap insurance. (See above chart.) Having supplemental Medigap coverage increases the Medicare expenditure by 59%.

Medigap policies make sure there is no deductible for the 92% of seniors who buy Medigap policies.

Figure 6.7   What Seniors Pay

drugs or doctor visits or laboratory work or tests) to meet their deductible.

- Savings on money currently spent on Medigap insurance premiums.
- Savings on money currently spent on Part D premiums.

These amounts would vary depending on the senior's age and location. Figure 6.7 shows Medicare methodologies and payment rates.

CHAPTER 7

Give Control to Consumers through HSAs

More individuals are buying into health savings accounts (HSAs), and more American companies are offering them to employees. Although as of the time of this writing, nearly half of all HSA buyers have been individuals, companies like Microsoft, IBM, Wendy's, and Wal-Mart are jumping on the HSA bandwagon.

Many seem to think these accounts can single-handedly save the American health care system. That is likely not the case, even though they can help America's health care consumers enormously.

Back to the Future

In 1992 in Washington, D.C., J. Patrick Rooney attended a speech on the power of compound interest, in which health care was mentioned in passing. Rooney thought of Einstein's quote that "The most powerful force in the universe is compound interest," and how it could be harnessed to make health care more affordable for American workers and companies.

If companies deposited this money into dedicated savings accounts owned by the employees, it wouldn't take long for most employees to build an impressive medical nest egg. Unspent money would roll over from year to year, accumulating interest as time went by. (Big medical costs during any given year would still be covered by the major medical insurance.)

This way, the employees—and not the employer's insurance company—would be the ones to benefit from the power of compound interest.

And benefit they would.

Through the magic of compound interest, employees who put $100 in a savings account drawing interest at a rate of 5 percent compounded annually would double the money in 15 years.

When Patrick Rooney attended the speech, Golden Rule was the nation's largest insurer for the individual market. Years earlier, it had offered the first health insurance plan with a $25 deductible. This tiny deductible reduced claim costs enough for the company to avoid a rate increase at the time.

Why?

Because when people had to spend some of their own money on health care, they spent it more carefully.

One Experience

Though the Washington, D.C., speaker had not developed his theory, its underlying premise was sound. A product that could deliver on the promise could be developed. While the professor's focus was directed to the compound interest, one couldn't help but see also the overall savings. Pat Rooney saw the potential savings to the public.

Within a few months, the world's first "medical care savings account" was developed. As conceived, it would add the power of *tax-free* spending to the power of compound interest. Shortly after the term was coined, Pat Rooney shortened it to "medical savings account," or MSA, a name that has stuck.

It took a few years to convince Congress to offer the tax benefits. But even without those tax benefits, beginning in 1993, employees of Golden Rule Insurance Company were offered MSAs. Employees had the choice of having these MSAs in lieu of standard insurance coverage. On the employee's behalf, the company offered to contribute annually $2,000 to each family policy (which carried a family deductible of $3,000) and $1,000 to each individual policy (which carried a deductible of $2,000).

With the company contributing these amounts to the employees' accounts, at the end of the year, the *most* any individual or family would have to pay out of pocket would be $1,000.

Employees liked knowing ahead of time how much they might have to pay out of pocket. Having such a firm cap on their expenses gave them confidence and peace of mind. They saw the company's contribution as "money I *can* spend for medical care, but if I *don't* spend it, that money is mine."

They liked that.

The first year, 83 percent of the employees elected to participate. By 1995, it was over 90 percent.

Did the plan work?

Even without the tax benefits, each family received an average annual refund of *$1,165.18*. Each individual received an average annual refund of *$658.11*. Just *10 percent* of the employees incurred expenses that exceeded their savings and needed to be covered by the major medical policy that covered them 100 percent.

So even *without* the tax benefits, the other 90 percent had unspent money left over.

These employees' medical needs were taken care of, and nine out of ten had extra money at year-end. At that time, employees could take any money left over once the year was over.

HSAs Today

What was named an MSA in 1993 was eventually enacted into law as an Archer Medical Savings Account, named after Representative Bill Archer (R-TX) who was then chairman of the House Ways and Means Committee. Today these accounts are called HSAs.

In the final days of 2003, President George Bush signed the federal legislation making HSAs tax free and available to all Americans with a qualified insurance plan (insurance to cover the big bills). By the end of 2007, more than 4.5 million citizens had tax-free HSAs, and the U.S. Treasury has predicted that 25 million Americans will have them by 2010.[1] Many American families with an HSA are now paying less each year for their health insurance premium, compared to a low-deductible, high-premium plan. (See Figure 7.1, which compares these two types of insurance.)

A Quick Overview

Anyone can set up an HSA once he or she buys qualified major medical health insurance (comprehensive insurance that covers hospital, doctor, and prescription drug costs). Sometimes you can buy the two products (the savings account and the major medical insurance) together from one company.

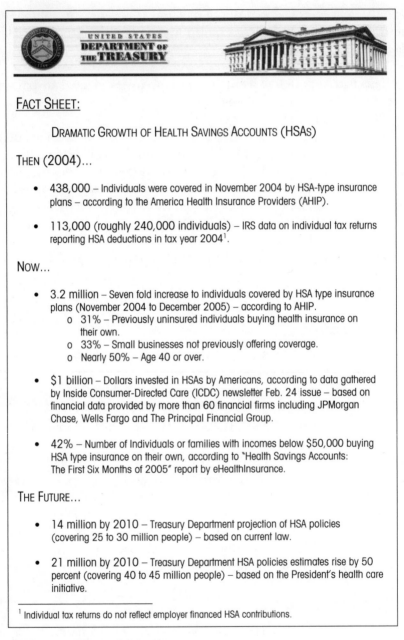

FACT SHEET:

DRAMATIC GROWTH OF HEALTH SAVINGS ACCOUNTS (HSAs)

THEN (2004)...

- 438,000 – Individuals were covered in November 2004 by HSA-type insurance plans – according to the America Health Insurance Providers (AHIP).

- 113,000 (roughly 240,000 individuals) – IRS data on individual tax returns reporting HSA deductions in tax year 2004[1].

NOW...

- 3.2 million – Seven fold increase to individuals covered by HSA type insurance plans (November 2004 to December 2005) – according to AHIP.
  - o 31% – Previously uninsured individuals buying health insurance on their own.
  - o 33% – Small businesses not previously offering coverage.
  - o Nearly 50% – Age 40 or over.

- $1 billion – Dollars invested in HSAs by Americans, according to data gathered by Inside Consumer-Directed Care (ICDC) newsletter Feb. 24 issue – based on financial data provided by more than 60 financial firms including JPMorgan Chase, Wells Fargo and The Principal Financial Group.

- 42% – Number of Individuals or families with incomes below $50,000 buying HSA type insurance on their own, according to "Health Savings Accounts: The First Six Months of 2005" report by eHealthInsurance.

THE FUTURE...

- 14 million by 2010 – Treasury Department projection of HSA policies (covering 25 to 30 million people) – based on current law.

- 21 million by 2010 – Treasury Department HSA policies estimates rise by 50 percent (covering 40 to 45 million people) – based on the President's health care initiative.

---

[1] Individual tax returns do not reflect employer financed HSA contributions.

Figure 7.1   HSA Fact Sheet

The purpose of the insurance is to protect you against big medical expenses, such as hospital stays, and to give you the peace of mind of limiting your total out-of-pocket medical costs. If during any given year your medical expenses rise to the level of your annual insurance deductible, the insurance kicks in to cover costs from that point forward.

Because the monthly premiums for these major medical policies can cost half what standard coverage costs, you can bank the monthly savings in your HSA to feather your medical nest egg.

Whatever the amount of your insurance deductible is, that's how much tax-deductible money you can put in the account each year, up to $2,850 for individuals and $5,650 for families. The smallest deductible is now $1,100 for an individual and $2,200 for a family. These are the 2008 numbers; the numbers change every year. If you were born before 1953, you can also make a $900 annual tax-free "catch-up" deposit to your HSA.

Health Care Freedom

An HSA offers consumers freedom they may be unaccustomed to. The money in an HSA can be used to pay any qualified health care bills below the insurance policy's deductible.

This may include expenses that insurance typically would not cover—expenses like contact lenses, over-the-counter medicines, or braces for your children. People can use these tax-free HSA funds to pay for a host of health care services, such as:

- Doctor visits
- Dental care (braces, or crowns, for example)
- Chiropractic care
- Vision care (including eyeglasses, contact lenses, and LASIK surgery)
- Auditory care (including hearing aids)
- Acupuncture treatments
- Prescription drugs and over-the-counter medications
- Diagnostic care (including X-rays and other imaging)
- Transportation to and from medical providers
- Medically supervised weight-loss programs
- Smoking cessation programs
- Long-term care costs (including long-term care insurance)

Most of us rack up a few medical bills during some years and more bills during others. During those years when health care spending is low, the money stays in the HSA accumulating tax-free interest—for when you might need it later.

This is *your* money—it doesn't belong to your insurance company or to your employer. You can spend it how you want, and it doesn't matter if you change jobs or move to another state. Your money goes with you. The money in the savings account may be used tax free for medical expenses. If withdrawn for other purposes before the age of 65, there is a 10 percent penalty on the money spent, and you must pay income tax on that amount as well.

With an HSA, you have no gatekeepers to contend with. No one is going to tell you what you can or cannot do with your money or which doctor you can or cannot see. With an HSA, you have the freedom to choose the care you want, free from any third party's predetermined network or parsimonious judgments.

"HSAs are a significant departure from the last four decades of health reform, which have been dominated by paternalist programs like Medicare, Medicaid, and managed care," says Dr. David Gratzer, a physician, writer, and Senior Fellow at the Manhattan Institute's Center for Medical Progress. Why? Because "HSAs seek to give Americans more control of their own health care."[2]

A Dollar-for-Dollar Comparison

Reason magazine editor Ronald Bailey has observed that HSAs "typically cost 20 percent to 60 percent less than conventional health insurance policies."[3]

But dollar for dollar, would *your* money be better spent in an HSA?

While every situation is unique, we can certainly compare averages. Using 2007 numbers, Figure 7.2 shows the savings that HSAs offer. For the purpose of this illustration, the average customer is in the 45- to 49-year age group and has no out-of-pocket costs beyond the fully funded deductible.

The Best Interest of the Consumer

In 2007, a traditional family health insurance premium costs (not counting additional co-pays or deductibles or co-insurance to the consumer) $12,106 dollars a year.[4] A family HSA-qualified health insurance plan costs (with cost variations in New York City versus Twin Falls, Idaho) $7,000 a year. (See Figure 7.2.)

Standard Family Insurance

$1,008.83	Average monthly premium in 2007

$12,106.00	**Total annual cost in 2007** **(according to the Kaiser Foundation)**

HSA Family Insurance ($3,500 Deductible)

$583.00	Average monthly premium

$6,996.00	Annual premium
+$3,500.00	Cost of fully funding the HSA

$10,496.00	**Total annual cost** **(premium plus funded HSA)**

Annual Difference

$12,106.00	Total annual cost of insurance plan
−$10,496.00	Total annual cost of HSA plan

$1,610.00	**Annual Savings with HSA Plan**

Figure 7.2   Standard Family Insurance

If you were a top executive in a large insurance company, which plan would you like to sell, the insurance that pays your company $12,000 a year, or the insurance plan that pays your company $7,000 a year?

How willing would you be as that executive to change your customer base to a $7,000 a year plan, from a $12,000 a year plan, and lose $5,000 a year in revenue per customer? Our guess is that the insurance executive is not so excited about losing $5,000 per customer per year. What is surprising is that an executive would actually admit this to a reporter.[5]

Wellpoint's chief of sales (Wellpoint is the largest of all the Blue Cross insurers) explains to *Forbes* magazine that their HSA-qualified health plan will not be marketed to large corporations like Bank of America or Kroger grocery stores because "such a move would hurt profit margins"—by obviously cutting insurance costs for employers and others.

Furthermore, because of the lower annual rate of increase in HSA premiums vs. traditional high-premium health plans, the revenue of large insurers takes another hit.

In the same *Forbes* article, Wellpoint's finance chief explains Wellpoint has a financial interest in higher health insurance costs: "Wellpoint's earnings would suffer if the upward march of health care costs (and the corresponding insurance premiums) collapsed from its 8% annual rate to the 2.5% inflation rate."

Since insurers make a percentage profit on their premiums, the higher the premiums, the higher their profits. Therefore, insurers have been complicit in letting hospitals ramp up prices radically, since their own profits increase when they have to charge higher premiums to cover higher hospital prices—giving the insurers higher profits.

These are two more reasons HSA-qualified health plans are in the best interest of the consumer, but not necessarily in the interest of insurers who have a traditional, high-premium health insurance base of business.

Ninety percent of enrollees will have a considerable portion of the $3,500 HSA deposit left unspent at year-end. (See Figure 7.2.)

These figures show that an HSA can help a family reduce its annual health care spending. And that's not even factoring in copays for doctor visits, costs for over-the-counter medicines, or costs for dental or vision care—all of which would be covered with tax-exempt HSA funds, but not by a standard insurance policy.

An IRA on Steroids

As John Goodman, head of the National Center for Policy Analysis, has said, HSAs are like "an IRA on steroids."[6] An HSA is an IRA on steroids, and more, for in addition to being a cost-effective way to pay for health care, it's a powerful tool for long-term investment. *Forbes* magazine has labeled the HSA a "super IRA."[7]

No other investment tool has so many tax advantages. The *New York Times* says that an HSA "gives you tax advantages every which way—you put in pretax dollars, it compounds free of taxes, and the accumulation is tax-free when you take it out to pay for medical expenses."[8]

Once you reach the age of 65, you can use your HSA funds for anything you want. You will need to pay normal income tax on the money you pull out for nonmedical expenses, but there is no withdrawal penalty at that point for using the funds for retirement, for remodeling, for travel, or for whatever else you may want to do.

Should you die with funds still in your HSA, the account transfers to your spouse or your surviving children, just like an IRA or any other retirement account.

HSAs give you flexibility. You can spend your HSA funds on your health care needs as they arise, or if you have the means and want to take maximum advantage of the savings opportunity, you can pay for health care services with other funds and rack up the HSA savings for later in life.

Here is Pat Rooney's personal example of saving money on laboratory work. My physician wanted some lab tests and I cooperated. His staff drew blood at his office and the lab sent the doctor the results. Then I got the bill for the lab work, over $900. The next time he wanted lab work, I said, "No, I'll go to my own laboratory and the results can be sent to you by fax." My cost then was a little over $200 for essentially the same lab work. My motivation was, "It's my money paying for the lab work."

The Truth Be Told

These savings incentives have led some to criticize HSAs as nothing more than a tax shelter for the privileged, saying that only the wealthy will benefit from HSAs.

THE TRUTH: HSAs were created to help ease the burden of expensive medical care for all Americans. Like Robin Hood, who stole from the rich and gave to the poor, HSAs steal wealth from the insurance companies and give it back to the people who deserve to keep it.

Some believe only the young will benefit from HSAs.

THE TRUTH: Younger people are usually healthier, so they will benefit from HSAs. And the earlier they start compounding interest, the more money they will have in the end. (The average age of enrollees in the individual insurance market is 46.5, which means, of course, that many are older than that.)

Some fear that people will ignore routine medical needs in order to save money.

THE TRUTH: This defies common sense. Families that love each other take care of each other, regardless of the cost. Relationships mean more to people than money. If there is a true medical need in a family, the money will be spent. However, people will become more conscientious with their health care. They will look for the best prices. Likely, they will not go to the doctor to get an antibiotic for every little sniffle.

The case can be made that people insured with HSAs will seek more preventive medicine in the form of annual checkups since these expenses are covered. If you are healthy—and you ensure that you stay healthy by getting annual checkups—you will save more money. Studies show that people with chronic conditions do a better job of managing their treatment and are more compliant in their care.

Our experience is that those who don't get health care don't get it for one reason: They truly can't afford it. And these people are currently uninsured.

And finally, some are afraid that only the *healthy* will benefit from HSAs.

THE TRUTH: The healthy are the ones who are overpaying the most for standard insurance, and we should expect them to flock to HSAs. They will be able to maximize their savings. But these accounts are also ideal for those at the other end of the spectrum who are suffering from chronic ailments. Once a chronically ill person hits the deductible amount of an HSA, his or her out-of-pocket expenses end. With traditional insurance, however, frequent copayments continue to mount even beyond the deductible. Usually, the co-payments do not count toward the deductible; and recently, there are a growing number of health plans on the market that have no upward limit or cap on the co-insurance. So if a plan pays a benefit of 80 percent and you pay 20 percent, you pay 20 percent of the big bill. Every HSA insurance policy has a maximum out-of-pocket amount that the insured pays, and no more than that. The insurance pays for everything else.

Evidence shows that *73 percent of Americans spend less than $500 per year on medical expenses*. There is no need for so many people to be throwing their money away on standard insurance. But neither should the sick, who really need the insurance, be forced to pay out-of-pocket co-pays *ad infinitum*.

Here's why HSAs are so appealing to people in poor health.

For an individual, the minimum insurance deductible allowable under the HSA law is $1,100; for a family, it's $2,200. So an individual or a family can have an HSA accompanied by insurance with these modest deductibles and contribute up to that amount to their HSA.

People who move to a $1,100 deductible from a full-coverage plan will save enough on the premium cost to have money to put the $1,100 in their savings account (if they are dealing with a fair insurer).

Now, this doesn't work dollar for dollar on the higher deductible plans, but on these deductibles people will save enough money on the cost of health insurance that they will have cash that they could put into their HSAs.

So where do you get the cash to fund your HSA? From the money you were previously spending on your health benefits! If you had the money to pay for health insurance in the first place, you have the money to buy the $1,100-deductible policy and deposit a $1,100 a year into your HSA.

The real advantage of the HSA for the unhealthy person is that he or she can take that $1,100 or $2,200 and use it to see any doctor.

After all, it's *your* money. There's no insurance company to dictate to you what doctor you spend that money on.

The very sick—those with chronic ailments—generally want to go to a specialist for their condition, the doctor who is best qualified to treat whatever condition they suffer from. With an HSA, the *patient* gets to choose that doctor; the doctor isn't chosen for him or her by some insurance company that wants to keep its costs down.

Remember, with an HSA, the sickly person is not deprived of *any* benefits. That person still has the same advantages he or she would have had on a normal, full-benefit health plan—except now there are no copayments! And for that first $1,100 or $2,200, the *patient* has complete power to choose whatever medical services he or she wants.

The physician whom a patient chooses may order more tests than a physician picked by an insurance company. The patient's physician may want blood tested every time the patient comes in, because the blood test provides so much information. The insurance company's physician may be more concerned with keeping costs down. The HSA approach transfers power to the customer.

A Word about Family Deductibles

Prior to the HSA legislation, insurance industry tradition was that insurance deductibles applied *to each and every person in the family.* So a $2,000 deductible meant $2,000 for a husband, $2,000 for his wife, and $2,000 for each of the children.

But the first HSA legislation allowed the entire family, instead of each individual, to be covered by one single $2,000 family deductible. The family deductible was our idea and was written into the first HSA law in 1996. These deductibles are still the norm among HSA plans.

Republicans versus Democrats

When that trial legislation was passed in 1996, it was severely restricted by Senator Edward "Ted" Kennedy of Massachusetts. Bill Archer has said a number of times that in one of their meetings to negotiate on the bill, Ted Kennedy turned to his staff and, speaking in a voice he thought low enough not to be heard, said: "We have to restrict this enough that it won't be too popular, because if we get millions of Americans with these savings accounts, we'll never be able to take it away from them."[9]

Unfortunately for Kennedy, Archer heard what he said.

The disagreements between the Republicans and the Democrats over health care have been disappointing. There is an expression for these people: "constitutional aginners," meaning people who are "agin" everything. The "aginnerness" on workable and good solutions to health care costs, in particular, between the Republicans and Democrats is deplorable.

It may surprise you to learn that the HSA legislation started out as Democratic legislation. Senator Tom Daschle (D-SD) and Representative Dick Gephardt (D-MO) were both on record as being in favor of it. In fact, the first U.S. Senate "Dear Colleague" letter about these accounts was signed by six U.S. senators, four of them Democrats. This 1992 letter is reprinted as Figure 7.3. (Daschle was at the time the Democratic leader in the Senate, Gephardt the Democratic leader in the House.) Both said publicly they were in favor of what were then called MSAs. The person who killed Democratic party support for HSAs, as far as the Democrats are concerned, was Senator Phil Gramm (R-TX).

Here's how that happened.

John Breaux
Louisiana

Committees:
Commerce, Science, and
Transportation
Finance
Special Committee on Aging

United States Senate

WASHINGTON, DC 20510-1803

WASHINGTON OFFICE:
(202) 224-4623

CENTRAL LOUISIANA OFFICE:
524 MURRAY STREET
ALEXANDRIA, LA 71301
(318) 473-7370

SOUTH LOUISIANA OFFICE:
THE FEDERAL BUILDING
705 JEFFERSON STREET, ROOM 103
LAFAYETTE, LA 70501
(318) 264-6871

NORTH LOUISIANA OFFICE:
WASHINGTON SQUARE ANNEX BUILDING
211 NORTH 3RD STREET, ROOM 102A
MONROE, LA 71201
(318) 325-3320

NEW ORLEANS AREA OFFICE:
HALE BOGGS FEDERAL BUILDING
501 MAGAZINE STREET, SUITE 1005
NEW ORLEANS, LA 70130
(504) 589-2531

September 8, 1992

Dear Colleague:

The United States is faced with a crisis in health care on two
fronts: access and cost control. So far, most of the proposals
before Congress attempt to deal with access but do not adequately
address the more important factor--cost control. We have
introduced legislation that will begin to get medical spending
under control by giving individual consumers a larger stake in
spending decisions.

We have introduced a bill, the Medical Cost Containment Act of
1992 (S. 2873), which would allow employers to provide their
employees with an annual allowance in a "Medical Care Savings
Account" to pay for routine health care needs. This allowance
would not be subject to income tax if used for qualified medical
expenses. Any money not spent out of a given year's allowance
could be kept by the employee in an account for future medical
needs during times of unemployment or for long term care. In
order to protect employees and their families from catastrophic
health care expenses above the amount in the Medical Care Savings
Account, an employer would be required to purchase a high-
deductible catastrophic insurance policy.

Unlike many standard third party health care coverage plans,
Medical Care Savings Accounts would give consumers an incentive
to monitor spending carefully because to do otherwise would be
wasting their "own" money. That is, money that they would
otherwise be able to save in their account for future needs.

Once a Medical Care Savings Account is established for an
employee, it is fully portable. Money in the account can be used
to continue insurance while an employee is between jobs or on
strike. Recent studies show that at least 50% of the uninsured
are uninsured for four months or less.

Today, even commonly required small dollar deductibles (typically
$250 to $500) create a hardship for the financially stressed
individual or family seeking regular, preventive care services.
With Medical Care Savings Accounts, however, that same individual
or family would have this critical money in their account to pay
for the needed services.

Figure 7.3 Medical Cost Containment Act

Medical Cost Containment Act (S. 2873)
Page 2

We feel that, while the Medical Care Savings Account concept does
not provide the total solution to the crisis in health care
access, it does begin to address the critical aspects of
increasing costs and utilization by consumers.

We hope that you will join us as cosponsors of this legislation.
If you have any questions please contact us or have your staff
contact Laird Burnett of Senator Breaux's staff at 4-4623.

Sincerely,

John Breaux

Richard Lugar

David Boren

Dan Coats

Tom Daschle

Sam Nunn

Figure 7.3   *(continued)*

When Gramm ran for president in 1996, he said all sorts of unkind things about President Bill Clinton. At the same time, Gramm endorsed the idea of MSAs. Every time Gramm spoke in condemnation of Clinton and in support of MSAs, a Democrat who was supporting MSAs would drop off!

Congressman Andy Jacobs (D-IL), the Democratic sponsor of the legislation, said at the time, "If you could get Phil Gramm to shut up, we could preserve medical savings accounts as a Democrat agenda." But of course, Phil Gramm wouldn't shut up, and eventually the Democrats opposed the plan.[10]

The sad truth is that today, HSAs have been embraced by the Republicans and opposed by the Democrats merely due to political considerations. It's certainly in the best interests of the public: Not only do HSAs encourage wiser spending, they help people who are not healthy, because they shift more power into their hands.

A Legitimate HSA Weakness

There is one legitimate weakness with an HSA. If people put the funds into the savings account on a monthly pro rata basis, at the end of the first month, they will have put in only one-twelfth of the annual deposit. If something happens right away, they will be underfunded for the deductible.

When an employer is involved, it's easy to say to employees: "Don't worry. If anything happens in the early months, we will make you a loan for the balance of the money that you would have accumulated in the first year." As the year progresses, the employer gets the money back from the employees' regular monthly deposits to the savings account.

But say it's an individual buying health insurance. A couple of insurance companies offer a supplemental indemnity benefit that will fill in the deductible if the person has medical expenses in the early months before the savings have accumulated.

Three Mistakes Employers Make

There are three common mistakes employers make when it comes to HSA plan design. The first is that the employer offers an HSA but does not put any money in the account. Guess what? Fewer employees will choose the HSA.[11]

As a general rule of thumb, if you are an employer planning on offering an HSA, unless you do not provide any health insurance, we do not recommend you offer an HSA unless you are going to contribute to the account.

Do not just pocket the savings from moving to an HSA-qualified health plan. Your employees will not like it. HSAs were not designed to be an insurance policy—they were designed by Congress to create savings from a lower premium insurance plan, and for those savings to be deposited, tax-free, in an account to meet the insurance plan's deductible.

A second common mistake made by employers is to make the smallest employer contribution to the HSA, while giving lower-deductible, higher-premium plans a larger contribution.[12] This is a mistake for several reasons. The HSA-qualified health plan premium costs less, so a premium increase of, say, 5 percent next year will be less than a 5 percent increase on a higher premium plan. For example, if an HSA family premium is $583 a month, while the average monthly premium for a family health plan in the United States is $1,008 a month, then a 5 percent increase on the HSA premium is a $29 a month increase, while a 5 percent increase on the $1,008 a month premium is $50.04 a month increase. Therefore, by subsidizing the higher-premium non-HSA plans, the employer is subsidizing the plans that will cost them more the next year.

Our recommendation is that employers equally subsidize all plans with the same dollar amount, and that they put their contributions into the account first, and any left over money should be applied to the insurance. This way, the employee contribution goes toward the premium, and the employer's contribution goes into the HSA.

Employers who choose to put their contribution into the HSA will find they are very popular, and it is a very clear and graphic way to show the employee just how much the employer is helping with the cost of health insurance every year.

Finally, employers and individuals should always choose an HSA-qualified health plan with 100 percent coverage above the deductible. That is, the out-of-pocket maximum is equal to the deductible. This means that if you are single and you have a $1,100 deductible, once you meet the $1,100 deductible, everything you spend on health care is covered 100 percent—prescription drugs, doctor visits, surgeries, everything.

This allows employees to know that the most they will ever pay in the year is the amount of their deductible, and they will be able to accurately calculate how much they will owe in a worst-case scenario (in this example, $1,100), which gives them comfort and the ability to calculate how much they will have to put into the HSA, on top of the employer's contribution, to be able to be covered 100 percent. Employers will find if they do not offer a plan with 100 percent coverage above the deductible, fewer employees will choose an HSA.

A Response to Mr. Rangel

Representative Charles Rangel (D-NY), now chairman of the U.S. House of Representatives Ways and Means Committee, criticized the concept of HSAs. Chairman Rangel was quoted in an article in *The Hill* newspaper as saying that HSAs would have little benefit to those with low income. Noting that 48 million Americans cannot afford health coverage under traditional insurance plans (the 48 million figure was used in the original article), Rangel said, "A lot of those people can't set aside money because they don't have enough income to take a deduction."[13]

Chairman Rangel's remark plays off the tax-deductible emphasis that has been given to HSAs. That misses the point. People don't *have* to set the money aside out of their earnings.

If they can buy typical health insurance or if their employer is buying it for them, the money is already going out the door. The cash will be there from the savings earned when they take a plan with a front-end deductible.

The important point regarding HSAs is that bringing consumer self-interest into the picture creates a miraculous saving on health care premiums. Skip the tax deduction. If you take a family health plan with a $2,200 deductible, you will save $2,200 on the cost of the health insurance. Then you will have $2,200 in cash in the HSA account—and you have traditional insurance coverage for costs above that.

Phooey. Which would you prefer: Spend $10,000 a year for health insurance, or spend $7,800 a year for insurance and have $2,200 that is yours to spend for health care—keeping any unspent portion if this your family's medical expenses for the year amount to less than $2,200. Any unspent monies in an HSA roll over year-after-year. An HSA is not like a flexible spending account (or FSA) where unless you spend the money, you lose it. With an HSA, the money in the account is yours from day one and you keep it until you spend it.

The savings are not entirely due to spending less on medical care. Part of the savings is a reduction in the cost of transactions. Consider this: If you're going to the doctor with insurance that has a $25 copayment and the doctor charges $75, you pay $25 and the doctor's office bills your insurance company for the remaining $50. It may cost as much for the insurance company to process that $50 payment to the doctor as it would to process a $2,200 bill. Having insurance pay these small bills is a lot less efficient than you paying them.

So, miraculously, your $2,200 deductible plan saves $2,200 or maybe even a little more on the cost of insurance.

Charlie Rangel said in the article that the Democrats will do to HSA expansion what they did to Social Security reform: Talk about it, then ignore it.

Chairman Rangel, please remember that HSAs started out as Democratic legislation. They began with your colleague on the U.S. Ways and Means Committee, Mr. Jacobs. HSAs were supported by Dick Gephardt, Senator Tom Daschle, and three other Democratic senators. Would you sabotage HSAs if the Republicans hadn't adopted the Democrats' idea?

Incidentally, Representative Pete Stark (D-CA) made a similar argument in an article that appeared in the journal *Business Insurance* in 2006. He said that HSAs are not much more than a tax shelter for the well-to-do.[14] But, Congressman, for people with modest incomes, a $2,200 deductible will create the savings to put $2,200 in the savings account.

What Does the Evidence Say?

Again, 73 percent of all Americans pay less than $500 in medical expenses annually, although they're paying much more than that for traditional health insurance.

But consumer research suggests the relatively healthy, younger, and better-off people are not the only ones buying HSAs. People from all income levels and age levels are buying them.

The online insurance brokerage eHealthInsurance.com analyzed the demographics of the people who bought HSAs through its web portal over a six-month period. This popular broker found:

1. More than 50 percent of HSA buyers were 40 years old or older.
2. Just less than 50 percent of HSA buyers were families with children.
3. More than 40 percent of HSA buyers had incomes of $50,000 or less.
4. In the individual market, 30 percent of the people who bought HSAs had previously been uninsured.[15]

Read number 4 again—no statistic could be more pleasing!

A Side Note

For years, some have claimed that you need to buy a high-deductible health insurance policy to get an HSA. In truth, you can meet the requirements in the law with a $2,200 family deductible. An insurance plan with a modest deductible may make better financial sense for you and your family. (The first $2,200 of deductible will usually reduce the cost of your insurance by $2,200, but any larger deductible beyond that produces diminishing savings.)

Find the deductible that works for you.

Before HSAs came along, there was no such thing as a "family deductible" in the world of insurance. Each member of the family had to meet his or her own health insurance deductible. That didn't work for many families, so Pat Rooney came up with the idea of the *family* deductible to consolidate the out-of-pocket risk for the family.

What Congress Still Needs to Do

Senator Orrin Hatch (R-UT) has introduced the best bill in Congress to expand, enhance, and generally make HSAs work even better. Below is a section-by-section analysis of what his bill specifically will accomplish.

Summary of S. XXXX
The XXXXX Act of 2007
Sen. Hatch introduced S. XXXX, the "XXXXXX Act of 2007," on January XX, 2008. A summary of the bill's provisions follows.

Purchase of Any Health Insurance with HSA Funds Allowed

Allows anyone with funds in an HSA account to pay for health insurance premiums of HSA-qualified policies. Under current law, people can only use their HSA account to pay for health insurance premiums when they are receiving federal or state unemployment benefits, or on a COBRA continuation policy from a former employer.

Greater Flexibility Using HSA Account to Pay Expenses

Allows all expenses incurred after HSA-qualified coverage begins to be reimbursed from the HSA account as long as they set up their account by April 15 of the following year. When people enroll in an HSA-qualified plan, some let a few months elapse between the time when their coverage starts (e.g., January) and when the health savings bank account is set up and becomes operational (e.g., March). However, the IRS does not allow for medical expenses incurred in that gap (between January and March) to be reimbursed with HSA funds.

Expanded Opportunities for Persons on Medicare

Allows Medicare beneficiaries enrolled only in Part A to continue to contribute to their HSA accounts after turning 65 if they are otherwise eligible to contribute to an HSA. Current law restricts HSA participation by Medicare beneficiaries, which means that once a person enrolls in Medicare they may no longer contribute to their HSA (although they may continue to spend money from an existing HSA). For most seniors, enrollment in Medicare Part A is automatic when receiving Social Security and is difficult to delay or decline enrollment. However, the current deductible for hospital coverage under Medicare Part A is over $1,000 per admission, nearly equal to the minimum deductible required for HSA-qualified plans.

Allows seniors enrolled in Medicare Medical Savings Accounts to contribute tax-deductible money to their accounts. Current law prohibits Medicare beneficiaries enrolled in Medicare MSA plans from adding their own money to their MSAs. Although created in the 1997 Balanced Budget Act, Medicare MSAs are a relatively new type of plan under the Medicare Advantage program. MSA plans allow seniors to enroll in a high-deductible plan and receive tax-free contributions from the federal government to HSA-like accounts. However, the government contribution is significantly lower than the plan deductible, and the beneficiary may not contribute any of their own money to fill in the gap.

Expanded Eligibility for Veterans

Allows Veterans to use VA medical services and retain their HSA eligibility. Current law prohibits veterans from contributing to their HSAs if they have utilized VA medical services in the past three months. The bill would remove those restrictions and allow veterans to contribute to their HSAs regardless of utilization of VA medical services.

Catch-up Contributions to Same Account Permitted

Allows both HSA-eligible spouses to make catch-up contributions to the same HSA account. Current law allows HSA-eligible individuals age 55 or older to make additional catch-up contributions each year. However, according to the IRS, even if both spouses are eligible to make catch-up contributions, the contributions must be deposited into separate HSA accounts. The bill would allow the spouse who is the account holder to double their catch-up contribution to account for their eligible spouse.

Clarification of FSA and HRA Rollovers to HSAs

Allows a one-time rollover of unspent funds from Flexible Spending Arrangements (FSAs) and Health Reimbursement Arrangements (HRAs). The Tax Relief and Health Care Act of 2006 allowed employers that previously offered FSAs to roll over unused FSA funds to an HSA as employees transitioned to an HSA for the first time. However, the IRS issued guidance earlier this year that did not allow the unused FSA funds to be rolled over to HSAs unless the employer offered a "grace period" that allows medical expenses to be reimbursed from an FSA through March 15 of the following year (instead of the usual "use or lose" by December 31). This bill clarifies current law to allow a one-time roll-over of funds regardless of whether an employer offers a grace period in its FSA plan in order to ease the transition from FSAs to HSAs.

Expanded Definition of "Preventive" Drugs

Allows HSA-qualified plans to include medications for chronic conditions as "preventive care." Current law allows "preventive care" services to be paid by HSA-qualified plans without being subject to the policy deductible. IRS guidance does not permit plans to cover services that treat existing conditions. The bill expands the definition of "preventive care" to include prescription and over-the-counter drugs that also prevent worsening of or complications from chronic conditions. This will provide additional flexibility to health plans that want to provide coverage for these medications and remove a perceived barrier to HSAs for people with chronic conditions.

Other HSA Provisions

The bill also makes several changes to the definition of "qualified medical expenses" in Section 213(d) of the Internal Revenue Code. The modification would affect all health care programs using the definition, including HSAs, Health Reimbursement Arrangements, and Flexible Spending Accounts. These changes include allowing Americans to deduct the cost of:

- Fees for "direct practice" physicians that bill their patients on a flat-fee basis in advance of receiving medical services on demand;
- Exercise and physical fitness programs, up to $1,000 per year; and
- Nutritional and dietary supplements, up to $1,000 per year.[16]

CHAPTER 8

Establish Fair Medical Prices

Do you know anything about medical prices?

Imagine you had no health insurance and were scheduled to enter the hospital next week to have gallbladder surgery. Do you have any idea what a reasonable charge by the hospital would be?

If you don't have any idea, you are very vulnerable to being gouged. And, unfortunately, that is just what's happening to people all across America today.

Which Price Tag?

There are actually three different prices that every informed medical consumer ought to know:

1. **The rate Medicare will pay for the service which is very close to the hospital's total cost.** Regardless of your age, you need to know what Medicare would pay for the services you receive. Medicare knows the cost for everything—even for childbirth. Hospitals almost universally complain that Medicare doesn't pay enough, that they lose money on Medicare, but that simply is not true: The reality is that the Medicare payment is designed by law to pay a little more than the cost incurred by an efficiently run hospital. (We'll discuss this more shortly.)
2. **The rate that the large HMOs will pay**, which in general is 4 or 5 percentage points higher than what Medicare will pay.
3. **The list price hospitals charge to the uninsured.** This price is often referred to as the "chargemaster" price.

What Medicare pays is not quite up to the reasonable charge for an uninsured person to pay, but he or she would now at least have enough information to conduct an informed discussion (or argument) with the hospital. (If you find yourself in this situation and at some point choose to work with an attorney, this will be valuable evidence to share in making your defense.)

President Bush signed Executive Order number 13410 on August 22, 2006 (reproduced herein as Appendix D), that gave each U.S. government agency, including Medicare, the option of making its payment rates public information. This executive order was based to a large extent on U.S. Senate bill, S. 2606, introduced by Senator Brownback (R-KS) and Senator Coburn (R-OK). (Figure 8.1 presents the "Dear Colleague" letter explaining S. 2606.)

To date, Medicare has not decided to release its payment rates to the public in a form that is readily usable or understandable. However, what Medicare has released is a step in the right direction.

Without using the Medicare payment rate benchmarks, how exactly can consumers find out, in a timely manner, what a reasonable price for their specific needs is?

Market forces work when those providing a service also provide a clear price and consumers can make their own cost–benefit decisions. How can you have a market if the price of the service is impossible to discover? Answer: You cannot have a functioning market.

In cases in which consumers do know the price of medical procedures (and they care enough not to pay unnecessarily high prices), their behavior changes radically, which has the effect of putting downward pressure on health care pricing by introducing competition for services based on price.

For example, in Minnesota, one woman had access to key information that changed her decision about when and where to have her daughter's tonsillectomy. She could have the outpatient procedure done by her doctor at the hospital where her brother works for $4,000. She also discovered that her doctor has surgical privileges at a surgery center, where the cost would be $1,500. She chose the surgery center, for the exact same procedure, with the exact same doctor, and saved herself $2,500. This mother cared about the price because her health insurance deductible was $5,000, and she was paying for it herself.

United States Senate
WASHINGTON, DC 20510

88% OF AMERICANS AGREE - COSPONSOR S. 2606

May 22, 2006

Dear Colleague:

A recent Zogby poll shows 88% of Americans support publishing Medicare prices for medical procedures. Why are these prices significant? First, reimbursement rates of the largest insurers are similar to Medicare rates. Second, those uninsured and with Health Savings Accounts (HSAs) often have difficulty determining health care prices because there is no reference point for those prices.

Publishing Medicare payments would provide a starting point for price comparison for many Americans. President George W. Bush agrees and recently directed the Department of Health and Human Services to make Medicare prices publicly available online by June 1st.

Last month, we introduced S. 2606, the Medicare Payment Rate Disclosure Act of 2006. This legislation tackles a key problem facing Americans today—the lack of transparency in our healthcare industry. The Medicare Payment Rate Disclosure Act of 2006 would empower citizens to act as informed consumers when purchasing their health care. Countless examples in our nation's history demonstrate that the American consumer possesses the ability to improve the cost-effectiveness and quality of products by making informed decisions in the marketplace. Yet the cost of health care remains largely inaccessible to Americans in our current system.

S. 2606 would enable greater price transparency at the consumer level. Under the Freedom of Information Act, Medicare reimbursement rates are publicly available today but are not easily accessible. If an individual wants to know what the Medicare reimbursement rate for a specific procedure was, they would have to look up the relative value of the service in the Federal Register and then use a complicated formula incorporating geographic data and a conversion factor for actual payment information. This confusing process makes it nearly impossible for consumers to have access to Medicare price data. Transparency is essential for Americans to have the ability to choose affordable health care services within their region. This bill ensures that there is a searchable location on the Internet where all consumers can go to view the Medicare reimbursement rates for all medical procedures and physical regions.

By removing these barriers for health care consumers that prevent them from comparing physician and hospital prices, Americans will obtain the knowledge to take charge of their health spending and to negotiate health care prices. This legislation is an important first step to accomplishing this objective. Please contact Melanie Benning with Senator Brownback at 224-6521, or Stephanie Carlton with Senator Coburn at 224-5754 if you wish to cosponsor.

Sincerely,

Sam Brownback
United States Senator

Tom Coburn
United States Senator

Figure 8.1   United States Senate Letter

What's a Reasonable Price?

What charge is reasonable for a person with no insurance to pay? To answer that, the first thing a person would need to do is estab-lish what Medicare would pay for the service.

Why?

There are two reference points for reasonable medical pricing, and both of them begin with the price that Medicare pays for services:

1. **A reasonable price according to a nationally recognized academic authority: Medicare plus 25 percent**

   The nation's preeminent authority on hospital pricing is Dr. Gerard Anderson of the Johns Hopkins School of Medicine in Baltimore. He provided wonderfully detailed testimony before the Oversight and Investigations Subcommittee of the Commerce Committee of Congress in June 2004.[1] His conclusion was that *Medicare plus 25 percent* is the reasonable payment an uninsured patient should pay to a hospital. (Dr. Anderson's testimony is in the public record and is printed in full in Appendix A.)

   Contrast this with what hospital authority Nathan Kaufman, SVP, Healthcare Strategy, recommended in a January 2007 presentation titled "Peak Performing Hospitals." In a section titled "Margin-Based Pricing Strategy," he advises that hospitals "Set retail charges at 3.5 times Medicare."[2] It's worthwhile to note that even those who want to charge excessively high rates do so in relation to Medicare. Medicare is the standard by which hospitals set their rates.

   Dr. Anderson testified that the only people paying these ever-increasing retail charges are those with limited bargaining power: the uninsured, international visitors, and some people with health savings accounts not in a doctor network.

2. **A reasonable price as established by a recent court case: Medicare plus 20 percent**

   There was a dispute between BayCare Health System Inc. of Southern Florida and an insurance network called Health Options. A pricing agreement between the two parties had been allowed to lapse after the two failed to agree on what constituted reasonable prices. So the hospital, no longer bound by a contract, chose to bill the insurance network the full chargemaster prices.

   The Florida legislature had put in place an independent tribunal to settle such disputes between insurance plans and hospitals. The two disputants took the matter to this independent tribunal, and the tribunal determined for them what constituted the right price: *Medicare plus 20 percent.*

An excerpt from a newspaper account discussing the case follows:

> Florida's largest health insurance company scored a huge victory in a billing dispute with the Tampa Bay area's main hospital group.
>
> In its claims dispute, BayCare argued that since there was no contract in effect, Health Options is required to pay what was billed and that those charges were, in fact, "usual and customary charges."
>
> However, state records indicate that BayCare didn't "provide a rationale for its assertion." Health Options reimbursed the facilities at 120 percent of the Medicare participating rate and provided a "detailed" reason why the level was usual and customary, state records show. The difference between what BayCare billed for emergency services and what Health Options reimbursed is about $1.45 million.[3]

What Can We Conclude?

It would seem that a reasonable price for health care for the uninsured is somewhere in the ballpark of 20 to 25 percent above what Medicare reimburses hospitals for specific services.

This information is part of the public record and is available to you and your attorney, should you need the assistance of one. And you very well may, even if you have insurance but go out of network. When hospitals are not part of the network with which an insurance company has contracts, they are considered "out of network," and the prices they charge for services can be considerably higher than they would charge an insurance company.

How to Defend Yourself against Hospital Harassment

Once *you* determine a reasonable price, don't expect your hospital to congratulate you for doing your homework.

When an individual questions a hospital about its prices, the hospital's normal response is to turn the bill over to its collection law firm, which then harasses the person by mail and telephone and threatens to destroy his or her credit reputation.

Here's some advice, should you find yourself in this awkward but all-too-common position.

To defend yourself, you *must* invoke the federal Fair Debt Collection Practices Act. There actually is a federal law with this title, and most states have adopted similar laws. You need to send a letter to the hospital and to the hospital's collection law firm advising them that you are protecting your rights under this act (either the state or federal act).

For your convenience, here is a sample letter you can use. Address the letter to the chief financial officer (CFO) of the hospital and send it by certified mail, return receipt requested. (You probably don't know the name of the hospital's CFO, but you can call the hospital and ask or look at the hospital's web site.) Send a copy of the letter to the collection law firm, again by certified mail with return receipt requested.

First Request Letter for UB-92 or UB-04

[date]
[Institution Name]
[Institution Address]
[Institution City, State, ZIP]
[CFO Name]

Re: [Patient Name], Account [Patient Account Number], Date Admitted [Admittance Date]

Dear Mr. [CFO Name]:

I am writing to request your full and thorough review of my account. I received your balance due notice indicating I owe $[Amount Due] on the account. Please be advised that I do not believe the charges to be a reasonable price for the services rendered.

I am exercising my rights under HIPAA (the Health Insurance Portability and Accountability Act) and demand that you provide me with a copy of the UB-92, UB-04, CMS-1500, or Form 837 used to make decisions on my behalf and made part of my designated record set. Under federal law (HIPAA), I am entitled to, and I am demanding, a copy of the financial responsibility agreement and principal admitting diagnosis, and treatment codes within

30 days of receipt of this letter. If you fail to provide either document, I will file a complaint with the Office of Civil Rights of the U.S. Department of Health and Human Services and forward my complaint to the U.S. House Oversight and Investigations Subcommittee.

I personally have a right by law to receive this information from you. The requested information should be sent to my attention at the address below. I will pay for any reasonable copy cost associated with this request. Thank you for your prompt assistance with this matter.

I recently was informed of my rights and now will use all legal avenues to protect myself from your unreasonable charges.

Please govern yourself accordingly.

[Your Name]

[Your Address]

Use If You Have *Not* Applied for Charity Care

[date]

[Institution Name]

[Institution Address]

[Institution City, State, ZIP]

[CFO Name]

Re: [Patient Name], Account [Patient Account Number], Date Admitted [Admittance Date]

Dear [CFO Name]:

I am writing to request your full and thorough review of my account. I received your balance due notice indicating I owe $[Amount Due] on the account. Please be advised that I do not believe the charges to be a reasonable price for the services rendered.

To protect my creditworthiness, I am submitting this letter under the Fair Debt Collection Practices Act (the "Act"). Accept this letter in accordance with applicable federal and state laws governing fair debt collection practices. Take notice I am **denying and disputing** any amount that you allege that I owe to [Hospital Name], and specifically deny that I owe any amounts for fees, costs, and expenses of medical supplies, services, diagnosis, or treatment in excess of their reasonable value.

(Continued)

I demand full and complete compliance with requirements of the Act, and any similar or related state laws, and will, if necessary, pursue all available remedies and relief provided by law.

I deny and dispute any amounts that you allege that I owe to [Institution Name] and specifically deny that I owe any amounts for the fees, costs, and expenses of medical supplies, services, diagnosis, or treatment in excess of their reasonable value. I demand that you verify the validity of this debt in writing within 30 days and submit a copy to me at the address below.

Do not contact me any further, except as expressly permitted by law, at my home or place of employment regarding this disputed debt.

I am also exercising my rights under HIPAA and demand that you provide me with a copy of the UB-92, UB-04, CMS-1500, or Form 837 used to make decisions on my behalf and made part of my designated record set. Under federal law (HIPAA), I am entitled to, and I am demanding a copy of the financial responsibility agreement and principal admitting diagnosis, and treatment codes within 30 days of receipt of this letter. If you fail to provide either document, I will file a complaint with the Office of Civil Rights of the U.S. Department of Health and Human Services and forward my complaint to the U.S. House Oversight and Investigations Subcommittee.

I recently was informed of my rights and now will use all legal avenues to protect myself from these unreasonable charges.

[Your Name]
[Your Address]

Use If You Have Applied for Charity Care

[date]
[Institution Name]
[Institution Address]
[Institution City, State, ZIP]
[CFO Name]

Re: [Patient Name], Account [Patient Account Number], Date Admitted [Admittance Date]

Dear [CFO Name]:

I am writing to request your full and thorough review of my account. I received your balance due notice indicating I owe $[Amount Due] on the account. Please be advised that I do not believe the charges to be a reasonable price for the services rendered.

To protect my creditworthiness, I am submitting this letter under the Fair Debt Collection Practices Act (the "Act"). Accept this letter in accordance with applicable federal and state laws governing fair debt collection practices. Take notice I am **denying and disputing** any amount that you allege that I owe to [Hospital Name], and specifically deny that I owe any amounts for fees, costs, and expenses of medical supplies, services, diagnosis, or treatment in excess of their reasonable value.

I demand full and complete compliance with requirements of the Act, and any similar or related state laws, and will, if necessary, pursue all available remedies and relief provided by law.

I deny and dispute any amounts that you allege that I owe to [Institution Name] and specifically deny that I owe any amounts for the fees, costs, and expenses of medical supplies, services, diagnosis, or treatment in excess of their reasonable value. I demand that you verify the validity of this debt in writing within 30 days and submit a copy to me at the address below.

Do not contact me any further, except as expressly permitted by law, at my home or place of employment regarding this disputed debt.

I am also exercising my rights under HIPAA and demand that you provide me with a copy of the UB-92, UB-04, CMS-1500, or Form 837 used to make decisions on my behalf and made part of my designated record set. Under federal law (HIPAA), I am entitled to, and I am demanding, a copy of the financial responsibility agreement and principal admitting diagnosis, and treatment codes within 30 days of receipt of this letter. If you fail to provide either document, I will file a complaint with the Office of Civil Rights of the U.S. Department of Health and Human Services and forward my complaint to the U.S. House Oversight and Investigations Subcommittee.

I further demand a copy of the [hospital name] charity care guidelines and the specific reasons for your nonprofit hospital denying my financial assistance application.

I recently was informed of my rights and now will use all legal avenues to protect myself from these unreasonable charges.

[Your Name]
[Your Address]

What's a UB-04 or a UB-92?

The UB-04 and UB-92 mentioned in the letters are summary bills. They are U.S. government standard forms used by all hospitals. Figure 8.2 presents an example UB-92. Hospitals are in the process of moving to a UB-04 as the standard billing form.

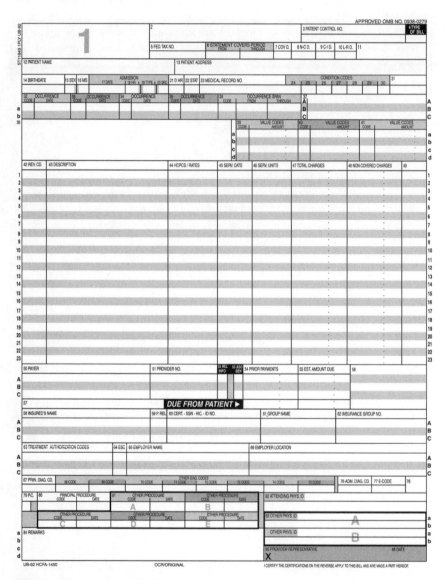

Figure 8.2   Sample UB-92

Where to Get the Medicare Information

The next step is to determine a *reasonable* charge for the services received. As mentioned earlier, a reasonable charge begins with what Medicare pays for those services. Medicare has so much information because it is able to demand a detailed report of costs from the hospitals.

Medicare has published a range of prices it pays for the top 31 inpatient and outpatient procedures in the United States. For gall-bladder removal, without complications and without laparoscope, the national average Medicare payment in 2006 was $15,967. The national average hospital charge for the same procedure in 2006 was $50,946. These numbers were released by the U.S. government because of the executive order signed by President Bush.

You can look up what Medicare would pay for any of these most common procedures by going to http://www.cms.hhs.gov/ HealthCareConInit/02_Hospital.asp. Also listed is the national average hospital charge for the same procedure.

That information is public information—if you know how and where to find it. If you don't know, call the offices of the Fairness Foundation, and someone there can look it up for you. The toll-free number is 800–742–3441. You'll likely need to leave a voice mail message, but your call will be returned within a day or two.

When you call, have in hand:

1. The name and location of the hospital in question.
2. The condition for which you received medical care.
3. The duration of your hospital stay, if you stayed overnight.
4. Your UB-92 or UB-04 form, so that you can read to us the DRG (Diagnostic Related Group) code from the lower right corner of the form. Or you can fax the form to 317–293–0603 after you leave a message or register on the web site.
5. Your daytime phone number (with area code), so we can call you back.

Or you can register online at www.hospitalvictims.org, with the five pieces of information listed.

Once you have advised the hospital that you are protecting your rights under the Fair Debt Collection Practices Act and you know what Medicare would pay for the service you received, you have the information with which to demand that the hospital reduce your charges to a reasonable amount. We suggest Medicare plus 25 percent.

Now You're a Royal Pain

From the standpoint of the hospital and its collection or law firm, someone with all this information in hand is not the typical patient. The case is no longer a routine collection account. By taking the suggested actions, you have stopped them from destroying your credit.

Typically, in this case, the collection law firm will give your case back to the hospital, telling it to work out with you what you actually owe. Only then will the collection law firm know what to pursue you for. That amount is in dispute, based on the Fair Debt Collection letter you have sent.

One very important point: If the collection firm continues to harass you after it has received your certified letter, its action is a violation of the law, and you can get penalties from the law firm for each violation. If you finally end up going to an attorney, you will need to provide him or her with a record of every instance of harassment you've experienced *after* the certified letter was sent and received by the hospital and its collection firm.

From the hospital's point of view, you have now become a pain in the rear, for you no longer fit into the routine collection procedures. Someone now has to talk with you and argue the reasonableness of the charges.

When you talk with the hospital about what you owe, be sure to quote to the hospital the precedents involved in the testimony of Dr. Gerard Anderson and the tribunal decision in Florida that Medicare plus 20 or 25 percent is reasonable. The hospital likely will claim that it charges the prices you've been charged to *everyone*. That is correct. The difference is what they will accept as payment.

"But those are *negotiated discounts* off a single price," the hospital representative may say. Phooey. The bottom line is that hospitals have different discounts for different payers, and all you're looking for is to be treated fairly.

You can find detailed information about the prices charged at many of the nation's larger hospitals online at www.hospitalvictims. org. This web site even lists the discounts these larger hospitals allow (on average) to people with insurance. This information can be valuable ammunition in your battle against the hospital.

Sounds Good, But Does It Work?

A nonprofit hospital in Florida recently settled two hospital bills for far less than it charged.

In the first case, the patient was billed $49,136, but the hospital accepted just *$4,686* as payment in full. That's less than one-tenth the sticker price!

The second case is only slightly less dramatic: The patient was billed $45,897, and the hospital accepted just *$6,000.19* as payment in full.

How did the hospital come to accept such a low payment? In both cases, the amount offered was the price Medicare would have paid, plus 32 percent. As you now know, "plus 32 percent" was on the generous side.

Do You Need a Lawyer?

In the unlikely event that the hospital decides to sue you, then by all means promptly get an attorney. You can find one in the bankruptcy pages in the yellow pages of your phone book. In most cases, the ad will tell you that there is no charge for the initial consultation with the lawyer.

A reminder: If the hospital's collection law firm has harassed you after you sent your Fair Debt Collection letter, your attorney can get a $1,000 penalty from them for each time you were harassed after the firm got your letter.

Show your attorney the Fair Debt Collection Practices Act letter you sent to the hospital and the collection law firm. Show your bill and the information you have gathered. If you haven't gotten the discount information already, have your attorney look at the hospitalvictims.org web site to find the discount your hospital normally offers to people with insurance.

Two useful legal documents appear in the appendixes of this book. The first, in Appendix B, is a memorandum of law that walks the reader through the legal precedents that prevent hospitals from charging unreasonable (or as Nora Johnson says, fantasy) prices. The second useful legal document is an actual complaint suing a hospital for unreasonable prices. It was filed by Amanda Marks against Hospital X of Florida, and appears in Appendix C.

The Key to Health Care Reform

If we are to control the cost of American health care, our first job is to stop our hospitals from price gouging the uninsured. This is the key for any substantive reform. If the hospitals don't get their houses in order, there can be no solution, for they set the practice for the entire health care industry.

While hospital executives readily agree their pricing is convoluted and illogical, out of self-interest they argue against what common sense suggests. Rather than agree to reform their pricing practices, hospital executives have answered, "Don't put the squeeze on us—what we need is a national solution for treating the uninsured." What do they mean by a "national solution"? We believe that it simply means "years of delay" before any meaningful reform.

Regrettably, hospital executives would rather change the subject and continue overcharging than do what fairness and justice demand.

CHAPTER 9

Make Medical Prices Transparent

AN INNOVATIVE APPROACH
TO PRICING HEALTH CARE

Before you buy anything, what's the first question we ask?

"What does it cost?"

We usually get a direct answer to our question, because sellers know we're not likely to buy until we have an answer.

But there is one thing we buy *without* getting the price ahead of time. And what is that?

Medical care.

Between a Rock and a Hard Place

Patti Brewer wished she had gotten the price ahead of time when she went to the hospital emergency room (ER) with what felt like a kidney infection. While there she was administered an IV and given CT (computed tomography) scans to check for a possible kidney stone, but no stone was found. The ER doctor prescribed an antibiotic for her and then sent her home.

Only *after* Patti received her care did she get an idea of how much it would cost. It turned out that the price was $8,224.

The hospital had charged her more than $5,000 for the scans, more than $600 for the IV, more than $400 for a blood analysis, and more than $200 for a urine analysis.

But Patti Brewer earned only $8 an hour as a data entry clerk, and she had no insurance. She told the hospital she couldn't possibly afford to pay that much and asked if they could work with her.

Apparently they could not.

"I have gotten nasty notices and threats to turn me over to the collection agency," Patti said later. "I told them I could send them $20 a month, but they said that would not do."[1]

The reason why Patti Brewer didn't get the price ahead of time—and the reason that virtually no one gets the price ahead of time—is that *the medical community wants to take advantage of us.* As one respected health care authority has said, "They do it because they can." In other words, they *profit* by obfuscating their billing process.

Why Not Be Honest?

Why can't medical prices be *transparent,* just like all other prices?

If we're to put an end to this nonsense, we have to familiarize ourselves the four *types* of medical prices:

1. The price for hospital care.
2. The price for the physician.
3. The price that the insurance company will pay to the hospital or doctor.
4. The price of ancillary services, such as anesthesia or laboratory.

Hospital lobbyists say there's no sense in providing hospital prices to the public because the public wouldn't understand them anyhow.

That's nonsense. Those who say such things are not trying to protect us or the general public—they're trying to protect the hospitals, so that after we go home from a hospital visit, they can send us a bill that's three or four times what it ought to be. And then they can send a collection agency to follow up.

Most of the time the hospitals do get the money out of us because most of us are afraid of having our credit rating damaged. The hospitals know this.

Cost Reporting

There is one thing that we all ought to know about, and that is something called an OSHPD (Office of Statewide Health Planning and Development) report. California requires its hospitals to report a ton of information, and they print it out in what is typically a four-page report, called an OSHPD report (pronounced *osh-pod*).

These reports are online and accessible to anyone with a computer. But how could this information be helpful to all of us who *don't* live in California? The value of these reports to all of us is that they reveal the average cost per patient day for each of the California hospitals which we can use in comparing costs of the hospital back home.

Now, what does "cost" mean? It means what the hospital is spending for everything. Everything includes depreciation—it's not just tangible costs going out the door, but it's also the cost of whatever the hospital is writing off. The OSHPD reports also reveal the total revenue, the net profit or net loss earned by each hospital. And it tells you how much each of these hospitals gets from Medicare.

OSHPD reports also tell how much the hospital gets from Medicaid and from the uninsured.

Truth Detector

"The uninsured and the indigent are almost never made to pay all of what they owe" for medical care, Federation of American Hospitals president Chip Kahn told a reporter for *The Hill* newspaper. According to the reporter, Kahn estimated that the uninsured pay for only about *10 percent* of the charges incurred.[2]

Really? What does the evidence say?

Let's see what the OSHPD reports show in California.

Do Hospitals Lose Money on the Uninsured?

The numbers shown in Figure 9.1 come directly from the OSHPD reports of four nonprofit in hospitals in California, the only state that requires its hospitals to fully disclose price information.

It's a shame that all states don't require this information. If they did, you could see exactly what the hospital in your town is taking in, what it's paying out, and how much profit it's making.

In general, according to these reports, about half of the hospitals make a profit on Medicare and about half lose money on Medicare. Generally, the hospitals lose money on Medicaid (which in California is called MediCal).

But, again, do they really?

	Amount Charged	Amount Collected	Actual Cost
San Gabriel Valley Medical Center	$9,056	$2,012	$1,399
Dominican Santa Cruz Hospital	$8,548	$2,950	$2,073
O'Connor Hospital	$7,610	$3,687	$2,220
St. Mary's Medical Center	$6,979	$4,200	$1,564

Amount Charged = How much the hospital charged its uninsured patients, per patient day

Amount Collected = How much of that charge the hospital was actually able to collect from its uninsured patients, per day

Actual Cost = The hospital's actual cost of caring for its uninsured patients, per patient day

Measure Per Patient Day in 2004

Figure 9.1   OSHPD Reports: Measure per Patient Day 2004

Who's Losing Money?

Looking deeper into a hospital's financial reporting, it's clear that hospitals report two types of costs: variable costs and fixed costs.

A fixed cost is the depreciation on a hospital's building and equipment. The hospital may have raised money—the public may have *provided* money to build the building and buy the equipment—but still it is able to count the subsequent depreciation of those fixed costs (building, materials, equipment). When a hospital reports its total cost, that sum includes depreciation—depreciation for buildings it often didn't pay for. Though it's nothing more than an accounting entry—no money is actually going out the door—hospitals still count depreciation as a cost. Medicare payments include both the variable and the fixed hospital costs.

Are We *Really* Too Dumb to Understand?

Hospitals have lobbyists because so much of the revenue comes from the U.S. government in Medicare payments—and they want to keep those payments as high as they can. These hospital lobbyists say that hospitals shouldn't disclose their prices because no one would understand them. They don't want to disclose their prices because they want to continue to be able to take advantage of the public.

Here are a couple more quick examples from California:

- Hospital A has a cost of $2,152 a day, and it's charging people who do not have insurance $9,724 a day. The hospital is actually collecting an average of $7,500 on that price. (The fact is, hospitals that run effective collection practices will succeed in getting most of that money.)
- Hospital B is charging $9,700 a day and collecting $9,200 a day. Hospital B usually gets this sum by using an independent law firm or collection agency that says to John Doe, "If you don't pay this, we will report it to the credit agency and your credit will become no good." People realize that if they want to buy virtually anything, they need to have a good credit reputation, so they will struggle and may put a second mortgage on their home to pay off the hospital.

We know this only because these hospitals happened to be in California, where such financial reporting is mandatory.

What do you think is happening elsewhere in the country where this information is not being made public? What's happening in *your* state?

What Needs to Change

The average American is not dumb, just ignorant of medical prices. We deserve to be educated. Here are the five things that need to happen for that education to take place:

1. Hospitals across the nation should be required to file a *federal* OSHPD report. The current Medicare cost reports provide only skeletal charge data. The public deserves to know more.
2. The Centers for Medicare and Medicaid Services (CMS), the federal agency that oversees these programs, should require an annual Medicare report that's similar to California's OSHPD report. In fact, CMS currently does get the information from hospitals, but CMS participates in the cover-up by failing to publish the information it has in a satisfactorily easy-to-use form.

3. Hospitals should give patients estimated charges for all non-emergency care in advance, in the same way we get estimates for car repairs.
4. Hospitals should be required to disclose what they charge for procedures *along with the actual cost* of the procedure.
5. Hospitals should publicly disclose what discounts they're offering to managed-care insurance companies and government insurance programs, just as they do in California.

Legislation Now Pending

Congress is currently considering a tool that would provide Americans much of this important information. It's called the Hospital Price Disclosure and Litigation Practice Act (HR 4450).

This legislation, if passed, would do two things:

1. It would require hospitals to disclose all of their prices to the uninsured prior to treatment, whenever possible.
2. In return, it would offer hospitals protection from lawsuits that might arise from bill disputes.

Here's how the act would work. Before an admission, the hospital must give uninsured patients three estimates to compare:

1. The price the hospital charges for the treatment.
2. The price the hospital accepts from its largest managed-care insurance plan (typically, Blue Cross).
3. The price the hospital accepts from Medicare.

After the treatment is performed, the hospital must then provide the uninsured patient with three more items of information:

1. An itemized list of the charges.
2. How much the hospital accepts from its largest managed-care insurance plan as payment for those same services (again, typically, Blue Cross).
3. How much the hospital accepts from Medicare as payment for those services.

Of course, if an admission is an emergency, there may not be time to discuss prices in advance. But anytime a hospital does provide a patient with this information and the patient agrees on the price in writing, then he or she cannot sue the hospital over the agreed price. After all, with the prices fully disclosed in advance, there should be no reason to sue.

Because hospitals are major economic players in every congressional district, chances are good that they have your representative's ear. But it is hoped that your representative will listen to reason and be willing to stand up for fairness on behalf of the average person. Contact your congressional office and say you want your representatives' support for the Hospital Price Disclosure and Litigation Practice Act (HR 4450).

Medicare Starts to Move

Finally bowing to years of pressure, Health and Human Services Secretary Mike Leavitt announced recently that CMS would begin reporting the prices of the 31 most common elective in-patient procedures. Why just 31? What's wrong with 50? What's wrong with 100?

We don't know what Secretary Leavitt is planning to report, but this is what CMS *should* report: exactly what OSPHD in California does. In other words, CMS should give the price that the hospital charges Medicare and the net price it collects from Medicare. (The artificial price, the price charged, doesn't mean a thing, but the net price does.)

What prices need to be transparent? These are the most important questions we need answered before we pay a medical bill:

- What is a hospital's gross price?
- What does it actually collect from Medicare?
- What does it actually collect from managed-care insurance?
- What does it actually collect from traditional insurance?
- And what does it collect from private-pay patients?

And Not Just the Hospitals

It is not just hospital prices that need to be disclosed. Doctors also ought to disclose their prices.

When you go into the doctor's office, you ought to be able to pick up a leaflet or sheet of paper that gives the prices. There also should be a report for ancillary services, such as laboratory work and the like. Patients should have ready access to the prices for everything. And if there are two prices, or three prices, or five, all the prices should be disclosed.

As hospitals and doctors disclose their prices, insurance companies also should report publicly the prices they negotiate with each group. Aetna has begun making available to its customers the prices the company actually pays to physicians in Cincinnati.

This is price transparency—this much, and nothing less.

Before we buy anything, one of the first questions we always ask is "What is the price?" We get a direct answer to this question from every other business, from the plumber to the car mechanic, from real estate agents to grocery stores. In no other part of life do you buy a product or service without knowing in advance—at least generally—what the price will be.

It's time for the medical community to give a straight answer as well.

CHAPTER

Build Risk Pools

AN INNOVATIVE APPROACH TO INDIVIDUAL HEALTH INSURANCE

It is estimated that about 1 million Americans can't get health insurance because of preexisting medical conditions.[1]

How can we help these people, in addition to those who just can't afford to buy insurance?

Since individuals can buy insurance only in the state in which they live, this question has largely been left to the states to answer. Most have chosen one of two paths: Some states simply force their insurance companies to accept all applicants, regardless of their health and their age. The other state practice is to offer a subsidized safety net for those who need the help. The first practice is called *guaranteed issue*. When it's the same price regardless of age, it's *community rating*.

The states that opt simply to provide a subsidized safety net for those people who are rejected by insurance companies seem to have a far better result for their citizens. Here are the reasons why.

New York State of Mind

Motivated by "compassion" and making insurance "fair," the state of New York decides to guarantee health insurance coverage to all citizens, regardless of their age or the condition of their health. Not content with this guarantee, though, the state goes further.

It mandates that every individual health insurance policy sold in the state must cover podiatry. New Yorkers who need health insurance *must* buy this benefit—*even* if they have healthy feet!

And they must also buy:

- Maternity care, even if they are male.
- Infertility treatment, even if they are not planning a family.
- Treatment for alcohol abuse, even if they do not drink.
- More than 30 other benefits, even if they don't particularly want or need them.

What does such compassion do to the price of health insurance? It shoots it sky high—making it unaffordable to those the state had hoped to help in the first place. In other words, it forces more people to go uninsured.

Though the insurance companies are being forced to sell insurance to all citizens in any state with mandated benefits, the citizens aren't forced to *buy* the policies. (An exception to this approach is the state of Massachusetts, where Governor Mitt Romney signed into law in April 2006 an effort to require citizens to carry health insurance, just like some states already require citizens to carry auto insurance. The question remains, though: Where will the citizens get the money? Health insurance costs much more than car insurance, especially in Massachusetts.)

The Council for Affordable Health Insurance has identified nearly 2,000 state-imposed health insurance mandates across the nation. The annual bill for all these state mandates is *$13.5 billion.*[2]

Somebody has to pay for these extra costs.

No Picnic in the Garden State

As bad as things are in New York and Massachusetts, individual health insurance rates are even worse in New Jersey. Thanks to the Garden State's regulatory mandates, New Jerseyans suffer the most unaffordable rates in the nation.

Courtesy of the state of New Jersey's web site, Figures 10.1 and 10.2 present a look at the rates currently being offered in the state.

Families that are buying health insurance on their own in New Jersey have four categories of standard plans to choose from, with at least four plans in each category. Plan A is the least expensive, Plan B a little more expensive, Plan C is still more expensive, and

January 2008 | New Jersey Individual Health Coverage Program Board | Standard Plans

SINGLE

SINGLE	Plan A/50				Plan B		Plan C		Plan D		HMO Plans						Standard Plan Rate Guarantee
	$1,000 Deduct	$2,500 Deduct	$5,000 Deduct	$10,000 Deduct	$1,000 Deduct	$2,500 Deduct	$1,000 Deduct	$2,500 Deduct	$1,000 Deduct	$2,500 Deduct	$15 Copay	$30 Copay	$40 Copay	$50 Copay	Split Copay	Deductible Coinsurance	
Aetna Life Insurance Company	886.00	728.00	-	-	1,044.00	904.00	1,189.00	1,022.00	2,228.00	1,915.00	-	-	-	-	-	-	12 mos
Aetna Health Inc.	-	-	-	-	-	-	-	-	-	-	1,181.50	805.20	-	-	-	432.90	12 mos
AmeriHealth HMO, Inc.	-	-	-	-	-	-	-	-	-	-	1,248.00	559.00	498.00	531.00	-	-	none
Celtic Insurance Company	1,219.00	1,080.00	-	-	1,528.00	1,375.00	4,419.00	3,352.00	6,009.00	5,288.00	-	-	-	-	-	-	3 mos
CIGNA HealthCare	-	-	-	-	-	-	-	-	-	-	1,208.34	-	-	-	-	-	none
Health Net of NJ	-	-	-	-	-	-	-	-	-	-	1,123.18	928.78	843.83	772.33	-	-	none
Horizon Blue Cross Blue Shield of NJ	1,205.84	1,039.39	657.58	429.26	1,323.13	1,129.76	,869.95	1,159.10	2,614.72	1,740.77	-	-	-	-	-	-	12 mos
Horizon HealthCare of NJ HMO Blue	-	-	-	-	-	-	-	-	-	-	585.70	487.40	-	-	481.06	303.09	12 mos
Oxford Health Insurance Company	605.41	493.70	424.63	366.91	923.30	734.36	,150.63	858.61	1,354.40	994.63	-	-	-	-	-	-	12 mos
Oxford Health Insurance Company (PPO)	-	-	-	-	-	-	575.51	442.04	624.43	-	-	-	-	-	-	-	12 mos
Oxford Health Plans	-	-	-	-	-	-	-	-	-	-	652.92	485.51	-	-	-	-	12 mos

ADULT & CHILD

ADULT & CHILD	Plan A/50				Plan B		Plan C		Plan D		HMO Plans						Standard Plan Rate Guarantee
	$1,000 Deduct	$2,500 Deduct	$5,000 Deduct	$10,000 Deduct	$1,000 Deduct	$2,500 Deduct	$1,000 Deduct	$2,500 Deduct	$1,000 Deduct	$2,500 Deduct	$15 Copay	$30 Copay	$40 Copay	$50 Copay	Split Copay	Deductible Coinsurance	
Aetna Life Insurance Company	1,531.00	1,254.00	-	-	1,793.00	1,529.00	2,025.00	1,739.00	3,847.00	3,307.00	-	-	-	-	-	-	12 mos
Aetna Health Inc.	-	-	-	-	-	-	-	-	-	-	2,128.90	1,450.80	-	-	-	780.10	12 mos
AmeriHealth HMO, Inc.	-	-	-	-	-	-	-	-	-	-	2,271.00	1,017.00	906.00	966.00	-	-	none
Celtic Insurance Company	2,133.00	1,890.00	-	-	2,675.00	2,406.00	7,734.00	5,865.00	10,517.00	9,255.00	-	-	-	-	-	-	3 mos
CIGNA HealthCare	-	-	-	-	-	-	-	-	-	-	2,175.01	-	-	-	-	-	none
Health Net of NJ	-	-	-	-	-	-	-	-	-	-	1,909.61	1,579.09	1,434.66	1,313.10	-	-	none
Horizon Blue Cross Blue Shield of NJ	2,136.62	1,841.86	1,165.15	760.64	2,344.62	2,001.76	3,317.87	2,056.73	4,639.85	2,607.08	-	-	-	-	-	-	12 mos
Horizon HealthCare of NJ HMO Blue	-	-	-	-	-	-	-	-	-	-	898.43	747.61	-	-	737.89	464.91	12 mos
Oxford Health Insurance Company	1,120.01	913.35	785.57	678.78	1,708.11	1,358.57	2,128.67	1,588.43	2,505.64	1,840.07	-	-	-	-	-	-	12 mos
Oxford Health Insurance Company (PPO)	-	-	-	-	-	-	,064.69	817.77	1,155.20	-	-	-	-	-	-	-	12 mos
Oxford Health Plans	-	-	-	-	-	-	-	-	-	-	1,240.55	922.47	-	-	-	-	12 mos

> These are monthly premium rates in effect for new business and renewals which occur during the month shown at the top of this page. Contact the carriers or your agent for rates for subsequent months.
> The PPO plan rates shown are listed according to the out-of-network benefit level. A PPO plan listed under Plan C, for example, means that the out-of-network coinsurance is based on Plan C (70%/30% coinsurance).
> Contact Oxford Health Insurance for details on the plan design for the available PPO products.
> Contact the HMO Carriers for information on the HMO Coverage subject to deductible and coinsurance.
> Contact the HMO Carriers for information on the HMO Coverage with a split copay.

Figure 10.1 Monthly Health Insurance Premiums for Single Individuals and One Adult with One Child Coverage in New Jersey, January 2008

Source: State of New Jersey Department of Banking and Insurance web site, New Jersey Individual Health Coverage Program Rates, Standard Plans, New Jersey Health Coverage Program Board, October 2007, Single and Family Plans, www.state.nj.us/dobi/division_insurance/lhcseh/lhcratepage_sp.pdf.

New Jersey Individual Health Coverage Program Board

Standard Plans

TWO ADULTS

TWO ADULTS	Plan A/50				Plan B		Plan C		Plan D		HMO Plans					Deductible Coinsurance	Standard Plan Rate Guarantee
	$1,000 Deduct	$2,500 Deduct	$5,000 Deduct	$10,000 Deduct	$1,000 Deduct	$2,500 Deduct	$1,000 Deduct	$2,500 Deduct	$1,000 Deduct	$2,500 Deduct	$15 Copay	$30 Copay	$40 Copay	$50 Copay	Split Copay		
Aetna Life Insurance Company	1,772.00	1,457.00	-	-	2,088.00	1,767.00	2,377.00	2,036.00	4,470.00	3,842.00	-	-	-	-	-	-	12 mos
Aetna Health Inc.	-	-	-	-	-	-	-	-	-	-	2,362.80	1,610.40	-	-	-	865.90	12 mos
AmeriHealth HMO, Inc.	-	-	-	-	-	-	-	-	-	-	2,496.00	1,118.00	-	996.00	1,062.00	-	none
Celtic Insurance Company	2,840.00	2,517.00	-	-	3,561.00	3,203.00	10,297.00	7,809.00	14,002.00	12,322.00	-	-	-	-	-	-	3 mos
CIGNA HealthCare	-	-	-	-	-	-	-	-	-	-	2,332.09	-	-	-	-	-	none
Health Net of NJ	-	-	-	-	-	-	-	-	-	-	2,021.52	1,671.63	1,518.74	1,390.06	-	-	none
Horizon Blue Cross Blue Shield of NJ	2,902.04	2,501.73	1,582.57	1,033.18	3,184.71	2,718.95	4,458.83	2,764.12	6,235.48	3,503.57	-	-	-	-	-	-	12 mos
Horizon HealthCare of NJ HMO Blue	-	-	-	-	-	-	-	-	-	-	1,252.66	1,042.37	-	-	1,028.82	648.20	12 mos
Oxford Health Insurance Company	1,210.82	987.40	849.26	733.82	1,846.60	1,468.72	2,301.26	1,717.22	2,708.80	1,989.26	-	-	-	-	-	-	12 mos
Oxford Health Insurance Company (PPO)	-	-	-	-	-	-	1,151.02	884.08	1,248.86	-	-	-	-	-	-	-	12 mos
Oxford Health Plans	-	-	-	-	-	-	-	-	-	-	1,305.84	971.02	-	-	-	-	12 mos

FAMILY

FAMILY	Plan A/50				Plan B		Plan C		Plan D		HMO Plans					Deductible Coinsurance	Standard Plan Rate Guarantee
	$1,000 Deduct	$2,500 Deduct	$5,000 Deduct	$10,000 Deduct	$1,000 Deduct	$2,500 Deduct	$1,000 Deduct	$2,500 Deduct	$1,000 Deduct	$2,500 Deduct	$15 Copay	$30 Copay	$40 Copay	$50 Copay	Split Copay		
Aetna Life Insurance Company	2,416.00	1,963.00	-	-	2,837.00	2,392.00	3,213.00	2,753.00	6,089.00	5,233.00	-	-	-	-	-	-	12 mos
Aetna Health Inc.	-	-	-	-	-	-	-	-	-	-	3,531.50	2,406.80	-	-	-	1,294.10	12 mos
AmeriHealth HMO, Inc.	-	-	-	-	-	-	-	-	-	-	3,519.00	1,576.00	-	1,404.00	1,497.00	-	none
Celtic Insurance Company	2,852.00	2,528.00	-	-	3,576.00	3,217.00	10,341.00	7,843.00	14,062.00	12,375.00	-	-	-	-	-	-	3 mos
CIGNA HealthCare	-	-	-	-	-	-	-	-	-	-	3,359.18	-	-	-	-	-	none
Health Net of NJ	-	-	-	-	-	-	-	-	-	-	2,696.03	2,229.39	2,025.49	1,853.87	-	-	none
Horizon Blue Cross Blue Shield of NJ	3,047.29	2,626.82	1,661.74	1,084.85	3,343.89	2,854.91	4,681.72	2,902.12	6,547.24	3,678.83	-	-	-	-	-	-	12 mos
Horizon HealthCare of NJ HMO Blue	-	-	-	-	-	-	-	-	-	-	1,773.90	1,476.11	-	-	1,456.92	917.92	12 mos
Oxford Health Insurance Company	1,725.42	1,407.06	1,210.20	1,045.69	2,631.41	2,092.93	3,279.30	2,447.04	3,860.04	2,834.70	-	-	-	-	-	-	12 mos
Oxford Health Insurance Company (PPO)	-	-	-	-	-	-	1,640.20	1,259.81	1,779.63	-	-	-	-	-	-	-	12 mos
Oxford Health Plans	-	-	-	-	-	-	-	-	-	-	1,958.76	1,456.53	-	-	-	-	12 mos

> These are monthly premium rates in effect for new business and renewals which occur during the month shown at the top of this page. Contact the carriers or your agent for rates for subsequent months.
> The PPO plan rates shown are listed according to the out-of-network benefit level. A PPO plan listed under Plan C, for example, means that the out-of-network coinsurance is based on Plan C (70%/30% coinsurance).
> Contact Oxford Health Insurance for details on the plan design for the available PPO products.
> Contact the HMO Carriers for information on the HMO Coverage subject to deductible and coinsurance.
> Contact the HMO Carriers for information on the HMO Coverage with a split copay.

Figure 10.2 Monthly Health Insurance Premiums for Two Adults and Family Coverage in New Jersey, January 2008

Source: State of New Jersey Department of Banking and Insurance web site. New Jersey Individual Health Coverage Program Rates, Standard Plans. New Jersey Health Coverage Program Board, October 2007, Single and Family Plans, www.state.nj.us/dobi/division_insurance/ihcseh/ihcratepage_sp.pdf.

Plan D is the most expensive. So, Plan B is a standard plan that is the least expensive of the middle two options.

New Jerseyans buying $1,000-deductible per-family health insurance on their own are forced to choose from only four Plan B options, which have premiums ranging from a low of $2,631.41 to a high of $3,576.00 *per month.* That is an annual cost of between $31,576.92 and $42,912. (See Figure 10.2, under Family, Plan B, $1,000 deductible, since these figures are so unbelievable every reader should check the table in 10.2 for themselves.)

The Plan B option is not even the most expensive one in New Jersey, not by a long shot. If a family wanted to consider a $1,000 per-family deductible plan from the Plan C category (the next higher level of benefits), the average of all Plan C premiums with a $1,000 per-family deductible is $4,6031.04 *per month, or $55,572.53 per year.* The next category of standard plans, Plan D, which is the most expensive category, has an average premium for a $1,000 per-family deductible of $6,467.58 *per month, or $77,610.98 per year.*

It makes economic sense for families whose employers do not provide health insurance in New Jersey to be uninsured, since it is clearly impossible for all but the most wealthy to afford the cost of insurance. So who in the individual insurance market in New Jersey is insured?

Only the very sick, who absolutely must have the insurance to shield them from even larger catastrophic costs. The rest just do without until they have a change in health that forces them to buy.

Ferrari Pricing

Dr. David Gratzer, MD, of the Manhattan Institute summed up the net effect of New Jersey's guaranteed issue and community rating mandates when he observed, "After a decade of such political meddling, the average monthly cost of a family policy in New Jersey bests the monthly lease of a Ferrari."[3]

That's no exaggeration. According to the New Jersey State Department of Insurance, a $1,000-deductible Plan B family health insurance plan for a New Jersey family averages $3,097.08 *per month.* That's no typographical error. A New Jersey family buying its own health insurance must spend more than *$37,000 each year.*

But here's the funny thing: Using figures obtained from eHealthInsurance.com, should these same families move across the state line into neighboring Pennsylvania, they would have 80 health insurance plans to pick from! Forty-three of these health plans cost less than $450 a month, and 27 of them cost less than $350 a month. Thirteen of these plans cost less than $300 a month. A $350 a month premium for an individual family health plan would cost *$4,200* a year![4] In other words, New Jersey families—who have a very limited choice of plans—are paying almost *9 times* the amount Pennsylvania families are paying.

One Way to Cope

We recently heard from a young man whose parents live in New Jersey. He said that his parents, who are slightly below Medicare age, are uninsured. They simply cannot afford health insurance, which would cost them more than $4,000 a month.

One solution is to "move" their home address on paper to Indiana, where the young man lives (or somewhere else a family member might live), and purchase insurance as a resident of a different state. As it turns out, people do it all the time. If this young man's parents bought their insurance in Indiana, then they could "move" back to New Jersey or anywhere else in the world and still keep it. They could move to England or France or Timbuktu and still carry the health insurance they bought in Indiana.

Why do this residency dance?

Because the health insurance that would cost this older couple $4,000 a month in New Jersey costs just over $735 a month in Indiana. That's a difference of more than *$3,000* a month! More important, it could mean for them the difference between having health insurance or going without.

Compassion versus Common Sense

In effect, states that pass laws guaranteeing insurance to all applicants put up a sign saying to everyone: "You don't have to buy health insurance until you need it, because we guarantee you can get it whenever you want it." When the healthy read this sign and get out of the insurance market until they really need it, the purchasers are only the ones who really need it, and the price is higher than hell.

It is a matter of compassion versus common sense. A state legislature feels compassion for those who can't get health insurance and mandates that insurance companies must take them. Then those who are healthy use their God-given common sense and don't buy insurance until they absolutely have to have it. (And then they wonder why it's so costly.) Meanwhile, the evidence shows that such misguided compassion actually creates more uninsured citizens than it helps.

We can't improve the common good by tossing common sense to the wind.

Casting the Net

But if guaranteeing health insurance to everyone isn't the answer, then what is?

Evidence shows that the states that have built safety nets to cushion the fall of those rejected by private insurers have chosen a better path.

These safety nets are *state risk pools*. A state risk pool is simply a government-subsidized health insurance plan for high-risk individuals. By providing access to health insurance for those who have applied for it and been turned down, state risk pools serve the same purpose as guaranteed-issue legislation. They provide access to health insurance for those who otherwise couldn't get it. But unlike the guaranteed-issue approach, risk pools do *not* cause the price of insurance to skyrocket out of reach for everyone. Typically, people getting their health insurance through the state risk pool will pay about 25 percent more than standard rates. (Figure 10.3 has a complete list of the 34 state risk pools and the information necessary to contact them.)

States that take this approach don't, as New Jersey and a few other states do, put up a sign that says "We guarantee you can get health insurance whenever you want it, so you can wait till you want it (and, in the meantime, save money)."

Double Incentive

Two additional factors make these safety nets an even *more* attractive path for states to take:

1. The federal government subsidizes the cost of state risk pools.
2. Many states pay for their risk pools by assessing the remaining cost to health insurance companies operating in the state.

So with the federal government and the state's private insurers helping fund the pools, neither the participants nor the taxpayers are left holding the whole cost.

Alabama (for portability only)
Alabama Health Insurance Plan
1-800-513-1384 or (334) 353-8924

Alaska
Alaska Comprehensive Health Insurance
Association
1-800-467-8725 or (907) 269-7900

Arkansas
Arkansas Comprehensive Health Insurance Pool
1-800-285-6477

California
California Major Risk Medical Insurance
Program
1-800-289-6574 or (916) 324-4695

Colorado
CoverColorado
(303) 863-1960

Connecticut
Connecticut Health Reinsurance
Association 1-800-842-0004

Florida (not open for new enrollees)
(850) 309-1200

Idaho
Idaho Individual High Risk Reinsurance Pool

Illinois
Illinois Comprehensive Health Insurance Plan
1-800-367-6410 or (217) 782-6333

Indiana
Indiana Comprehensive Health Association
1-800-552-7921 or (317) 614-2000

Iowa
Iowa Comprehensive Health Association
(877) 793-6880

Kansas
Kansas Health Insurance Association
1-800-290-1366 or (316) 792-1779

Kentucky
Kentucky Access
(866) 405-6145

Louisiana
Louisiana Health Insurance Association
1-800-736-0947 or (504) 926-6245

Maryland
Maryland Health Insurance Plan
(888) 444-9016

Minnesota
Minnesota Comprehensive Health Association
(952) 593-9609

Mississippi
Mississippi Comprehensive Health
Insurance Risk Pool
(601) 362-0799

Missouri
Missouri Health Insurance Pool
1-800-843-6447 (All but NW Missouri)
1-800-645-8346 (NW Missouri)

Montana
Montana Comprehensive Health Insurance
Association
(406) 444-8200

Nebraska
Nebraska Comprehensive Health Association
(402) 343-3574 or (877) 348-4304

New Hampshire
New Hampshire Health Plan
(800) 578-3272

New Mexico
New Mexico Medical Insurance Pool
(505) 622-4711

North Dakota
Comprehensive Health Association Of
North Dakota
1-800-737-0016 or (701) 282-1235

Oklahoma
Oklahoma Health Insurance High Risk Pool
1-800-255-6065 or (913) 362-0040

Oregon
Oregon Medical Insurance Pool
(503) 373-1692

South Carolina
South Carolina Health Insurance Pool
1-800-868-2500, ext. 42757,
or 1-803-788-0500, ext. 42757

South Dakota
South Dakota Risk Pool

Tennessee
TennCare Program
Contact Tennessee area county medical
assistance offices, or (615) 741-8642

Texas
Texas Health Insurance Risk Pool
1-888-398-3927

Utah
Utah Comprehensive Health Insurance Pool
1-800-705-9173 or (801) 442-6660

Washington
Washington State Health Insurance Pool
1-800-877-5187

West Virginia
AccessWV
1-866-445-8491

Wisconsin
Wisconsin Health Insurance Risk Sharing Plan
(608) 441-5777

Wyoming
Wyoming Health Insurance Pool
(307) 634-1393

**Congress recently passed an
additional $49 million for state
high risk pool administration.**

Figure 10.3   The 34 State Risk Pools

As of late 2007, 34 states had established risk pools. These safety nets are currently serving about 200,000 people nationwide.[5] But more need the help that risk pools offer—every state should have such a safety net.

State safety nets work; guaranteed-issue laws do not.

The Problem for Small Businesses

The bad news is that while the damage that guaranteed-issue laws inflict on individuals is limited to a handful of states, *federal* guaranteed-issue legislation in place is financially crushing small businesses and their employees all across the nation.

When the Health Insurance Portability and Accountability Act (HIPAA) went into effect at the end of 1996, it required that any group health insurance policy sold to a small business (defined as a business with 50 employees or less) *must* accept every employee who wants to be included in the plan, regardless of the employee's health or age.

Again, this sounded like a compassionate way to ensure high-risk employees could get coverage. But as with state guaranteed-issue programs, the HIPAA requirement has some unintended consequences: The rates for coverage rose *100* percent! That's right—the price of health insurance for small businesses has *doubled* under the weight of the new HIPAA requirement.

Just as individuals are dropping insurance rather than paying for unaffordable state mandates, small businesses are dropping employee health care coverage altogether rather than pay for a federal mandate that has become crippling. Among the small businesses that continue to offer benefits, more and more employees are dropping out, unable to cover their share of the cost.

The good news is that there's a way that state risk pools can help small businesses too.

A Future Answer for Small Businesses

One obvious solution to this dilemma would be to reinstate normal risk selection and let declined employees go into state risk pools at rates of no more than the normal price for insurance plus 25 percent. (States commonly cap the risk pool premium rates.)

The normal rate plus 25 percent for those in the state risk pool is still a good deal less than *double* the normal rate, which companies now are paying.

When we know that guaranteed acceptance has caused rates for small businesses to double, wouldn't it be better to have normal rates and just let the few who are declined pay higher rates in the state risk pool? To help an employee rejected by private insurers, small employers could offer to cover the extra cost necessary for the employee to enter the state risk pool. *That way an employer might pay more for a small number of employees but not double for every one.*

A More Immediate Answer

One way that small companies can skirt this oppressive HIPAA requirement today is by dropping their group health insurance coverage and encouraging their employees to buy individual policies— which typically cost *half* the price of small-group policies. (Except, of course, in those states like New Jersey or New York, which have elevated individual rates due to guaranteed-issue laws.)

Employers who choose to go this route can use a portion of their former health care spending to pay part of the employees' cost.

How might that work?

Let's say a business has 10 employees, and all apply for individual health insurance. Two of those 10 are denied coverage and go into the state risk pool. Let's assume these two pay 25 percent more than what others would pay to get insurance. Remember, this is 25 percent more than the normal *individual* insurance rate, which is already half the current available small-group rate. Additionally, that increased premium only applies to the two employees who are declined, and not to all 10, as before. The employer can now afford to make an incremental contribution toward the increased cost of individual insurance for the two employees in the state risk pool.

List Bill

To lower the cost of health insurance for a small employee group, the expedient action is, for the employees who want health insurance, to buy individual insurance in the marketplace. We would normally think that buying as a group would be less costly. Generally, a group purchase for a small group is double the cost of individually purchased insurance since HIPAA came along. You can shop around and learn for yourself. Small group under HIPAA, which requires *guarantee issue,* is 2 to 50 employees, not necessarily 50 insured.

The employees can buy in the individual market and the employer can pay part or all of the cost by additional compensation. If a couple of the employees have a health problem in the family, those individuals can go to the high-risk pool in the state where they will pay a higher premium. But it's just those few who will pay the higher individual premium for themselves and their family. The employer is entitled to pay whatever compensation the employer wishes, so the employer may add extra compensation for those who have to go to the state risk pool. The criterion generally used to determine whether the insurance is "group" and comes under HIPAA is whether payroll tax is paid. If the employer and employee paid payroll tax, it generally isn't considered group insurance, rather it is individually owned insurance. There can be a list bill covering the employees, so the employer may take the premiums out of the paychecks and remit to the insurance company. The employer is then remitting employee money.

The Rest of the Story

State risk pools are only part of the solution we seek. The states that have erred by adopting guaranteed-issue legislation—New York, New Jersey, Maine, Vermont, and Massachusetts—do not receive federal money to subsidize their mistake, as they do not have state risk pools that can be subsidized. So, the uninsured trapped in these states—the people who need coverage most—have no reasonably priced safety net to fall back on. This would all change, obviously, if people could just buy the health insurance offered in another state.

CHAPTER

11

Build a National Marketplace

AN INNOVATIVE APPROACH TO INDIVIDUAL HEALTH INSURANCE

In Lawrenceville, a town in southern Illinois just nine miles from the Indiana border, with fewer than 6,000 residents in the 1940s, choices for shopping were limited. Across the border was the larger town of Vincennes, Indiana, which was three to four times the size of Lawrenceville. Everyone from Lawrenceville went to Vincennes to shop, where they were sure to find more choices and better prices. They would even go to Vincennes for groceries. If a person needed a suit, he or she went across the border to Indiana to buy it.

Pat Rooney, one of the co-authors of this book, grew up in Lawrenceville, Illinois. His family did what we have just described.

Today, when we want to buy something from another state, we do it without giving the matter a second thought. The Commerce Clause of the U.S. Constitution allows us this freedom. In this age of Amazon.com and eBay, we can buy most things across state lines.

But probably not health insurance.

Most people don't realize that even today, in the twenty-first century, Americans cannot cross a state line to buy health insurance. Congress passed a law in 1945 declaring insurance not to be interstate commerce, shortly after the Supreme Court had determined that it was. At issue was the question of who should regulate health insurance, the federal government or the states, and Congress voted to vest regulatory power with the states.

But Congress can easily allow the cross-state purchase of insurance without assuming federal regulatory control of the industry. After all, we buy cars in other states. We get credit cards and mortgages in other states. *We ought to be able to buy health insurance wherever we can get the best coverage and the best price.*

Do You eBay?

Dennis Hastert, formerly the Republican Speaker of the House of Representatives, took the initiative to call on experts (including one of the authors of this book) to help create legislation and a market for selling health insurance nationally. He had spoken with Meg Whitman, the head of eBay, and Speaker Hastert wanted health insurance to be sold over the Internet the way other products are sold.[1]

John Shadegg, a Republican congressman from Arizona, worked on the legislation that would allow this to happen. So far, the bill has been reported "do pass" out of the Commerce Committee in the U.S. House of Representatives, but it has not yet been brought to the floor of the House for a vote. That bill's number in the current Congress (the 110th) is HR 4460, but in the 109th Congress, when it nearly came up for a vote, its bill number was HR 2355. The reason it did not come up for a vote on the floor of the U.S. House is opposition from Republican Congress members from New Jersey and New York who don't want to offend their home state insurance regulators.[2]

Nothing Matters More

Why is this matter so important? Because it would enable people to buy health insurance where they could get the best buy—and therefore, be able to be insured.

In the last chapter, we looked at New Jersey and Pennsylvania and saw how individual health insurance rates differed from one side of the river to the other. We saw how state mandates are driving up the cost of health insurance unmercifully in states like New Jersey and New York. *Nothing would help the consumers in these states more than letting them go beyond state borders to buy the insurance coverage they want for the price they can afford.*

The beauty in this approach is that we don't need to change the laws in New Jersey or New York or any other state. These states can continue to regulate the insurance companies that market in their states as much as they want to. And if the people of these states want to pay for all the benefits mandated by their state, they're free to do so. But if the citizens want to pursue other options—get more choices and better prices—then they would be free to do that as well.

Roadblocks to Freedom

It turns out that many state insurance commissioners oppose giving their citizens such freedom. Why? Because *they* want to be able to tell the consumers in their state what health insurance coverage they can or cannot buy rather than let the consumers make their own choice.

The BlueCross BlueShield Association is in league with this opposition. And why is that? Because there are several states, particularly in the Northeast, where BlueCross is the dominant force in the health insurance market. Even if it's an unaffordable market, it's *their* market, and they want to keep it. BlueCross BlueShield's opposition to this bill is well known and understood in Washington, D.C.

This collusion between state regulators and large insurers is the same story of business trying to get government to protect its market share that has taken place throughout history. In 1908, Henry Ford began selling Model Ts at the low price of $825. Many other auto manufacturers were making cars at the time, but their vehicles were being sold at closer to *$10,000*. Knowing they couldn't compete with the $825 price tag coming out of Detroit, manufacturers in neighboring states sought protection from their state legislatures. The legislators didn't disappoint them: Several states pronounced the Model T unsafe and unfit to drive on their roads. Of course the charge was baseless, but the companies felt they needed such legislation to protect them from financial ruin.

Thankfully, the federal government finally stepped in and passed a law requiring all states to accept the Model T and any other vehicle that met the safety standards.[3]

It's time for history to repeat itself.

There is no reason why large insurance companies and their cronies in state government should be allowed to shut out legitimate competition from other states. It wasn't right when the automakers did it in the early twentieth century, and it isn't right for the large insurance companies to do it today in the twenty-first century.

Marketplace freedom would be a freedom for customers, not for insurance companies. Customers would become free to buy health insurance across state lines.

Health Care Choice Act

The legislation that can achieve this progress is called the Health Care Choice Act (HR 4460) introduced by Congressman Shadegg and has 43 cosponsors, as of this writing, in the 110th Congress. This act would allow people to buy health insurance that is approved and being sold in another state. The policy must conform to state law where the health insurance policy is filed, not to the state where the insurance purchaser lives.

The Health Care Choice Act protects consumers by ensuring a level of financial stability among the insurance companies and by ensuring an independent review mechanism for all who purchase coverage under the terms of this legislation.

What would this proposed legislation do for the insurance market? Well, what did it do for the automobile market?

Not in My Backyard

Critics say interstate commerce will create fly-by-night insurers operating in less regulated states that will take advantage of consumers.

"The best analogy for what to expect here is probably our experience with interstate banking," the *Wall Street Journal* has said, "which has indeed resulted in operators moving to friendly climes like Delaware and South Dakota but which has also proven nothing but a boon to consumers. A national market has allowed the growth of big, financially stable institutions that have earned consumer trust."[4]

The BlueCross Association says interstate commerce would jeopardize the risk pool (the overall pool of money that makes insurance possible by allowing the healthy to subsidize the sick). But as we've clearly seen, the healthy are already out of the insurance pool in the high-cost, heavy-mandate states. "A larger national market can only improve matters," the *Wall Street Journal* argues.

"Choice and competition are the great taskmasters that relentlessly deliver lower prices and higher quality to American consumers," comments Sally Pipes of the Pacific Research Institute, a West Coast think-tank.[5] "This is as true for automobiles as it is for artichokes, computers as it is for camping gear. The only exceptions are when government policies limit choice and thwart competition, which is exactly the case with individual health insurance regulations that restrict Americans' choice of health insurance based on the state in which they reside. It's time to end the states' monopolies."

An Idea for the People

In the current monopolistic environment, millions of Americans are afraid to move, switch jobs, or start their own businesses for fear of losing their health insurance.

That fear would go away if they were allowed to shop nationwide for policies that would follow them wherever they went.

America's policymakers must decide whom they're going to serve: the special interests or the people. The special interests may not want change, but the people clearly do. A Zogby International poll has shown that 72 percent of Americans think people should have the option of buying a policy that is approved and available in another state. According to Zogby, "A majority of people in every sub-group—including at least two-thirds in most—supports this. Hispanics (86%) and African Americans (85%) are the most likely to be in support, as are four in five single adults and people with annual household income of $15,000–$24,999 and $35,000–$74,000." Further, "more Republicans (20%) than Democrats (12%) or independent voters (13%) are opposed."[6]

The small-business community represents the largest portion of the uninsured population. In a recent National Federation of Independent Business member ballot, *80 percent* of the members said that individuals and the self-employed should be allowed to purchase health insurance coverage across state lines.[7]

J. Kevin A. McKechnie, the staff director of the HSA Council, part of the American Bankers Association, talks about mandates imposed on health insurance plans by states. Writes McKechnie: "[I]nvolving government in health care choices brings politics to the doctor's office. That's why dance therapy and hair replacement procedures are mandated as covered benefits in some states. They're expensive, of dubious medically necessity, and arise less from considerations of public health than from good lobbying. If you think health care is expensive now, wait until the government makes it 'free.'"[8]

Let's Get It Done

Dennis Hastert has said that his goal is simply to "give Americans the ability to choose the health insurance product that best meets their needs. The Health Care Choice Act will modernize the healthcare marketplace. Consumers will no longer be constrained by the options in their hometown or state but will be able to shop on the Internet and buy the insurance that best meets their individual or family needs."[9]

Just as is with the case of health savings accounts, the Health Care Choice Act will not single-handedly fix all the problems in American health care, but it is the one reform that could accomplish much very quickly. It's common sense. It's long overdue. We need to get it done.

Until we modernize the sale of individual health insurance in America, the only affordable alternative for many is to establish residency in an affordable state, buy insurance there, then move back to the state in which they currently reside, while keeping the insurance they bought elsewhere.

Consumers should be free to buy health insurance wherever *they can get the best coverage for the best price.*

CHAPTER

Make Basic Health Care Cheaper and More Convenient

AN INNOVATIVE APPROACH TO HEALTH CARE DELIVERY

Imagine that your daughter awakes one morning with a bad sore throat. You think she may have strep and need an antibiotic.

At this point, you can do one of two things:

1. You can call the pediatrician's office and try to schedule an appointment for late morning or early afternoon, probably at the cost of $75 or $100. (That's provided you can get in today.) You'll then need to call your office to let them know you will be out for the day. Once you arrive at the doctor's office, you will wait half an hour before your daughter is seen. Once the doctor prescribes an antibiotic, you will need to stop by the drugstore on the way home to get the prescription filled.

2. For $40, you can take your daughter right away to the new quick care clinic located inside Wal-Mart, where no appointment is necessary. Once you arrive, your daughter is seen if not immediately, then in minutes. The nurse practitioner is much more qualified than a registered nurse and is closer in training to a doctor. He or she prescribes an antibiotic, and you get the prescription filled while you're still at Wal-Mart. Now you are free to stay at home with your daughter, or you can make other arrangements for her and go to work.

Which of the two sounds like the better deal to you?

The reality is that most of our health care needs are simple. Wal-Mart knows this, and that's why it is experimenting with primary care clinics inside stores in select markets. And Wal-Mart is not the only retailer sticking its toes in the health care pool. A major innovation in health care has come on us ever so quietly. This innovation is the quick care clinic.

It's a giant step in the right direction.

What Is a Quick Care Clinic?

Quick care clinics go by many names—MinuteClinics, RediClinics, Quick Care, Take Care, and 30-Minute Clinics—but basically they all operate the same way.

A neighborhood store—whether it's a big-box retailer, a drugstore, or a grocery store—leases some of its interior space to an outside company that specializes in operating retail health clinics. Staffed by a nurse practitioner or physician's assistant (who operates under the oversight of a physician), the in-store clinic offers customers a limited range of basic tests and treatments at a lower cost than what is charged at a doctor's office. Using medical software to follow established clinical protocols, quick care clinics focus on the diagnosis and treatment of common illnesses. Most also administer vaccinations, perform diagnostic screenings, and conduct physical exams.

These clinics typically treat a predefined set of minor illnesses, from ear infections, to strep throat, to bladder infections. Often the price of each treatment is listed on a message board, much like the daily special at your local restaurant. If the symptoms indicate a more serious condition, the patient is referred to a doctor's office.

Quick care clinics operate just like a doctor's office, insofar as they are covered by most insurance plans and can write prescriptions when necessary. Unlike a doctor's office, however, when you go to a quick care clinic in a nearby retail store:

- No appointment is necessary.
- Most visits take about 15 minutes.
- The cost is significantly less.

These benefits are hugely appealing to most people.

The Customer Is King

The retail stores that house these new quick care clinics are interested in having more customers and doing more business. That's the critical difference between these clinics and regular doctor's offices.

They know right off that their ability to get more customers and take in more money is *price sensitive.* The public that goes to Wal-Mart or Target or CVS is a price-sensitive public. These are people who are not going to the Mayo Clinic for their health care. They've been going to the physician they've known for 10 years—but they've had to make an appointment every time, and many times they have to sit and wait despite their appointment.

Not so at the quick care clinic. When they go to the MinuteClinic at CVS, the sign says loud and clear: "No appointment needed."

Wal-Mart is happy with the early results its clinics have delivered. "We'll certainly grow this business if it makes sense," Wal-Mart spokeswoman Sharon Weber has said. "I can tell you the customers have been very pleased."[1]

Take Care clinics, another of the major players in this newly emerging market, claims on its web site to have already served 100,000 patients. It proudly boasts a 98 percent customer satisfaction rate.[2] That's impressive. How would you rate the convenience and affordability of the care you've been getting from *your* doctor?

Calling Dr. Nurse

Many people frequently get care for ailments that are pretty ordinary. If they get a prescription, it's probably one they've gotten half a dozen times before. Most of the time, what people need is someone to check their vital signs to make sure there's nothing more serious going on and to write the prescription for them. A quick clinic run by a nurse can do that just fine.

A business colleague whose sister is a nurse calls his sister when he has minor medical issues. Whether its sniffles or sunburn, she provides him with guidance that takes care of the problem. The rest of us would do just as well to have a nurse on hand, at lower prices, for minor matters. Quick care clinics become our sister-nurses and allow us to be seen quickly for a lower price. No long waiting times (that can lead to more serious health problems). Also, no frivolous trips to absurdly expensive hospital emergency rooms.

Quick care clinics will be a great blessing to the future of American health care. They will permit most of us to see a medical professional without having to wait or go to the hospital emergency room. (It is estimated that 25 to 40 percent of all emergency room visits are for nonemergency needs.) It doesn't take a shrewd consumer to appreciate the amount to be saved between a $40 quick clinic visit and a $240 emergency room (ER) visit for a nonemergency need.

Insurance companies complain all the time about all the patients who go to the emergency room, and Medicaid, the health plan for the very low income, ends up spending a lot of its money at the ER. Now people can go to a quick care clinic, get quicker medical care, and save money for *whoever* is paying.

"You've Got Care"

"The cost savings represented by the [quick care clinic] format can be significant," said Dr. Jack Rowe, the chief executive of Aetna Inc. "When you are able to treat a simple health problem with high-quality care in a clinic setting, everyone wins. The patient receives convenient quality care and payers have lower costs."[3]

William R. Brody, M.D., the president of Johns Hopkins University, agrees: "The [quick care clinic] model of care represents an effective means of making quality health care services accessible to a wide audience of patients."[4]

Steve Case made a fortune by founding the popular computer service America Online. Recently, he invested a sizable part of that fortune—$500 million—in a company that will invest in quick care clinics. "There should be new options for providing health care," he said. "Why should a parent whose child has an ear infection have to take time off work to get that child treatment? Why can't we have clinics in convenient locations—retail stores, pharmacies, or grocery stores—open at convenient times?"[5]

Quick care clinics can help uninsured individuals, self-insured employers, and health care insurers cut their health care costs dramatically. In addition to saving patients millions of dollars, they can save them frustrating hours of waiting time.

This is a marvelous blessing for the American people. We should all stand up and applaud.

Do It Right the First Time

AN INNOVATIVE APPROACH TO WELLNESS

*Big insurers liked managed care because it meant they could make
money by not paying for medical care.*

Dr. Paul Ellwood

In the early 1990s, Dr. Paul Ellwood and Professor Alain Enthoven
provided the intellectual steam for Hillary Clinton's health care
plan. Ellwood led the Jackson Hole Group, which was a discussion
and planning group, on health maintenance organizations for the
nation. They met in Ellwood's home in Jackson Hole, Wyoming.
That was the time Mrs. Clinton was developing her health plan for
the nation.

Dr. Ellwood is the father of health maintenance organizations
(HMOs). In the Jackson Hole discussions, Ellwood asserted that
there needs to be a gatekeeper to control costs.

Perhaps the most illuminating discussion on controlling costs
was the considerable debate regarding the publishing of doctor's
fees. It was proposed that the insurance plan could authorize a
fee level and allow the patient to go to the doctor of the patient's
choice. The idea was universally rejected by the people who made
up the planning group.

The reason for the rejection was "the physician of the patient's choice" would do more than the physician of the insurance company's choice. *The insurance executives absolutely did not want the physician who might do more.* More tests would run up the costs for the HMO, and the insurance executives did not want to pay for doing more. That's why they felt the need for a gatekeeper: to keep the patients and doctors from "doing more."

The Right Goal

In 2004, the Harvard Business School published an excellent article titled "Solving the Health Care Conundrum," by Michael Porter and Elizabeth Olmsted Teisberg.[1] In the article, the authors put much emphasis on "doing it right the first time." They simply said that getting the right diagnosis and the right treatment the first time not only improves outcomes for the patient but *can dramatically reduce costs.*

How did managed care get it so wrong?

According to Porter and Teisberg, "[Managed care] treated health care as if it were a commodity."

The discussion in the Jackson Hole Group about letting the patient choose the physician fits right in with Porter and Teisberg. Porter and Teisberg argued that if we are ever to reform American health care, we must change the nature of competition within it.

The Right Kind of Competition

"Competing on cost alone makes sense only in commodity businesses, where all sellers are more or less the same," the authors reported.

Clearly, that is not true in health care. Yet, that perverse assumption —which neither buyers nor sellers really believe—underlies the behavior of the system participants. Payers, employers, even providers pay insufficient attention to achieving better outcomes and improving value over time, which are what really matter.

The fundamental problem with American health care, they said, is that competition exists between health plans and networks, but not at the level of disease. "[Competition] should occur in the prevention, diagnosis, and treatment of individual health conditions or co-occurring conditions," they argue. "It is at this level that true value is created—or destroyed—disease by disease and patient by patient."

And this becomes all the more important as diagnoses and treatments become increasingly specialized, they said:

> Prostate cancer, for example, is now understood to be six different diseases that respond to different treatments. Providers should compete to be the best at addressing a particular set of problems, and patients should be free to seek out the providers with the best track records given their unique circumstances. In the current environment, where patients' treatments are determined by the networks they are in, network providers are all but guaranteed the business.

That just makes no sense for the patient. In the long run, it costs more.

It Is Your Health

It's not humanly possible for one physician to know everything. When a physician doesn't have an answer, the patient should have access to someone who does. Though a specialist may cost more money, patients will save money in the long run by getting it right the first time.

Hence, when these authors say that "doing it right the first time" can improve outcomes and reduce costs, that makes good sense.

Lose the Gatekeepers

Does losing the gatekeepers make good sense? Not to the managed-care gatekeepers, who want to limit us to routine, cheap medical care.

Phooey.

No one wants routine, cheap medical care for the sake of saving money. We want *effective* medical care so we can get well and get on living. We don't just want to recover from whatever ails us; we want to get well *soon*.

But this is the opposite of what most insurance companies want. Some of the health insurance industry has a managed-care mentality to manage medical care and save the company money. They save money by restricting the care and keeping the patient on the cheapest medication.

Is that the kind of medical care you want?

Get Well Soon

With a health savings account (HSA), we have a cash fund that *we* control, which *we* can spend at our own discretion for medical care. If we have a major bill that's in excess of our deductible, the insurance takes over.

As a practical matter, with an HSA, it becomes impossible for insurance companies to get us to shift to *their* doctors after we have gone through our deductible. The HSA gives us a degree of control we didn't have before.

A new study by Frank Lichtenberg of Columbia University deals with patient outcomes in choosing drugs. His evidence concludes that the newer, more expensive drugs may indeed cost more, but their purpose is to get the patient well sooner.[2] It makes sense: The reason for discovering the new drugs is that they will be more effective and will get John or Jane Doe well more quickly.

Patients, of course, aren't interested in buying the "newest thing" just because it's new. We're only interested in the best results. For most ailments, the generic drug is just fine, and it's cheaper. But if a new, more expensive medication will get us well *sooner,* then that *is* what we want.

Who wants a gatekeeper telling us no, we *must* use something cheaper to keep *their* costs down? That's not the right approach. In the end, we're learning it's not even the cheapest approach.

We don't want to live forever, but we do want to live in comfort as long as we're here.

Wrapping It All Up

We can summarize the thoughts expressed in the previous chapters in this way:

- America does not need to give a tax exemption for health insurance that mainly benefits those with the higher incomes. We can, and we should, stop the tax exemption of employer-provided health benefits and replace it with a cash grant to everyone to apply to the purchase of health insurance. Those who have an employer-provided health benefit still generally have to pay a lesser part of the health benefit costs. The cash grant would cover most of cost with a remainder paid by the individual, just like present employer-provided health benefits.

- The high prices charged by nonprofit hospitals (the majority of the hospital industry) should be stopped. What is going on is shameful. Hospitals are not really in competition, for generally there is only one large hospital in a community, perhaps two or three at most, that all hire the same consultant showing them how to raise their prices. Hospitals are large employers, so members of Congress are reluctant to make hospitals unhappy. How can competition solve this? There is no real competition. Though we don't like going the regulatory route, it appears that taking tax exemptions away from price gougers may be the only way. As it is, the hospitals get away with the excessive prices and pay their chief executives huge amounts of money.

- Medicare could save tons of money by permitting seniors to utilize medical savings accounts (called health savings accounts [HSAs] for people under 65); for people over age 65, they are still called medical savings accounts [MSAs]). The nation's preeminent authority on Medicare, Roland E. King, who helped design Medicare and the diagnosis-related group (DRG) payment system, says there are no good reasons not to permit seniors to have MSAs with no risk adjusting of the money allocated.

- Health savings accounts are a simple idea. They can create a lot of satisfaction and a lot of savings. They permit customers to self-insure for the small bills and have major medical insurance for the big bills. They are not for the "healthy and wealthy," as some would argue. People already have deductibles and copayments; look at Medicare as an example. The copayments can amount to big money over time. With an HSA, the person has a known out-of-pocket risk that can be filled with pretax dollars. (In other words, the deposit to the savings account is tax deductible.)

All of these ideas and policy recommendations will make medical care better and more affordable.

A P P E N D I X A

Public Testimony of Dr. Gerard Anderson

Review of Hospital Billing and Collection Practices, Subcommittee on Oversight and Investigations, The Energy and Commerce Committee, United States House of Representatives, June 24, 2004, 1:30. P.M.

Witness Testimony from Dr. Gerard Anderson, Professor, Department of Health Policy & Management and International Health, Bloomberg School of Public Health, Johns Hopkins School of Medicine:

> Mr. Chairman, members of the Committee; my name is Dr. Gerard Anderson. I have been working on hospital payment issues for many years. Between 1978 and 1983, I worked in the Office of the Secretary in the U.S. Department of Health and Human Services. In 1983, I was one of the primary architects of the Medicare Prospective Payment legislation. Following passage of the Medicare Prospective Payment legislation, I joined the faculty at Johns Hopkins, where I have been for the past 21 years. At Johns Hopkins, I direct the Johns Hopkins Center for Hospital Finance and Management, the only academically based research center focusing exclusively on hospitals. I am also a professor of Health Policy and Management and professor of International Health in the Bloomberg School of Public Health and Professor of Medicine in the School of Medicine at Johns Hopkins University.

I would like to begin my testimony by highlighting several milestones in hospital payment policy. Because of the evolution of hospital payment policy, self-pay patients are currently being charged 2 to 4 times what people with health insurance coverage pay for hospital services. These are not market rates and need to be lower. After reviewing the milestones, I will then make a series of specific suggestions to the committee that will make the current hospital payment system more equitable to the self-pay patients. My preferred option is that hospitals be limited to what Medicare pays plus 25 percent.

Critical Milestones That Have Led to Market Failure in Hospital Payment

One hundred years ago most hospital care was either free or very inexpensive. In 1900, hospitals could provide little clinical benefit for most illnesses and were primarily places for housing the poor and insane who were sick. Hospitals were primarily philanthropic organizations. They were established primarily in poor urban areas.

Beginning in the 1920s, the ability of hospitals to improve the health status of patients increased dramatically. For the first time, rich and poor Americans sought out hospital care when they became seriously ill. Anesthesia expanded access to surgery, and antibiotics made it easier to treat infections.

Physicians had a wider range of services to provide to hospitalized patients. New drugs and new equipment became available and better and more highly trained personnel were required to provide these services. The cost of providing hospital care began to accelerate. In order to recover these higher costs, hospitals began to charge patients for services. Hospitals developed a charge master file. Initially, there were only a few items on the list. It listed specific charges for each service the hospital provided. A hospital day had one charge, an hour in the operating room had another charge, and X-ray had a third charge, and so on. As the number of services the hospital offered increased, so did the length of the charge master file. There are now over 10,000 items on most hospital charge master files.

Before 1929, there was no health insurance and patients paid the hospital directly. In 1929, Baylor Hospital in Dallas, Texas, began a program selling health insurance to school teachers in the Dallas

County School district. Baylor created this health insurance system because many of its patients were having difficulty paying hospital bills. It became the prototype BlueCross Plan. As the depression worsened in the 1930s, the ability of people to pay their hospital bills also worsened. BlueCross and other types of insurance programs proliferated. These insurers paid charges based on the charge master file.

During this period, the charges were based on the cost of providing care plus a small allowance for reserves. The markup over costs was typically less than 10 percent.

Private health insurance received a major boost during World War II when Congress made health insurance tax exempt. After World War II, private insurers continued to pay the charges that hospitals had established. Over time, the ability of hospitals to improve the health status of their patients increased, the kinds of services provided by hospitals increased, and the costs of hospital care began increasing at two to three times the rate of inflation. By 1960, the typical hospital had established a list of prices for approximately 5,000 separate items. There were no discounts; everyone paid the same rates. The rates that insured and self-pay people paid were similar.

Hospitals set their prices for these 5,000 items on a few criteria. The most important factor was costs. Charges were typically set at a given markup over costs, usually 10 percent. The hospital would estimate how much it cost to deliver a service and then charge 10 percent more. The ability of hospitals to estimate cost for individual services, however, was extremely limited by cost accounting. No hospital really knew how much it cost to provide a particular service because cost accounting techniques were not sufficiently detailed.

Market forces determined charges for only a few services. Childbirth, for example, was one service for which patients could engage in comparative shopping. Pregnant women had almost nine months, advance warning that they would be admitted to the hospital and their families could therefore engage in comparative shopping. In theory, they could compare differences in the out-of-pocket costs and the perceived quality between two hospital delivery rooms. Thus, hospitals kept delivery room charges at or below actual costs.

For most services, however, *it was often impossible for consumers to engage in comparative shopping* because *either* admission was an emergency or their doctor had admitting privileges in only one hospital. For most admissions, they had no idea what services they would use during their hospital stay. They could not engage in comparative shopping if they did not know what services they were going to need. In addition, for most people, insurance paid the full bill and so patients had no financial incentive to engage in comparative shopping.

Medicare Becomes Involved

When the Medicare program was established in 1965, Congress decided that the Medicare program would pay hospital costs and not charges. This was the method of payment used primarily by BlueCross. Congress recognized that charges were greater than costs and that the Medicare program would be able to exert little control over charges. A very detailed hospital accounting form called the Medicare Cost Report was created to determine Medicare's allowable costs.

In order to allocate costs between the Medicare program and other payors, the Medicare program required hospitals to collect uniform charge information. Uniform charges were necessary in order to allocate costs to the Medicare program. The Medicare Cost Report could determine allowable costs for the entire hospital; however, it needed a way to allocate these costs specifically to the Medicare program. Charges are used to allocate costs to the Medicare program. If, for example, 40 percent of the charges were attributed to the Medicare program, then the cost accounting system would allocate 40 percent of the costs to the Medicare program.

In order to prevent fraud and abuse, the Medicare program required hospitals to establish a uniform set of charges that would apply to everyone. Otherwise, the hospital could allocate charges in such a way that would result in more costs to the Medicare program.

Hospitals continued to have complete discretion on how they established their charges. The Medicare program did not interfere with how hospitals set charges for specific services. One hospital could charge $5 for an X-ray and another hospital $25 for the same X-ray. A number of studies conducted at the time showed wide variation in hospital charges.

People with insurance generally had little reason to scrutinize their bills because they had first dollar coverage. Insurance paid the full hospital bill. Also, patients did not know what services they would need and so they did not know what prices to compare. Insurance companies did little to negotiate with hospitals regarding hospital charges in the 1960s and the Medicare and Medicaid programs did not pay on the basis of charges.

In the 1970s, market forces still had a small impact on hospital charges. In reality, the hospital had virtual carte blanche to set the charges. The number of separate items that had a charge associated with them doubled from 5 to 10,000 at the typical hospital, where it is today.

Two major changes occurred in the 1980s that had a major impact on hospital charges. First, Medicare created the Prospective Payment System which eliminated any need for using hospital charges to allocate hospital costs. Second, most insurers began negotiating discounts off of charges or using some other mechanism to pay hospitals. As a result, any market forces that existed to limit what hospitals could charge were almost completely eliminated.

In 1983, the Medicare program moved away from paying costs and instituted the Prospective Payment System (DRGs). As the Medicare Prospective Payment System became operational, the need for the Medicare Cost Report and therefore the need for a uniform charge master file to allocate costs became less and less important. Today, because nearly all of the Medicare program uses some form of prospective payment, the requirement of a uniform charge master file by the Medicare program is virtually unnecessary.

Managed-care plans began to negotiate with hospitals in the early 1980s. They wanted discounts off of charges in return for placing the hospital in their network. They successfully negotiated sizeable discounts with hospitals. As insurers began to compete with managed-care plans in the mid-1980s, they also began to move away from paying full charges and started negotiating their own deals. Some insurers decided to pay on a per-day basis, others decided to pay discounted charges, or a negotiated rate. Nearly all private insurers and managed-care plans stopped using full charges as the basis of payment by 1990. They simply could not compete in the marketplace if they paid full charges.

Cost Shifting and Market Failure

As each segment of the market developed a different way to pay hospitals, this lead to a phenomenon known as "cost shifting." As the Medicare program instituted the Prospective Payment System

(DRGs), the Medicare program began to limit the amount that Medicare would spend. Faced with constraints on Medicare (and soon thereafter Medicaid) spending, the hospitals began to engage in "cost shifting."

To do this the hospital industry increased prices to commercial insurers. Given that most commercial contracts were written to reimburse hospitals based on the hospital's own charges, it was a relatively simple matter for hospitals to raise their prices. When commercial insurers tried to raise prices to the employers, however, employers began to examine alternatives. Employers slowly and then rapidly embraced managed care. Managed care expanded rapidly using their market power to negotiate discounts off of charges with hospitals. Soon commercial insurers asked for similar discounts. Private insurers continued to pay more than Medicare, however, in most cases.

Without the federal government, state governments, private insurers, or managed-care plans paying full charges, the regulatory and market constraints on hospital charges were virtually eliminated. By 1990, the only people paying full charges were the millions of Americans without insurance, a few international visitors, and the few people with health savings accounts. These individuals had limited bargaining power and were asked to pay ever-increasing prices. Effectively, there was market failure in this aspect of the hospital market.

Without any market constraints, charges began increasing much faster than costs. In the mid-1980s, charges were typically 25 percent above costs. Without any market constraints, it is now common for charges to be two to four times higher than costs. Charges are also two to four times what most insurers pay. Most insurers, including Medicaid, Medicare, and private payers, pay costs plus/minus 15 percent. Over the past 20 years, the difference between what the hospital charges and what it costs to provide care has grown steadily in nearly all hospitals.

Hospitals have been able to increase charges because self-pay individuals *have limited bargaining power when they enter a hospital.* They first must find a team of physicians willing to treat them who also have privileges at that hospital. Then they must negotiate with the hospital. Often, they wait until they are ill before they seek medical care. This further diminishes their bargaining power because it is now an emergency. Often, the hospital wants prepayment. Because most self-pay persons have limited resources and cannot make full payment in advance, this further diminishes their bargaining power.

Perhaps the most important constraint on their bargaining power, however, is that they do not know what services they will ultimately need. They do not know how long they will remain in the hospital, what X-rays or lab tests they will need, and therefore they cannot know in advance what services they will require and which of the 10,000 prices they should negotiate.

Costs, and What Insurers Pay in Pennsylvania

Using the most recent data available I compared what insurers pay and what hospitals charge in Pennsylvania. As noted earlier, charges vary considerably from hospital to hospital. Pennsylvania collects data on what hospitals charge and what insurers pay in Pennsylvania for different illnesses (www.phc4.org). For example, I looked at the charges that Philadelphia area hospitals charged for medical management of a heart attack in 2002. The average charge was over $30,000. Most insurers paid less than $10,000.

Why Are Charges So Much Higher than What Insurers Pay?

There are three main reasons why hospitals set charges two to four times what they expect to collect from insurers and managed-care plans. The first is that Medicare outlier payments are partially based on charges. The second is that bad debt and charity care is typically calculated at full charges. The third is that some self-pay patients actually pay full charges.

In the Medicare program, a small proportion of patients are much more expensive than the average patient. These are known as outlier patients. Medicare pays for these patients outside of the DRG system. Medicare continues to use charges as part of the formula used to determine outlier payments.

Recent investigations have shown certain hospital systems manipulating the payment system in inappropriate ways to overcharge the Medicare program for outlier patients. One aspect of this fraud was the exceptionally high amounts these hospitals charged. Lowering the charges would diminish the overcharges in the Medicare program for outlier payments and would reduce the level of fraud.

Second, hospitals routinely quantify the amount of bad debt and charity care they provide. This helps with fund raising and is used to meet charitable obligations. However, by valuing bad debt and charity care at full charges, these numbers vastly overestimate the amount of bad debt and charity care the hospital actually provides.

There are three groups that still pay charges. The first are people who have health savings accounts. Some of these individuals may be able to negotiate discounts although most pay full charges. It is extremely difficult for one person to negotiate with a hospital, especially in an emergency situation. The hospital holds all of the cards. Lowering the charges will benefit people with health savings accounts.

The second category is international visitors. These are typically affluent individuals who need a procedure that can be performed most effectively in the United States. These individuals are willing to pay full charges, even at inflated prices.

There are compelling arguments to charge international visitors higher prices than Americans. Most can afford to pay and, in addition, they have not subsidized the hospital sector in the United States through tax payments and other public subsidies. On the other hand, in most other countries Americans are usually treated free of charge if they have an emergency. An American injured while traveling in Canada, Australia, France, and the like. would be treated free of charge or receive a very small bill. Although there is no data that I know of that would allow us to compare the cost of care provided to Americans traveling abroad to the cost of care provided to foreigners receiving care in the United States, I expect it would be similar. In that case, it seems unfair to charge foreign visitors so much more for a service when Americans receive care free of charge overseas.

Impact on the Uninsured

The third, and by far the largest group that is asked to pay full charges is the uninsured. There are 43 million Americans who are uninsured. The uninsured can theoretically negotiate with hospitals over charges, but they have little bargaining power. My review of hospital practices suggests that less than 1 in 20 uninsured patients actually negotiates a lower rate.

Many uninsured people are unable to pay full charges. In fact, most studies suggest that less than 1 in 10 uninsured people pay a portion of their charges and relatively few pay full charges. In fact, in most hospitals only 3 percent of total revenues comes from people who are uninsured. Self-pay patients represent a very small proportion of hospital revenues.

The toll on the uninsured, however, can be substantial. There are numerous reports that show hospitals attempting to collect payments from the uninsured. The people who do not pay are sent to collection agencies and some are driven to bankruptcy. One study found that nearly half of all personal bankruptcies were related to medical bills (M.B. Jacoby, T.A. Sullivan, E. Warren, "Rethinking the Debates over Health Care Financing: Evidence from the Bankruptcy Courts," NYU Law Review 76, May 2001: 375). Another survey (D. Gurewich, R. Seifert, J. Pottas, "The Consequences of Medical Debt: Evidence from Three Communities," The Access Project, February 2003) found that hospitals were routinely requiring upfront payments, refusing to provide care, or encouraging uninsured patients to seek new providers if they did not have health insurance. Many respondents found the terms the hospitals were offering were difficult to maintain given the hospitals' inflexible collection processes and their own financial situations.

Nearly all hospitals do this to some extent. For example, a series of stories in the *Wall Street Journal* examined the collection procedures at Yale-New Haven Hospital. The *Wall Street Journal* found that in 2002, the Yale-New Haven Hospital was lead plaintiff in 426 civil lawsuits, almost all of which concerned collections or foreclosure lawsuits against individuals, compared with 93 lawsuits at a similarly sized local hospital. Yale-New Haven Hospital also frequently engaged in aggressive collections measures, such as wage garnishment, seizure of bank accounts, and property liens. In 2001, the hospital filed 134 new property liens in New Haven, almost 20 times the number filed by the city's other hospital.

Benefits of Lower Charges

If charges were lowered, there could be two beneficial outcomes. First and most important, fewer self-pay individuals would declare bankruptcy. Second, more self-pay patients would be able to pay their bills if the charges were more in line with prevailing rates.

Guiding Principles for Setting Rates

The question therefore becomes what is a reasonable rate for hospitals to charge self-pay patients given that neither market forces nor regulations constrain hospital charges.

I propose four guiding principles. First, the rate should not interfere with the marketplace. The rate that self-pay individuals should pay should be greater than what insurers and managed-care plans are currently paying hospitals. Second, the charges should not be substantially higher than what insurers and managed-care plans are currently paying hospitals. Individuals with limited bargaining power should not be asked to pay exorbitantly high rates because they lack market power. Third, the rate should be transparent to patients. Patients should know the prices they will be asked to pay when they enter the hospital. Fourth, the system should be easy to administer and to monitor.

Two Payment Alternatives

I have two specific suggestions for Congress to consider.

The first is to mandate that the maximum a patient can pay is the amount paid by Medicare plus 25 percent. I call this DRG plus 25 percent. The rationale for allowing hospitals to charge 25 percent more than Medicare is based on three factors. First, private pay insurers pay an average of 14 percent more than Medicare for a similar patient. I then add 1 percent for prompt payment. Finally, an additional amount (10 percent) is added because the amount paid by private insurers is an average and some commercial insurers pay more than the average. Adding the three factors together results in a proposed payment rate of DRG plus 25 percent.

The advantages are that the DRG plus 25 percent rate is easily monitored and adjusts for complexity of the patient. It would be continually updated by Medicare as Medicare updates the PPS rates. The disadvantage is that the rate is not market determined. In most markets, however, it would be above what insurers and managed-care plans are paying.

A second option is to allow hospitals to charge the maximum they charge any insurer or managed-care plan on a per-day basis. The advantage is that it is market determined.

There are four disadvantages. First, it will require regulations and auditing to verify the rate is the maximum they charge any insurer or managed-care plan. Second, in order to make the rate transparent, it will be necessary to keep the rate in place for an extended period of time, probably a year. This interferes with the marketplace. Third, it will require hospitals to tell all insurers and managed-care plans who was the worst negotiator. This also interferes with the marketplace.

Fourth, it requires all negotiations to be on a per-day basis. Any other payment system would be too complicated. This interferes with the marketplace.

Balancing the pros and cons of both options, I recommend the DRG plus 25 percent option. It complies with all four principles—it is above what insurers are paying, it is a reasonable amount, it is transparent, and it is easy to monitor and verify.

Rate Is Too Low

Insurers may argue that they are entitled to more substantial discounts over self-pay individuals for two reasons—prompt payment and volume discounts. The prompt payment argument has some validity. A two-month delay in payment at a 6 percent interest rate is equivalent to a 1 percent savings. This is built into the DRG plus 25 percent payment.

The volume discount argument is more complicated. In my opinion it has limited financial impact, especially on medical services. Most insurers and managed-care plans do not guarantee a certain volume of patients and certainly they do not guarantee a certain case mix of patients. Instead, they agree to put the hospital on a preferred list of hospitals. The patient and the physician still make the final decision regarding which hospital to select. The choice, therefore, is fundamentally different from a purchase in the manufacturing or retail sector where a large volume of goods or services is actually purchased.

The second part of the volume argument, however, is probably more important. The same medical services will be used if the patient is self-pay or insured. The patient will use the same set of laboratory tests, spend the same time on the operating table, require the same nursing hours, and so on. The medical services are what is most expensive in a hospital and this does not depend on the volume of patients that an insurer has.

Incentives to Purchase Health Insurance

Some individuals with high incomes choose to self-insure. An important and difficult question is whether these individuals should be able to get the benefits from these lower rates.

One argument is that these individuals have voluntarily chosen to go without health insurance and they should pay a much higher rate if they get sick. A second argument is that these individuals should be given financial incentives to purchase health insurance and that lowering the hospital rates for them will only induce them to go without coverage.

Although there is merit in both arguments, the question is what is a fair rate for them to pay when they get sick? When they need hospitalization they should pay a rate that is somewhat higher than people with health insurance coverage pay. The DRG plus 25 percent criterion meets this objective. This group of people should not be asked to pay for the bad debts of other self-pay patients any more than the insured population. And, if the rates were reasonable, they would be more likely to pay.

Simplification of Payment System

The medical care system could be simplified if such a change were enacted. One major change would be the elimination of the Medicare Cost Report. A second simplification is that it would be easier to calculate any discounts that hospitals are offering to low-income individuals.

The Medicare Cost Report was created in 1965 with the passage of the Medicare legislation and the decision by the Congress to pay costs. The Medicare cost report is now a document that is over 6 inches thick and requires many hours for hospitals to complete. However, with the passage of the Medicare Prospective Payment legislation in 1983 and subsequent adoption of additional Prospective Payment Systems for outpatient care and the like, there is no longer a compelling reason for maintaining the Medicare Cost Report. Any information the Congress needs from hospitals to set hospital payment rates could be summarized in a few pages. The only relevant information is the profit of hospitals and some information used to calculate graduate medical education and disproportionate share payments.

Hospitals often give discounts to low-income self-pay patients. It is therefore key to understand what is the basis for the discount. A discount from full charges is not really a discount if it is still greater than what insurers and managed-care plans would pay. A true discount would be below what public and private payers are expected to pay. If the payment system for self-pay patients were simplified (DRG plus 25 perent) then it would be easier for them to determine if they are really getting a discount and how much they were expected to pay. Currently, the self-pay person does not know the real extent of the discount or how much they will pay.

Summary

In summary, what should be done?

1. Both Congress and the hospital industry should recognize that hospital charges are not determined by market forces. The only people paying full charges are those with limited or no bargaining power.
2. The maximum that self-pay individuals should have to pay for hospital services should be DRG plus 25 percent.

I would be happy to answer any questions.

APPENDIX B

Memorandum of Case Law Precedents Showing Hospitals Can Charge Only Reasonable Prices

Memorandum of Law in Support of Plaintiff's Motion to Compel

It is clearly settled law in the State of Florida that hospitals may legally charge only a reasonable price for health care when a definite price term is not agreed on prior to service. In *Payne v. Humana Hospital Orange Park*, 661 So.2d

(Continued)

1239 (1st DCA 1995), the Florida District Court of Appeal addressed this precise issue, and stated:

> A patient may not be bound by unreasonable charges in an agreement to pay charges in accordance with "standard and current rates." When a contract fails to fix a price furthermore, a reasonable price is implied. Humana thus is limited to reasonable compensation.

Id. at 1241 (internal citations omitted). Pursuant to an open price term, a hospital simply does not possess an "unbridled license to fix any exorbitant or unreasonable price [it] may wish." Fla. Stat. 672.305(2)[1] at Comment 219. The mere fact that a hospital has offered a price that it declares is reasonable, does not make it so. Reasonableness of a hospital's charges for medical care are not proven by a mere proffer of their bill. (See *Albertsons, Inc. v. Brady,* 475 So.2d 986 (Fla. 2d DCA 1985)). When a hospital presents a patient with a bill pursuant to an agreement to pay undisclosed prices for healthcare, that bill is construed to be an offer to settle the outstanding hospital account for the prices listed. The Florida Fourth District Court of Appeal, when discussing the reasonableness of medical billing, stated that "services are rendered with the expectation that the patient will pay a reasonable amount in return." *A.J. v. State,* 677 So. 2d 935 at 937 (Fla. 3d DCA 1974)

As with any offer, and pursuant to the statutory mandate of reasonableness contained in Fla. Stat. 672.305(2), a patient may dispute the hospital's assertion that the billed rates are reasonable, and may decline to accept the hospital's offer to settle the account for the rates billed. The Florida Fourth District Court of Appeal has summarized this issue as follows:

> Fees are not typically discussed at the time of treatment. The patient's obligation is not to pay whatever the provider demands, but only a reasonable amount. A medical bill constitutes the provider's opinion of a reasonable charge for the services and an offer to settle for that amount. The patient is not legally bound by the provider's estimate; the patient may contest the reasonableness by counter-offering to pay a lower amount.

A.J. v. State, 677 So. 2d 935 at 937 (Fla. 3d DCA 1974). When a patient contests the reasonableness of a hospital charge, the factors in making a determination of reasonableness have recently been clearly articulated by the federal courts in Florida, relying primarily on state cases. In *Colomar v. Mercy Hospital, Inc.,* 461 F.Supp 2d 1265 (S.D. Fla. 2007), after recognizing that "Florida law is settled that when the price term in a contract for hospital services is left 'open' or undefined, then the courts will infer a reasonable price,"[2] the court stated that "no single factor can be used to determine the reasonableness of [a] hospital['s] charges. Rather, several non-exclusive factors are relevant to the inquiry." The Court then set forth the following reasonableness factors:

As discussed in more detail below, those factors include but are not necessarily limited to: (1) an analysis of the relevant market for hospital services (including the rates charged by other similarly situated hospitals for similar services); (2) the usual and customary rate [the hospital] charges and receives for its hospital services; and (3) Mercy's internal cost structure.

Colomar v. Mercy Hospital, Inc., 461 F.Supp.2d 1265 (S.D. Fla. 2007) at 1269. The court went on to expressly refute the commonly raised argument that the unreasonableness of a hospital's charges can only be proven by market analysis, and that differential pricing for the uninsured is irrelevant. The Mercy Court stated succinctly that "a market analysis is not the only way to evaluate reasonableness" and went on to state that:

The reality is that the rates hospitals charge for services do not always accurately reflect the value of the services, especially when the hospital routinely accepts much less for them. When that is the case, then simply looking at the rates charged relative to other hospitals can give a false sense of value. That is, if other hospitals grossly overcharge for services relative to their costs, then a mere side-by-side comparison of hospitals' unreasonable charges would make them appear reasonable. Such consistency, standing alone, is not synonymous with reasonableness.

Id. Florida statute and the line of cases in both the state and federal courts firmly establish that unless price terms are expressly agreed upon, hospitals are entitled only to reasonable compensation. *See Mercy Hospital, Inc. v. Carr*, 297 So. 2d 598 (Fla. Dist. Ct. App. 1974); *Albertsons, Inc. v. Brady*, 475 So. 2d 986 (Fla. Dist. Ct. App. 1985); *Payne v. Humana*, 661 So. 2d 1239 (Fla. Dist. Ct. App. 1995); *A.J. v. State*, 677 So. 2d 935 (Fla. Dist. Ct. App. 1996); *Hall v. Humana*, 686 So. 2d 653 (Fla. Dist. Ct. App. 1996); *Greenfield v. Manor Care Inc.*, 705 So. 2d 926 (Fla. Dist. Ct. App. 1997); *Colomar v. Mercy Hospital, Inc.*, 461 F.Supp. 2d 1265 (S.D. Fla. 2007). To determine the reasonableness of a hospital's prices, Florida courts will consider all relevant evidence of reasonableness or unreasonableness, which will include but not be limited to a hospital's costs in rendering the care, the amounts customarily accepted as payment in full for the care, and the rates charged in the relevant market

(Continued)

for the care *See Colomar v. Mercy Hospital,* Inc., 461 F.Supp. 2d 1265 (S.D. Fla. 2007).

Certificate of Service

We hereby certify a true and correct copy of the foregoing was sent via U.S. mail and facsimile (305) 347–4050 on October____, 2007 to Alan D. Lash, Lash & Goldberg L.L.P, Bank of America Tower, 100 Southeast 2nd Street, Suite 1200, Miami, Florida 33131.

Respectfully submitted this____day of October, 2007 by:

Law Offices of Matthew Dietz, P.L.

2990 SW 35th Avenue

Miami, Florida 33133

Telephone: 305/669–2822

Facsimile 305/442–4181

e-mail: mwalrath@usdisabilitylaw.com

Michael D. Walrath, Esq.

Florida Bar No.: 0019328

APPENDIX C

An Example of a Legal Complaint against a Hospital for Unreasonable Charges

IN THE COUNTY COURT IN AND FOR
MIAMI-DADE COUNTY, FLORIDA
CIVIL ACTION
CASE NO.: 07-17753-CC-25-04

Amanda Marks

PLAINTIFF,

v.

Hospital X, a Florida nonprofit
Corporation.
DEFENDANT.

Complaint

COMES NOW, the Plaintiff, Amanda Marks, by and through the undersigned counsel, and sues Defendant, Hospital X (hereafter "Hospital X"), for causes of action, and in support thereof states as follows:

(Continued)

Parties and Jurisdiction

1. Plaintiff, Amanda Marks, is a resident of Baltimore, Maryland, who was treated at Hospital X in Miami while on vacation, on March 19, 2004.
2. Defendant, Hospital X, is a Florida nonprofit corporation with its principal place of business located at undisclosed address Miami, Florida.
3. Venue is proper in this court because this is where Plaintiff's causes of action arose.
4. Hospital X has imposed its unfair, deceptive, and unconscionable rates on the Plaintiff through billing her at her residence, Baltimore, Maryland.
5. The Plaintiff brings this action under Florida law and does not rely on any federal claim or cause of action.
6. Hospital X made the decision to engage in these discriminatory and unconscionable pricing and billing and collection practices at their corporate headquarters in Florida.
7. The amount in controversy is less than $15,000, as Ms. Marks' bill in its entirety is $9,047.68.

Introduction; Background

8. Hospital X is based in Miami, Florida, and operates 935 licensed beds. Hospital X's official "corporate mission" is "Healthcare excellence, Ethical behavior, Accountability, Respect and caring, Teamwork and Service before self." The fact is that Hospital X fulfills its mission only to those consumers whose rights are protected by powerful governmental or private third-party payers, while treating all unrepresented self-pay patients who do not qualify for Charity Care in an unconscionable, uncaring, and unfair manner, in violation of Florida law.
9. Most hospitals nationwide—including Hospital X—have an established and admitted differential billing policy for goods, services, and medical care which charges a reasonable fee for services rendered to patients who are represented by private or public health insurance; and a disproportionately and unconscionably higher fee for services rendered to unrepresented self-pay patients.[1] "The uninsured pay nearly three times more for hospital services than health insurers pay, and the gap between what they are charged and what insurers pay has soared since 1984."[2] There are approximately 45 million U.S. residents without health insurance, 3.7 million in the State of Florida. *Id.* All of these consumers enter express or implied Agreements to pay for the medical care rendered, but in every instance, price terms are left open.

10. Patients without insurance who are not Medicare or Medicaid recipients and are not granted Charity Care, an extreme minority of patients served, are the only patients charged the full "charge-master" rates while deep discounts are given to those with insurance (either by private insurers or government programs such as Medicare and Medicaid).[3] These rates are not reasonable, are usually several hundred percent higher than the "discounted" rates which Hospital X customarily accepts for its services, and bear no relationship whatsoever to the hospital's costs.

11. When asked how the charge-master rates are derived, a veteran CFO of a California Health System stated that "there is no method to this madness" and that "cockamamie formulas" were typically employed.[4]

12. Charge-master rates, in reality, serve as nothing more than the starting point for negotiations with those entities powerful enough to be afforded the privilege of negotiating in the first place, a privilege which is to be afforded all parties entering into a contract.

13. Testimony before Congress, as well as guidelines promulgated by the American Hospital Association, suggest that a reasonable rate for medical care is twenty-five percent (25%) above Medicare rates.[5]

14. Efficiently run hospitals are capable of operating under a cost plus 5 percent charging structure, because self-reported "costs" contemplate all aspects of cost, such as utilities, salary expenditures, insurance, facility maintenance, administrative costs, and the like. Hospital X charged Amanda Marks $9,047.68, which is approximately 345 percent above Hospital X's approximate costs of $2,623.83, and 273 percent above the reasonable rate.[6] Hospital X bills a reasonable amount for identical medical care when rendered to the overwhelming majority of its patients, which in the instant case would have been $3,312.59 for identical goods, services, and care.

15. In most cases, Hospital X seeks to collect on the bills sent to an uninsured by having its collection agents continuously harass the patients at home and at work, placing liens on the person's home, garnishing wages, and seizing bank accounts of those that cannot pay these unconscionable rates.

16. Hospital X has attempted to collect these unconscionable amounts from Amanda Marks by sending threatening letters and by repeated telephone calls to her home. Hospital X's collection tactics are as coercive, threatening, and unfair as the amounts billed.

17. The hospital industry agrees that this is a serious problem. The Florida Hospital Association, as long ago as 2003, admitted that uninsured

(Continued)

patients are "the single-most important health care issue."[7] Since that time, the gap between the charges to the uninsured and those represented by third-party payers has widened. However, Hospital X has done little or nothing to change its billing policies toward the uninsured. One argument historically raised as justification for this unfair and deceptive pricing practice was that hospitals are prohibited by the Medicare rules and regulations from offering discounts to uninsured patients. This is patently untrue, and the HHS Office of the Inspector General dispelled this myth on February 19, 2004, when his office issued its official report stating that "No OIG authority prohibits or restricts hospitals from offering discounts to uninsured patients who are unable to pay hospital bills."[8]

18. As a result of Hospital X's unconscionable, deceptive, and unfair practices, Hospital X profits handsomely. In the instant case of the $9,047.68 billed to Amanda Marks, the profit to Hospital X is $6,423.85. A responsibly run hospital can be operated on a 5 percent profit margin, therefore a 25 percent profit margin, in accordance with testimony before Congress, more than adequately compensates Hospital X, and would amount to a profit of $692.54. The difference between the two amounts is nothing less than unsubstantiated and unnecessary profiteering, amounting to $5,731.31 in windfall profits in the instant case.

19. Hospital X's unfair, discriminatory, and unconscionable practices are directly against public policy and extensively damage society as a whole. The 44 million U.S. residents without health insurance cost U.S. taxpayers between $65 billion and $130 billion per year in lost productivity mainly because these uninsured citizens cannot afford medical services, and therefore forgo medical attention until their health has degenerated to an emergency situation.[9] This trend ignores all of the known benefits of early detection and treatment, exacerbating medical conditions and their expense to society, while simultaneously leading to decreased quality of life and shorter life spans for the uninsured. "Lack of health insurance causes roughly 18,000 unnecessary deaths every year in the United States."[10]

20. The public has started to demand change from the hospital industry in its billing and collection practices. The House Subcommittee on Oversight and Investigations launched an investigation into these hospital billing and collection practices. Rep. James Greenwood, the chairman of the subcommittee, revealed that "[i]n the worst instance, hospitals simply apply outrageously high charges—higher than what Medicare pays, higher than private payers—and then will relentlessly

and sometimes mercilessly pursue poor people for their money, even to the point of having them arrested." In an article entitled "Hospitals Sued for Charging Uninsured Patients More Than Insured Patients" on News Channel Five's Internet news web site, Democratic Senator and Presidential hopeful Barack Obama of Illinois was quoted as saying "It makes no sense that people without health insurance pay more than people with insurance for the same operation."[11]

21. Hospital X's unfair policy of charging the uninsured inflated rates for medical services and goods results in one of three situations: (1) the uninsured pays the unconscionable rates, directly profiting Hospital X by several hundred percent more than is reasonable; (2) the uninsured will not or cannot pay these unconscionable rates, allowing for-profit hospitals to claim these inflated rates as bad debt, with positive tax implications; or (3) Hospital X grants Charity Care, reporting the amount of "charity" at the inflated rates, seeking governmental reimbursement in the form of disproportionate share payments and the like, and appearing to meet charitable obligations when such obligations are actually not met. The end result is added profits, tax write-offs for for-profit hospitals, government reimbursements worth millions of dollars annually, and inflated charity figures which are used in meeting community benefit obligations and fund-raising efforts for nonprofit hospitals.

22. Hospital X charged, and/or collected from Amanda Marks, inflated rates for medical services and goods simply because she is not represented by a powerful public or private insurance carrier. Hospital X is able to charge uninsured, self-pay patients these unfair and unconscionable rates because: (a) uninsured individuals lack the "bargaining power" of insurance companies; (b) typically an uninsured arrives at the hospital under emergent circumstances and cannot "shop around" for less costly medical care; and (c) because uninsured patients typically lack the ability to enforce their legal rights, leaving a hospital with little or no incentive to obey the law.

23. While some in the hospital industry have undertaken voluntary initial reforms to prevent discriminatory pricing, Hospital X has not, and continues to bill all uninsured patients at inflated, "full charge-master" rates.

24. This lawsuit is brought to enjoin Hospital X from engaging in discriminatory and unconscionable pricing, and unfair and deceptive billing and collection practices, and to obtain appropriate damages for the Plaintiff.

(Continued)

Specific Factual Allegations

25. On or about March 19, 2004, the Plaintiff sought emergency medical treatment at Hospital X, located at undisclosed address Miami, Florida. Amanda Marks did have health insurance when she received medical services at Hospital X; however Hospital X failed to bill the carrier, and now pursues Amanda Marks as a self-pay patient.

26. For her less than one-day hospitalization for a mild seizure, believed to be a well-known side effect of the prescription medication Welbutrin, Hospital X charged Amanda Marks $9,047.68. The costs incurred by Hospital X in providing the medical care rendered to Amanda Marks were approximately $2,623.83.

27. Hospital X charged Amanda Marks $9,047.68, which is 345 percent above its costs of approximately $2,623.83.

28. The rate at which Hospital X charged and billed Amanda Marks for the medical services and goods she received is not reasonable, and far exceeds the rate that Hospital X charges for identical care when rendered to the vast majority of its patients.

29. Hospital X charges and receives between one percent (1%) and twenty-five percent (25%) above costs for its hospital services when rendered to the vast majority of its patients, yet charged Amanda Marks 345 percent above its costs for the services rendered while the amounts billed to the majority of its patients are labeled "discounted."

30. The reasonable price for the medical care rendered to Amanda Marks by Hospital X is $3,312.59, which would yield a reasonable profit of $692.54, yet Hospital X charged Amanda Marks $9,047.68, which yields an unconscionable and unreasonable profit of $6,423.85. The amount billed is 273 percent above the reasonable amount billed for identical medical goods, services, and care when rendered to the majority of Hospital X's patients.

31. The actual profit to Hospital X in the instant case is approximately 928 percent above the reasonable profit of approximately $692.54, generated when Hospital X bills a reasonable amount for identical services when rendered to the vast majority of its patients.

32. Hospital X will receive $5,731.31 in unjustified windfall profit, the difference between the actual profit as billed and the reasonable profit, if permitted to collect on this unconscionable debt. This windfall profit is pursuant to Hospital X's unilaterally set and wholly unsubstantiated charge-master price list, and their unsupported assertion that the billed amount represents the reasonable value of the care rendered.

33. Ms. Marks is damaged because the alleged debt has been reported to credit reporting agencies and has damaged Amanda Marks's credit.

Hospital X attempted to collect, or authorized its collection agents to contact Amanda Marks and to collect on this unconscionable debt. Hospital X or Hospital X's agents attempted to do so by contacting Amanda Marks on numerous occasions via mail and telephone.

34. Amanda Marks is aggrieved by the collections process and the threat of uncertainty of the outcome of legal action to recover the full, unreasonable amount billed.

35. Amanda Marks is aggrieved by Hospital X's unfair differential pricing practice, which inflates the cost of their services to Amanda Marks by 273 percent, because this practice provides a significant disincentive to seek necessary medical care, lowering Amanda Marks's quality of life, severely jeopardizing Amanda Marks's health and well-being, and statistically reducing Amanda Marks's life expectancy.

36. Ms. Marks makes only $7,000 to $9,000 per year, and would make a perfect candidate for charity care. However Ms. Mark's request, as well as those of the undersigned, to submit a charity care application have been refused or ignored.

37. Ms. Marks and the undersigned have repeatedly requested copies of the UB-92, UB-04, CMS-1450, CMS-1500, or Form 837 which will be used to calculate the hospital's charges. This form will be used to determine the reasonableness of the hospital's charges. These requests have either been refused or ignored.

38. Upon admission to the hospital Ms. Marks informed the hospital that she possessed valid health insurance coverage. Mt Sinai refused or otherwise failed to properly bill Ms. Marks under her then-existing health insurance policy three years ago.

39. Now, approximately three years after Ms. Marks had switched health insurance companies, Hospital X proceeded to bill Ms. Marks at an undiscounted, self-pay rate.

40. Ms. Marks's insurance company at the time of service refuses to now pay this amount because over three years had elapsed between the time of service and billing and Ms. Marks is no longer insured by them.

41. Ms. Marks's current health insurance company also refuses to pay these costs because she was not covered by them at the time of service.

Count 1

Violation of Florida's Deceptive and Unfair Trade Practices Act

42. Plaintiff re-alleges paragraphs 1 through 41 of this Complaint as if fully set out herein.

(Continued)

43. Florida's Deceptive and Unfair Trade Practices Act, Fla. Stat. §501.201, et seq. ("FDUTPA"), prohibits "unfair methods of competition, unconscionable acts or practices, and unfair or deceptive acts or practices in the conduct of any trade or commerce." §501.204.

44. The stated purpose of FDUTPA is to protect consumers from "those who engage in unfair methods of competition, or unconscionable, deceptive, or unfair acts or practices in the conduct of any trade or commerce." §501.202.

45. Hospital X conducts trade or commerce as defined by FDUTPA because it "advertised, solicited, provided, offered, or distributed by sale or otherwise, a good or service or thing of value." §501.203(8).

46. Plaintiff is an "interested person" and a "consumer" as defined by FDUTPA, Section 501.203(6) and (7), because the Plaintiff is an individual who is affected by a violation of the Act.

47. Plaintiff sought and received medical services and goods at Hospital X, and was the victim of an unfair, deceptive, unconscionable, and unlawful trade practice which resulted in Plaintiff being billed rates that are drastically higher than those charged for identical services when rendered to the vast majority of Hospital X's patients.

48. Plaintiff was damaged by this violation because the amounts remain due and owing, and because Plaintiff's credit has been damaged accordingly and is damaged by the collections process and the uncertainty of future damages.

49. The rates at which Hospital X billed Amanda Marks for medical services and goods far exceeded the industry norm, was approximately 273 percent greater than the rates charged to the majority of its patients, and was approximately 345 percent above Hospital X's actual cost of providing the medical goods, services, and care.

50. Area hospitals render identical care to the vast majority of their patients at reasonable prices, hundreds of percent less than the rates billed to Amanda Marks, making the most common price or "normal price in the industry" a reasonable price.

51. Hospital X's unfair, deceptive, unconscionable, and unlawful practices benefits it by millions of dollars annually, and damaged the Plaintiff as it does all self-pay patients receiving medical care from Hospital X.

52. Hospital X's conduct violates FDUTPA, and was conceived, devised, planned, implemented, approved, and executed within Florida, who has an interest in prohibiting violations of FDUTPA in furtherance of its legislative intention of protecting Florida's consumers.

53. Plaintiff sustained damages as a direct and proximate result of Hospital X's unfair, deceptive, and unconscionable practices. FDUTPA, Section 501.211(2) provides Amanda Marks a private cause of action against

Hospital X, and entitles her to recover her actual damages, plus attorney's fees and costs.

54. Plaintiff is damaged, and has suffered and will continue to suffer irreparable harm if Hospital X collects or continues efforts to collect on this debt, and continues to engage in differential, discriminatory, and unfair pricing, and unfair and deceptive billing and collections practices.

55. Amanda Marks is aggrieved by the collections process and the threat of uncertainty of the outcome of legal action to recover the full, unreasonable amount billed.

56. Plaintiff has no other adequate remedy at law for these damages.

WHEREFORE, Plaintiff, Amanda Marks, demands judgment against Hospital X for compensatory damages, pre- and post-judgment interest, attorney's fees, injunctive relief, costs incurred in bringing this action, and any other relief the Court deems just and proper.

Count II

Declaratory Relief: Unjust Enrichment

57. Plaintiff re-alleges paragraphs 1 through 41 as if fully set forth herein.

58. Plaintiff conferred a benefit on Hospital X by visiting and seeking medical services, goods, and care at Hospital X, thereby offering the Defendant an opportunity to make a reasonable profit on said care.

59. Hospital X appreciated and was fully aware of the benefit conferred upon it by Amanda Marks, as it serves patients in the regular course of business and accepts as payment a reasonable profit for services rendered to the majority thereof.

60. Hospital X solicited and accepted the benefit conferred upon it, and sought to unlawfully maximize this benefit by charging Amanda Marks rates for medical services and goods that exceed Hospital X's actual cost by approximately 345 percent The rates charged were not reasonable, regular, or usual and customary for like medical services, but were instead approximately 273 percent higher than the reasonable rates billed for identical services when rendered to the majority of Hospital X's patients.

61. Hospital X will be unjustly enriched by the rates it charged and has attempted to collect from Amanda Marks, in the amount of $5,731.31, and it would be inequitable to allow Hospital X to reap the benefit of these inflated charges.

62. Hospital X continues to unjustly enrich itself in this fashion when collecting from other self-pay patients, and Amanda Marks has no adequate remedy at law to stop Hospital X from continuing to "overcharge" self-pay patients,

(Continued)

and as a result will suffer irreparable harm without appropriate injunctive relief to prevent this ongoing and future unjust enrichment.

63. Plaintiff is entitled to an order declaring that Hospital X's practices are unjust and against public policy, requiring Hospital X to cease collection on all amounts they have billed as a result of these unconscionable charges and policies, a determination that collection of such amounts constitute unjust enrichment, and that Hospital X recalculate outstanding self-pay accounts to reflect a reasonable rate as determined by this Court.

WHEREFORE, Plaintiff demands judgment against Hospital X for compensatory damages, pre- and post-judgment interest, attorney's fees, declaratory and injunctive relief, costs incurred in bringing this action, and any other relief the Court deems proper and just.

Count III

Breach of Implied Covenants of Reasonableness, Good Faith, and Fair Dealing

64. Plaintiff re-alleges paragraphs 1 through 41 as if fully set forth herein.
65. The written agreement(s) between the Plaintiff and Hospital X do not include specific set amounts for any of the governing prices, nor any other price terms whatsoever.
66. Hospital X breached the express terms of the Agreement between Amanda Marks and Hospital X, which states that the hospital will bill "ussual and customary rates." Instead, hospital charged rates unique to self-pay patients, wholly unlike the usual and customary charges billed for services rendered to the vast majority of its patients.
67. There is an implied covenant of reasonableness, good faith and fair dealing in all agreements between Hospital X and its patients, including the agreement with the Plaintiff, regarding the charges for medical services and supplies.
68. In addition to breaching the express terms of the agreement, Hospital X breached the implied covenants by charging the Plaintiff unreasonably, unlawfully, and excessively high rates for medical services, supplies, and care pursuant to a contract with an open price term.
69. Amanda Marks is aggrieved by the collections process and the threat of uncertainty of the outcome of legal action to recover the full, unreasonable amount billed.

WHEREFORE, Plaintiff demands judgment against Hospital X for compensatory damages, pre- and post-judgment interest, attorney's fees, declaratory and injunctive relief, costs incurred in bringing this action, and any other relief the Court deems proper and just.

Count IV

Breach of Contract Pursuant to Florida Statute §672.305

70. Plaintiff re-alleges paragraphs 1 through 41 as if fully set forth herein.
71. Plaintiff impliedly entered a contract with Hospital X requiring payment for care rendered, but leaving open the specific price term.
72. Fla. Stat. §672.305 allows parties to conclude a contract with an "open price term," but requires the party setting the price to insert a reasonable price and to fix that reasonable price in good faith. Fla. Stat. §672.305 specifically comments that the party setting the price may not fix any unreasonable price they may wish. *Id.* at Comment 2.
73. Pursuant to Fla. Stat. §672.305, the open price term must be interpreted to import reasonable rates, roughly equivalent to those charged to the majority of other patients, and reasonably related to Hospital X's costs in providing said supplies, services, and care.
74. Hospital X breached its contract with the Plaintiff, as it breaches all contracts with similarly situated self-pay patients, by charging unreasonable, excessive, and unconscionable rates instead of reasonable ones.
75. Hospital X breached the express terms of the contract which obligated Hospital X to pay "ussual and customary rates" because instead of charging Amanda Marks ussual and customary rates, Hospital X charged prices unique to self-pay patients and wholly different than those charges billed for services rendered to the vast majority of its patients.
76. Amanda Marks is damaged by Hospital X's breach, and must be placed in the position she would have been in, but-for that breach. Specifically, Plaintiff was overcharged by $5,731.31, and has had the full, unconscionable amount billed reported to collections. Ms. Marks' bill should be reduced to the reasonable amount for the services and care rendered, and should even then only be responsible only for the amount of her deductible under her then existing insurance policy.
77. Amanda Marks was and is damaged by the ongoing nature of Hospital X's breach, in that it provides a significant disincentive to seek medical care, reducing Ms. Mark's quality of life, endangering Ms. Marks' health and safety, and statistically reducing her life expectancy.
78. Amanda Marks is aggrieved by the collections process and the threat of uncertainty of the outcome of legal action to recover the full, unreasonable amount billed.

WHEREFORE, the Plaintiff, Amanda Marks, demands judgment against Hospital X for compensatory damages, pre- and post-judgment interest, attorney's fees, declaratory and injunctive relief, costs incurred in bringing this

(Continued)

breach of contract action, and any other relief the Court may deem proper and just. Plaintiff reserves the right to request punitive damages in this action in accordance with Fla. Stat. §768.72(1).

Count VI

Declaratory Judgment; Laches

79. Amanda Marks hereby incorporates the allegations set forth in paragraphs 1 through 41 as though fully set forth herein.
80. Amanda Marks has substantial financial interests which are affected by her contract with Hospital X, and the interpretation thereof.
81. Amanda Marks is in doubt regarding her rights, status, and equitable relations under the contract that she entered into with Hospital X and seeks a declaration thereof.
82. At the time of service which is the subject of this cause, Amanda Marks was insured by MPA National Teamsters, BlueCross BlueShield (hereafter BlueCross BlueShield).
83. Upon admission to Hospital X, Ms. Marks immediately disclosed to Hospital X that she was insured by BlueCross BlueShield.
84. More than a year after her hospitalization at Hospital X, Amanda Marks switched insurance companies, initiating a policy with Kaiser Permanente.
85. Amanda Marks, knowing that she was insured and that she informed Hospital X of the same, interpreted her responsibilities and rights under her agreement with Hospital X to obligate her only for the deductible amount of her then existing insurance coverage.
86. Any future claims for any amount in excess of Ms. Marks' deductible payment under her then existing insurance policy are barred by the doctrine of Laches, because:
    a. There was conduct on the part of Amanda Marks putting Hospital X on notice that she had insurance coverage. Upon admission to the hospital Ms. Marks informed the hospital that she possessed valid health insurance coverage under BlueCross BlueShield. Hospital X refused or otherwise failed to properly bill Ms. Marks under her then existing BlueCross BlueShield health insurance policy at the time of service, or to bill Ms. Marks within a reasonable time after her hospitalization.
    b. Amanda Marks will be substantially injured if relief is accorded to Hospital X via future collection of this debt.
    c. Amanda Marks will continue to be substantially injured if such a suit is not barred because Hospital X or its collection agencies or attorneys

have reported the alleged debt to reporting agencies, thereby destroying Plaintiff's credit, which will ultimately result in a Judgment against Ms. Marks for substantially more than her known obligations.

d. Hospital X unreasonably delayed the assertion of their known right to collect amounts billed to Amanda Marks from her then-existing insurer until such time that Ms. Marks was no longer insured by the same.

e. BlueCross BlueShield has refused to pay Hospital X for the amounts due pursuant to Ms. Marks' hospitalization on or about March 19, 2004, because such amounts were claimed more than three years after the date of service, at such time when Ms. Marks was no longer an insured.

f. Amanda Marks had no knowledge that Hospital X had failed to enforce their known rights in the collection of the alleged debt from BlueCross BlueShield until she received a bill for the undiscounted charge-master rates, approximately three years after the date of service.

g. To date, more than three years after the date of service, Hospital X has not yet filed suit or otherwise attempted to formally collect the amount allegedly owed by the Plaintiff.

h. Because of Hospital X unreasonable three-year delay in acting upon their known rights, Ms. Marks alleged debt has exponentially increased because Hospital X has attempted to collect on her account at full charge-master rates as a self-pay patient, making her allegedly responsible for $9,047.68 instead of the comparatively small deductible amount which Ms. Marks would have been obligated to pay under her then-existing insurance policy.

WHEREFORE, Amanda Marks respectfully requests that this court provide a declaration of her rights, status, and equitable and legal rights under her Agreement with Hospital X, and judicially declare and clarify said rights, status and equitable relations, as follows:

1. Provide guidance of the Court in defining the undisclosed price term as being the amount for which Amanda Marks would have been responsible as a deductible payment under her then-existing insurance plan.

2. Reform the contract to allow Amanda Marks to pay, in full discharge of her obligations, the deductible payment under her then-existing insurance policy.

3. Declare any future suit brought by Hospital X, or any other collection agency or attorney, in relation to Amanda Marks hospitalization on

(Continued)

or about March 19, 2004, in excess of the amount due as a deductible under her then-existing insurance policy to be barred by the doctrine of Laches.

Award such further relief as this Court deems just and fair.

Jury Demand

Plaintiff hereby demands a trial by jury on all issues so triable.

Respectfully submitted this ____day of August, 2007 by:

Law Offices of Matthew Dietz, P.L.

2990 SW 35th Avenue

Miami, Florida 33133

Telephone: 305/669–2822

Facsimile 305/442–4181

e-mail: mwalrath@usdisabilitylaw.com

Michael D. Walrath, Esq.

Florida Bar No.: 0019328

APPENDIX D

Executive Order

PROMOTING QUALITY AND EFFICIENT HEALTH CARE IN FEDERAL GOVERNMENT-ADMINISTERED OR -SPONSORED HEALTH CARE PROGRAMS

By the authority vested in me as President by the Constitution and the laws of the United States, and in order to promote federally led efforts to implement more transparent and high-quality health care, it is hereby ordered as follows:

Section1. Purpose. It is the purpose of this order to ensure that health care programs administered or sponsored by the Federal Government promote quality and efficient delivery of health care through the use of health information technology, transparency regarding health care quality and price, and better incentives for program beneficiaries, enrollees, and providers. It is the further purpose of this order to make relevant information available to these beneficiaries, enrollees, and providers in a readily useable manner and in collaboration with similar initiatives in the private sector and nonfederal public sector. Consistent with the purpose of improving the quality and efficiency of health care, the actions and steps taken by Federal Government agencies should not incur additional costs for the Federal Government.

Sec. 2. Definitions. For purposes of this order:

(a) "Agency" means an agency of the Federal Government that administers or sponsors a Federal health care program.

(b) "Federal health care program" means the Federal Employees Health Benefit Program, the Medicare program, programs operated directly by the Indian Health Service, the TRI-CARE program for the Department of Defense and other uniformed services, and the health care program operated by the Department of Veterans Affairs. For purposes of this order, "Federal health care program" does not include State-operated or -funded federally subsidized programs such as Medicaid, the State Children's Health Insurance Program, or services provided to Department of Veterans' Affairs beneficiaries under 38 U.S.C. 1703.

(c) "Interoperability" means the ability to communicate and exchange data accurately, effectively, securely, and consistently with different information technology systems, software applications, and networks in various settings, and exchange data such that clinical or operational purpose and meaning of the data are preserved and unaltered.

(d) "Recognized interoperability standards" means interoperability standards recognized by the Secretary of Health and Human Services (the "Secretary"), in accordance with guidance developed by the Secretary, as existing on the date of the implementation, acquisition, or upgrade of health information technology systems under subsections (1) or (2) of section 3(a) of this order.

Sec. 3. Directives for Agencies. Agencies shall perform the following functions:

(a) Health Information Technology.
(1) For Federal Agencies. As each agency implements, acquires, or upgrades health information technology systems used for the direct exchange of health information between agencies and with nonfederal entities, it shall utilize, where available, health information technology systems and products that meet recognized interoperability standards.

(2) For Contracting Purposes. Each agency shall require in contracts or agreements with health care providers, health plans, or health insurance issuers that as each provider, plan, or issuer implements, acquires, or upgrades health information technology systems, it shall utilize, where available, health information technology systems and products that meet recognized interoperability standards.

(b) Transparency of Quality Measurements.

(1) In General. Each agency shall implement programs measuring the quality of services supplied by health care providers to the beneficiaries or enrollees of a Federal health care program. Such programs shall be based on standards established by multi-stakeholder entities identified by the Secretary or by another agency subject to this order. Each agency shall develop its quality measurements in collaboration with similar initiatives in the private and nonfederal public sectors.

(2) Facilitation. An agency satisfies the requirements of this subsection if it participates in the aggregation of claims and other appropriate data for the purposes of quality measurement. Such aggregation shall be based on standards established by multi-stakeholder entities identified by the Secretary or by another agency subject to this order.

(c) Transparency of Pricing Information. Each agency shall make available (or provide for the availability) to the beneficiaries or enrollees of a Federal health care program (and, at the option of the agency, to the public) the prices that it, its health insurance issuers, or its health insurance plans pay for procedures to providers in the health care program with which the agency, issuer, or plan contracts. Each agency shall also, in collaboration with multi-stakeholder groups such as those described in subsection (b)(1), participate in the development of information regarding the overall costs of services for common episodes of care and the treatment of common chronic diseases.

(d) Promoting Quality and Efficiency of Care. Each agency shall develop and identify, for beneficiaries, enrollees, and providers, approaches that encourage and facilitate the provision and receipt of high-quality and efficient health care. Such approaches may include pay-for-performance models of reimbursement consistent with current law. An agency will satisfy the requirements of this subsection if it makes available to beneficiaries or enrollees consumer-directed health care insurance products.

Sec. 4. Implementation Date. Agencies shall comply with the requirements of this order by January 1, 2007.

Sec. 5. Administration and Judicial Review.

(a) This order does not assume or rely on additional Federal resources or spending to promote quality and efficient health care. Further, the actions directed by this order shall be carried out subject to the availability of appropriations and to the maximum extent permitted by law.

(b) This order shall be implemented in new contracts or new contract cycles as they may be renewed from time to time. Renegotiation outside of the normal contract cycle processes should be avoided.

(c) This order is not intended to, and does not, create any right or benefit, substantive or procedural, enforceable at law or in equity against the United States, its departments, agencies, or entities, its officers, employees, or agents, or any other person.

THE WHITE HOUSE

110TH CONGRESS
1ST SESSION

S. 173

To amend title XVIII of the Social Security Act to establish
Medicare Health Savings Accounts.

IN THE SENATE OF THE UNITED STATES

JANUARY 4, 2007

Mr. INHOFE (for himself and Mr. DEMINT) introduced the
following bill; which was read twice and referred to
the Committee on Finance.

A BILL

To amend title XVIII of the Social Security Act to establish
Medicare Health Savings Accounts.

*Be it enacted by the Senate and House of Representatives of the United
States of America in Congress assembled,*

Section 1. Short Title.

This Act may be cited as the "Medicare Health Savings Accounts Act of 2007."

Sec. 2. Establishment of Medicare Health Savings Accounts.

(a) ESTABLISHMENT.—

(1) IN GENERAL.—Title XVIII of the Social Security Act (42 U.S.C. 1395 et seq.) is amended—

    (A) by redesignating part E as part F; and

    (B) by inserting after part D the following new part:

PART E—MEDICARE HEALTH SAVINGS ACCOUNTS

ENTITLEMENT TO ELECT TO RECEIVE BENEFITS UNDER MEDICARE HEALTH SAVINGS ACCOUNTS

SEC. 1860E–1. (a) IN GENERAL.—The Secretary shall establish procedures under which each eligible beneficiary (as defined in subsection (b)) shall be entitled to elect to receive benefits under a Medicare Health Savings Account under this part instead of benefits under parts A, B, or D.

(b) ELIGIBLE BENEFICIARY DESCRIBED.—An eligible beneficiary described in this subsection is an individual who—

    (1) is entitled to benefits under part A or enrolled under part B;

    (2) has a health savings account (as defined in subsection (d) of section 223 of the Internal Revenue Code of 1986), or certifies that they will use funds provided under this part to establish such an account; and

    (3) is enrolled under a high deductible health plan (as defined in subsection (c)(2) of such section, except that section 223(c)(2)(A)(ii)(I) of such Code shall be applied by substituting 'the amount in effect under clause (i)(I)' for '$5,000').

(c) BENEFITS TO BE AVAILABLE IN 2008.—The Secretary shall establish the procedures under subsection (a) in a manner such that Medicare Health Savings Accounts are available for years beginning on or after January 1, 2008.

(d) PRESERVATION OF ORIGINAL MEDICARE FEE-FOR-SERVICE BENEFITS.—Nothing in this part shall be construed to limit the right of an individual who is entitled to benefits under part A or enrolled under part B to receive benefits under such part (or under part C or D) if an election to receive benefits under Medicare Health Savings Accounts under this part is not in effect with respect to such individual.

(e) RULE OF CONSTRUCTION.—Nothing in this part shall be construed as preventing an individual from depositing personal funds (subject to the contribution limitations under section 223 of the Internal Revenue Code of 1986) into a Medicare Health Savings Account.

MEDICARE HEALTH SAVINGS ACCOUNTS PROGRAM

SEC. 1860E–2. (a) IN GENERAL.—The Secretary shall establish a program to be known as the Medicare Health Savings Accounts program (in this part referred to as the 'Medicare HSA program').

(b) AMOUNT PROVIDED TO ENROLLEES.—

(1) AMOUNT.—The Secretary shall establish procedures to ensure that, for each plan year an individual is enrolled in the Medicare HSA program, the Secretary shall provide to such individual an amount that is equal to 95 percent of the annual MA capitation rate (as calculated under section 1853(c)(1)) with respect to that individual for the Medicare Advantage payment area the individual is in.

(2) PERMISSIBLE USE OF AMOUNT.—The Secretary shall establish procedures to ensure that the amount provided under paragraph (1) is used only for the following purposes:

(A) As a contribution into a health savings account established by such individual, as described in paragraph (2) of section 1860E–1(b).

(B) For payment of premiums for enrollment of such individual under a high deductible health plan described in paragraph (3) of such section.

(3) NOTIFICATION OF AMOUNT PROVIDED.—The Secretary shall ensure that, not later than the date that is 90 days before the date on which payment of the amount provided under paragraph (1) is made to an individual enrolled in

the Medicare HSA program, such individual receives notification of such amount. Such information shall be made available on the web site of the Centers for Medicare & Medicaid Services (based on the age and geographic location of the beneficiary) and through 1–800–MEDICARE.

(4) PAYMENT.—Payment of the amount provided under paragraph (1) shall be made from the Federal Hospital Insurance Trust Fund and the Federal Supplementary Medical Insurance Trust Fund (including the Medicare Prescription Drug Account within such Trust Fund) in such proportion as the Secretary determines appropriate.

(5) RECOVERY OF AMOUNT PROVIDED IN CASE OF TERMINATION.—

> "(A) IN GENERAL.—In the case of a termination of an election to receive benefits under this part as of a month before the end of a plan year, the Secretary shall provide for a procedure for the recovery of amounts provided attributable to the remaining months in such year.
>
> (B) PENALTY.—
>
>> (i) IN GENERAL.—In addition to the amount recovered under subparagraph (A), if the Secretary determines there was fraud involved in such termination, the Secretary may apply a civil money penalty of not more than 25 percent of the amount recovered.
>>
>> (ii) CIVIL MONEY PENALTY.—The provisions of section 1128A (other than subsections (a) and (b)) shall apply to a civil money penalty under this subparagraph in the same manner as they apply to a civil money penalty or proceeding under section 1128A(a).
>
> (C) PAYMENT FOR ITEMS AND SERVICES.—The Secretary shall establish procedures under which providers of services and suppliers (as defined in sections 1861(u) and 1861(d), respectively) are required to accept as payment for items and services provided to an individual enrolled in the Medicare HSA program under this part the amount that would otherwise be paid under the original Medicare fee-for-service program under parts A and B.

**"ELECTION OF BENEFITS UNDER MEDICARE HSA
PROGRAM; TERMINATION OF ELECTION**

"SEC. 1860E–3. The Secretary shall establish procedures for the election of benefits, and the termination of such election, as appropriate, under the Medicare HSA program."

(2) CONFORMING REFERENCES TO PREVIOUS PART E.— Any reference in law (in effect before the date of the enactment of this Act) to part E of title XVIII of the Social Security Act is deemed a reference to part F of such title (as in effect after such date).

(b) AMENDMENT OF INTERNAL REVENUE CODE OF 1986.—

(1) IN GENERAL.—Paragraph (7) of section 223(b) of the Internal Revenue Code of 1986 (relating to medicare eligible individuals) is amended to read as follows:

"(7) MEDICARE ELIGIBLE INDIVIDUALS.—The limitation under this subsection for any month with respect to an individual shall be zero for any month such individual is entitled to benefits under part A, B, or D of title XVIII of the Social Security Act."

(2) EFFECTIVE DATE.—The amendment made by this subsection shall apply to taxable years beginning on or after January 1, 2008.

(c) SUNSET OF MSA PROVISIONS.—Section 1851(a)(2)(B) of the Social Security Act (42 U.S.C.1395w–21(a)(2)(B)) is amended—

(1) by striking "MSA.—An MSA plan," and inserting the following: "MSA.—

"(i) Subject to clause (ii), an MSA plan,"; and

(2) by inserting after clause (i), as added by paragraph (1), the following new clause:

"(ii) Beginning on January 1, 2008, the plan described in clause (i) shall not be available as a Medicare Advantage plan under this part."

The Common Sense Guide to

HEALTH SAVINGS ACCOUNTS

*What You Need to Know
About High Deductible Health Plans
And Health Savings Accounts*

Written by:

**Roy Ramthun, President
HSA Consulting Services, LLC**

TABLE OF CONTENTS

HOW TO USE THIS GUIDE

This guide is intended to help individuals and families better understand health savings accounts (HSAs), how the health plans that make people eligible for HSAs compare to traditional health insurance, and how to determine whether an HSA is right for you or your family. A worksheet is included to help you compare the financial features of the HSA to a traditional policy. In addition, a detailed comparison of a traditional PPO policy and an HSA plan prepared by the *Washington Post* is re-printed in Appendix 3.

The guide examines the finer details of HSAs and the health insurance policies that accompany them. In each section, a "Buyer's Guide" provides advice, reminders, and things to consider when examining an HSA. The "Buyer's Guide" is intended to provide additional insight into the finer details of HSAs and how they work.

Additional help is provided through answers to frequently asked questions, definitions of terms that are commonly used with HSAs, and a description of additional resources available through the Internet.

Every attempt will be made to keep this guide current with any changes in the laws, regulations, or operational details of HSAs. In addition, the section "Frequently Asked Questions" will be updated as additional clarification is needed and further questions arise.

INTRODUCTION

Increasingly, individuals and families are considering health insurance policies with higher deductibles than traditional policies. Sometimes, employers are asking their employees to enroll in these plans, either as an option or the only health insurance plan available to employees. Individuals and families purchasing health insurance on their own can sometimes only find affordable health insurance if they choose a policy with a high deductible.

Some, but not all, of the newer health insurance policies with high deductibles may qualify individuals and families for a new type of trust or custodial account that has certain tax advantages, called a "health savings account" or "HSA." An HSA offers a way to put aside money to pay for your routine medical expenses and help you save money on taxes. HSAs are designed to fill in the gaps for "catastrophic" insurance policies that cover larger medical bills.

Most of us know that we can lower or premiums on our auto or homeowners insurance by raising our policy deductible. But few of us actually put the savings into a "rainy day" fund in case we actually have to pay our deductible when we have a claim. HSAs offer a way of putting money into that "rainy day" fund for health care. The tax benefits that come with the HSA make the opportunity that much better.

This guide will provide useful information about: (1) which types of high-deductible health insurance policies qualify for HSAs and which do not; (2) how to set up and use an HSA; and (3) tips on how to help you find good resources to answer your questions.

Health savings accounts do not solve some or all of the problems with obtaining health insurance. However, for many individuals and families, HSAs can make health insurance more affordable while providing an alternative way of financing their medical coverage.

HISTORICAL BACKGROUND

In 1996, federal legislation included a demonstration project which created Archer medical savings accounts (MSAs). MSAs have many similarities to HSAs, including their coordination with high deductible health insurance policies and tax advantages. However, these accounts were limited in scope and available only to self-employed individuals and employees of small businesses.

In 2003, federal legislation removed the limitations on MSAs and re-named them "health savings accounts." HSAs are now available to any individual or family with HSA-qualified insurance. There are no limitations on who may have an HSA based on income or employment status. However, dependent children cannot have their own HSAs but may be covered by the HSAs of their parents. In December 2006, additional changes were made to the HSA program that improved account funding opportunities.

"HSA-QUALIFIED" HEALTH INSURANCE

The term "HSA-qualified" insurance refers to health insurance policies with deductibles higher than traditional policies. HSA-qualified plans generally have lower premiums, higher deductibles, and higher out-of-pocket spending limits, but in other ways resemble traditional health insurance plans. However, not all policies with high deductibles make individuals eligible to contribute to an HSA. In order for a high-deductible policy to be an "HSA-qualified" policy, the policy must meet certain requirements relating to deductibles, out-of-pocket expenses, covered benefits, and preventive care. Plans that meet these requirements are called "high-deductible health plans" or "HDHPs."

Deductibles

In order for a high-deductible health insurance policy to be "HSA qualified," the policy must have an annual deductible that is at least $1,100 for self-only coverage or $2,200 for family coverage beginning in 2007. The policy can have an annual deductible as high as $5,500 for self-only coverage or $11,000 for family coverage in 2007. If a high-deductible policy has an annual deductible below or above these amounts in 2007, it is not an HSA-qualified policy.

> *NOTE: The amounts are adjusted annually for inflation and may increase from one year to the next. For 2008, the minimum deductibles will be the same as in 2007. However, the maximum annual deductible will increase to $5,600 for self-only coverage and $11,200 for family coverage in 2008.*

Policies offering "family coverage" can apply a single "umbrella deductible" to the entire family. For example, a family has a policy that has a deductible of $4,000 that applies to all medical expenses incurred by the family members. This means that one family member could incur all $4,000 of medical expenses before the deductible is satisfied. Other policies have "embedded deductibles" for individual family members. For example, a family has policy that has an "umbrella deductible" of $5,000 but has "embedded deductibles" of $2,500 for each family member. This means that when any family member has incurred $2,500 of medical expenses, that family member will have satisfied their individual deductible. However, a $2,500 deductible could still apply to other family members until $5,000 in medical expenses has been incurred by all the family members combined.

> *NOTE: Family policies must have "embedded deductibles" for individual family members that are at least $2,200 per person or the policy is not "HSA-qualified."*

Buyer's Guide: Make sure your policy has a deductible that meets the requirements, especially as the required amounts change over time. The level of deductible you choose will impact your premium and savings opportunity. Higher deductibles can lower your premium significantly and provide savings that you can put into your HSA each year. However, you may not want to choose policies with the highest deductibles, at least initially, because the amount you can contribute to your HSA to cover the deductible is limited each year. Over time, you may accumulate enough funds in your HSA to lessen the impact of higher deductibles. In addition, individuals age 55 or older can make additional contributions to their HSAs, each year, which may allow them to accept policies with higher deductibles.

Based on a 2007 survey by America's Health Insurance Plans (AHIP), annual premiums for best-selling HSA-qualified plans in the individual market averaged about $2,100 for individual coverage and $4,600 for families (see Table 1). Premiums for large employer-based HSA-qualified plans averaged about $2,800 for single coverage and $7,000 for family coverage. By contrast, premiums for all employer-based plans overall averaged $4,500 and $12,100, respectively, based on data from the Kaiser Family Foundation/HRET's 2007 survey of employer-sponsored health benefits.

Table 1.   Features of Individual Market Best-Selling HDHPs (AHIP Survey)

	Single	Family
Premium (Age 30–54)	$2,106	$4,616
Deductible	$2,668	$5,264
Out of pocket maximum	$3,449	$6,881
Lifetime maximum	$3.8 million	$3.9 million

Limits on Out-of-Pocket Expenses

"HSA-qualified" policies must also limit annual out-of-pocket expenses paid by the individual or family for covered benefits under the plan. After the individual or family reaches this out-of-pocket limit, the plan must pay 100 percent of the cost of benefits covered under the plan for the remainder of the plan year. For 2007, the out-of-pocket limit cannot be any higher than $5,500 for self-only coverage or $11,000 for family coverage. Out-of-pocket limits can be as low as $1,100 for self-only coverage or $2,200 for family coverage beginning. If a high-deductible policy has an out-of-pocket limit above or below these amounts, it is not an HSA-qualified policy.

NOTE: The amounts are adjusted annually for inflation and may increase from one year to the next. For 2008, the limit on out-of-pocket expenses will increase to $5,600 for self-only coverage and $11,200 for family coverage.

It is possible for the out-of-pocket limit to be as low as the policy deductible, in which case the plan pays 100 percent of covered benefits after the deductible is met. Other policies charge co-insurance (e.g., 20 percent) for covered benefits received after the deductible is met, up to a higher limit on total out-of-pocket expenses. Under HSA-qualified policies, the deductible, co-pays, and co-insurance amounts paid under the plan *must* count toward meeting the out-of-pocket limit on expenses.

Buyer's Guide: Make sure your policy has a limit on out-of-pocket expenses that meets the requirements. The out-of-pocket limits for HSA-qualified plans can offer two significant benefits to individuals and families when compared to traditional policies, especially for those with high medical expenses. First, some traditional policies do not have a limit on out-of-pocket expenses, leaving individuals and families exposed to unlimited and unpredictable expenses each year. Second, the deductible, co-pays, and co-insurance amounts paid under an HSA-qualified plan *must* count toward meeting the out-of-pocket limit on expenses. Under some traditional policies, the deductible and co-pays do not count toward meeting the out-of-pocket limit.

The level of out-of-pocket limit you choose will impact your premium. Some policies offer out-of-pocket limits as low as the deductible, meaning after you have met your deductible, the plan pays 100 percent of covered benefits. However, policies with higher limits may have lower premiums. Over time, you may accumulate enough funds in your HSA to lessen the impact of higher out-of-pocket limits. In addition, individuals age 55 or older can make additional contributions to their HSAs each year, which may allow them to accept policies with higher out-of-pocket limits.

Covered Benefits

There is a common misperception that HSA-qualified policies are "bare bones" insurance policies. This is generally not the case. Typically, the covered benefits under HSA-qualified policies are identical to traditional policies. The major difference is the amount of the deductible and the limit on out-of-pocket expenses.

High-deductible insurance policies are subject to the same insurance laws and regulations as other policies (HMOs, PPOs, indemnity policies, etc.). This means that the same benefit mandates, premium regulations, and consumer protections prescribed by each state (and the federal government) apply to these high-deductible policies. As with traditional policies, HSA-qualified policies must be approved for sale by the state insurance department.

The only exceptions to this are policies offered by companies (typically larger companies) that self-insure their company benefits. However, these policies are regulated by a federal law known as "ERISA," which allows companies to offer policies to their workers providing the same benefits regardless of which state the employees work.

One key difference between traditional plans and HSA-qualified plans is that the deductible must apply to all covered benefits under an HSA-qualified plan, including the cost of prescription drugs. This means that an individual or family could meet their deductible solely through prescription drug expenses. If you take a lot of prescription medicines, you may pay more out of your own pocket (or use HSA funds) than the $15 or $20 co-pays you are used to paying, but you may also hit your deductible faster and reach higher levels of insurance coverage more quickly (e.g., 80 or 100 percent coverage).

As with traditional policies, HSA-qualified policies may have different levels of covered benefits depending on whether they are provided by "in-network" or "out-of-network" physicians, hospitals, and other medical providers. The limits on deductibles and out-of-pocket expenses described above apply only to covered benefits from "in-network" providers.

Just like traditional policies, HSA-qualified policies may put limits on covered benefits, such as the number of visits, limit payments to "usual, customary, and reasonable" (UCR) amounts, use formularies or preferred lists for prescription drugs, and require prior authorization before services are provided. These limitations should be described in any insurance policy contract. *Be sure to read the policy contract and determine if the coverage is what you and your family need based on your family's history of medical care use.*

All consumers should learn as much as possible about the scope of coverage under the plan. In particular, you should not assume that once the plan's deductible or out-of-pocket limit is met, all remaining medical expenses will be paid by the plan. While individuals who expect to rely on the plan's coverage because they have high medical bills should understand how the plan will handle their particular expenses, everyone should *understand what the plan will and will not cover* once their deductible and out-of-pocket limits are met. As is the case with any type of health insurance, benefits are subject to the definitions, limitations, and exclusions described in the policy and are payable only if determined by the plan that they are medically necessary. However, such decisions may be subject to plan reconsideration and external appeal.

Buyer's Guide: As with any insurance contract, the amount of covered benefits affects your premium. Pay close attention to the details of what is covered and under what circumstances, what is *not* covered (or "excluded") and under what circumstances, and the types of medical providers from which covered benefits are available. Make sure you understand what expenses count toward satisfying your policy deductible and out-of-pocket limits.

If you are chronically ill and take several prescription medications, you may satisfy your HSA-qualified policy deductible with your drug expenses alone. Although this means that you pay the total cost of your prescriptions while your deductible is in effect, you will pay only the negotiated cost of your medicines, not the full retail price. This is one of the benefits of your HSA-qualified policy. Another benefit is that since these prescription expenses count toward meeting your deductible, you may hit your deductible and out-of-pocket limits faster than under a traditional policy, which means your policy could pay 100 percent of covered benefits sooner than a traditional policy.

Preventive Care

HSA-qualified plans may provide coverage for preventive care on a first dollar coverage basis (i.e., without having to apply these expense to the policy deductible). HSA-qualified plans are not required to cover preventive care services, but most policies do offer at least some coverage for preventive care. Plans may cover 100 percent of preventive benefits or charge co-pays for the benefits. Plans may cover a limited or unlimited amount of preventive care benefits.

Each qualified plan determines what services are considered "preventive care" under the plan. Federal regulations allow plans to cover services such as the following:

- Periodic health evaluations, including tests and diagnostic procedures ordered in connection with routine examinations, such as annual physicals.
- Routine prenatal and well-child care.
- Child and adult immunizations.
- Tobacco cessation programs.
- Obesity weight-loss programs.
- Screening services (see attached Appendix 1).

Some, but not very many, prescription drugs can be covered as "preventive care" under your policy. Two examples of types of drugs that may be covered as "preventive care" are drugs known as:

1. **Statins** that lower your cholesterol levels to prevent heart disease (e.g., Lipitor, Crestor, Mevacor, Zocor, Cholestin, Pravachol, etc.).
2. **Angiotensin-converting enzyme (ACE) inhibitors** that can help prevent (or prevent reoccurrence of) a heart attack

or stroke (e.g., Capoten, Lotensin, Vasotec, Altace, Zestril, Accupril, etc.).

NOTE: Birth control pills and devices are not considered "preventive care" for HSA-qualified plans.

Buyer's Guide: Look for a policy that provides coverage of preventive care services that you will (or should) use. This will save you money in the long run and will help you maintain and improve your health. Make sure you understand the details of the preventive care services covered by your plan. Some services that are considered "preventive care" may not be covered by your plan.

Some plans may charge co-pays for certain preventive services. Of course, you can use your HSA funds to pay these co-pays. Pay special attention to whether any prescription drugs are covered as "preventive care" and under what circumstances. If you are unsure, ask your insurance plan for a more detailed explanation. If you are chronically ill, it is unlikely that your medications will be considered "preventive care."

Is Your Policy HSA-Qualified?

If your policy does not meet the requirements described above regarding deductibles, out-of-pocket limits, and covered benefits (including preventive care), it cannot be HSA qualified. You must generally rely on your health insurance carrier to determine whether your policy meets the requirements and is "HSA qualified." HSA-qualified policies generally include a statement that they meet the requirements for HSAs or are determined to be a "High-Deductible Health Plan" (HDHP). Although unlikely, some older insurance policies may meet the requirements to be "HSA qualified."

Buyer's Guide: If you believe your current policy meets the HSA requirements, you should ask your insurance carrier to tell you *in writing* whether your policy is HSA qualified. If the carrier is unwilling or unable to do so, you *should not* make your own determination. It is recommended that you contact your state insurance department and/or seek legal advice from a qualified professional who can help you make a determination. If you obtain your HSA-qualified policy through your employer, you can generally rely on the company's determination.

How to Find an HSA-Qualified Policy

Companies are increasingly offering HSA-qualified policies to their workers. If your employer does not offer an HSA-qualified policy or you do not currently have an HSA-qualified policy but would like to obtain one, contact a local insurance agent or ask your current insurance company about switching to an HSA-qualified policy. You may also want to contact the state insurance department for assistance, if needed. There are also many resources available on the Internet if you search on terms like "health savings account" or "HSA."

Buyer's Guide: Almost every health insurance company sells HSA-qualified policies. Ask any sales representative, agent, or broker about their experience selling HSA-qualified policies. Choose one that sells a lot of HSA-qualified policies, not just a few. Ask for references of companies or individuals to whom they have sold HSAs. If you do not currently have health insurance coverage or have a medical condition, *you may be subject to medical underwriting and exclusions for pre-existing conditions* when purchasing an *HSA-qualified policy. HSA-qualified policies offer no greater protection against medical underwriting and/or pre-existing medical exclusions than traditional policies.*

Other Coverage

To be eligible to contribute to an HSA, not only must you have HSA-qualified insurance, but you must also *not* have any other first dollar coverage that could disqualify you. Other types of coverage that might disqualify you include:

- A traditional HMO, PPO, or indemnity policy, including coverage under a spouse's policy.
- A flexible spending account (FSA) or health reimbursement arrangement (HRA), including a spouse's FSA or HRA.
- Medicare.
- Medicaid.
- Tricare.
- VA benefits (if received within the past three months).

General purpose HRAs and health care FSAs are not HSA-qualified plans. However, certain types of FSAs or HRAs can be compatible with an HSA. For example, if your employer offers a "limited purpose" FSA or HRA that only reimburses dental, vision, and/or preventive care expenses, you can still be eligible for an HSA. These types of plans are desirable because it offers another tax-preferred way of paying for these expenses without using your HSA funds.

Certain types of insurance will not jeopardize your eligibility for an HSA. The following types of insurance may offer medical benefits but generally will not disqualify you if they are in place along with the HSA-qualified plan:

- Auto.
- Accident.
- Dental only.
- Vision only.
- Insurance for a specific disease or illness, as long as it pays a specific dollar amount when the policy is triggered.
- Hospital indemnity.
- Long-term care.
- Disability.
- Wellness programs offered by your employer, if they do not pay for significant medical benefits.
- Work site employee assistance programs (EAPs), if they do not pay for significant medical benefits.

Buyer's Guide: It is possible for you to be eligible for an HSA even though the rest of your family is not. This is possible even if you have "family coverage" that covers the rest of your family members. However, you should be particularly careful when a family member (except dependent children) has "other coverage" because it could jeopardize your ability to have and contribute to an HSA. Although HSA-qualified policies can be used as "secondary insurance," your primary insurance may eliminate your ability to contribute to an HSA account.

Be especially careful when your spouse has other insurance coverage or an FSA or HRA through his/her employer. It is not good enough to say you will never use their coverage or account to pay for your medical expenses—your spouse's plan/account must not allow your expenses to be paid (and should state this in writing). It is acceptable for your spouse's coverage/account to cover your children's medical expenses. Since dependent children cannot establish their own HSA accounts, any other coverage they may have is not relevant.

It may be worthwhile to consider purchasing a supplemental "hospital indemnity" or "accident" policy. They can be relatively inexpensive but will help you pay your medical bills if you have to pay your entire deductible all at once because you are hospitalized. This will help keep the funds already deposited in your HSA for other medical expenses.

HEALTH SAVINGS ACCOUNTS

Individuals that have HSA-qualified insurance policies (and no other first dollar coverage that disqualifies them) are eligible to establish HSAs and make contributions each year. Contributions provide certain tax advantages as described below. Funds deposited in the account roll over automatically each year and may be invested without paying taxes on earnings. Account funds may be used tax free to pay for qualified medical expenses. Accounts may be established with qualified institutions such as banks and credit unions.

Making Contributions to Your HSA

Contributions to HSAs may be made by individuals, employers, and other individuals (including family members). Employers can make fixed dollar or "matching" contributions. Contributions made by employers and employees through payroll deduction are treated the same way as payment of health insurance premiums for tax purposes—these contributions are not counted as "income" when determining income and employment taxes. This means that HSA contributions made through your job can reduce both you and your employer's income and FICA taxes.

Source of HSA Contribution	Tax Status
Employer	No income or payroll taxes (FICA) applied
Employee, through payroll deduction	No income or payroll taxes (FICA) applied
Employee, but not through payroll deduction	Deductible on employee's income taxes
Family member or friend	Deductible on recipient's income taxes

Contributions can also be made outside of your employment. In this case, you pay no income taxes on your contributions. In addition, the amount you contribute to your HSA reduces your taxable income. For example, if your income is $42,000 and you make a $2,000 contribution to your HSA, the amount of your income that is taxed is only $40,000. You are not required to itemize deductions to take the deduction for your HSA contributions. However, you do have to complete the standard Form 1040 (you cannot file the form 1040-EZ).

> *NOTE: HSA contributions are also deductible from state income taxes in all states except[1] Alabama, California, New Jersey, and Wisconsin. The following states have no state income tax: Alaska, Florida, New Hampshire, Nevada, South Dakota, Tennessee, Texas, Washington, and Wyoming.*

Contributions may also be made by other individuals, such as family members. For example, parents may want to help their children that have recently graduated from college and are now on their own to fund their HSAs. In these situations, the person receiving the funds (i.e., the son or daughter) receives the tax deduction on their income taxes. These contributions may also be exempt from gift taxes for the person making the contribution (e.g., the parents).

The amount that can be deposited into an HSA each year is set by the U.S. Treasury Department using a formula specified in law. For 2007, the amount you can deposit is limited to:

- $2,850 for individuals with self-only coverage.
- $5,650 for those with family coverage.

> *NOTE: The amounts are adjusted annually for inflation and may increase from one year to the next. For 2008, the annual contribution limit will increase to $2,900 for individuals and $5,800 for families.*

Individuals age 55 or older may make additional "catch-up" contributions each year. For 2007, the maximum additional contribution is $800.

---

[1] As of August 31, 2007.

NOTE: For 2008, the maximum "catch-up" contribution will be $900 per person. For 2009 and future years, the maximum additional contribution is $1,000 per person. These amounts are set in federal law and are not adjusted for inflation.

If your employer makes contributions to your account, the company decides how frequently to make the contributions (e.g., every payday, monthly, quarterly, etc.). If you make contributions through payroll deduction, the contributions will probably be deposited in your account with every paycheck, or at least monthly. Once the money is deposited in your account, it belongs to you. Your employer cannot tell you what to do with the funds after that point.

If the amount of contributions being made by your employer and/or by you through payroll deduction do not add up to the maximum amount you are allowed to contribute for the year (including catch-up contributions), you can deposit the difference into your HSA and deduct this amount on your income tax return. For example, if you have self-only coverage and your employer agrees to contribute $1,000 to your HSA and you have another $1,000 deposited to your account through payroll deduction, you can make an additional deposit of $850 to your HSA. If you are age 55 or older, you could also make a catch-up contribution for the year.

You do not have to wait to incur medical expenses before you make this contribution (e.g., $500 in the example above) to your account. Contributions can be made at any time of the year and as late as the income tax filing deadline (usually April 15) in the following year. However, funds must be deposited into your HSA before they can be used to pay for or reimburse your medical expenses. If you do not deposit the funds first, you will not receive credit for the deposits and therefore not qualify for the income tax deduction for HSA contributions.

If your HSA-qualified coverage begins in any month other than January, you can still make the full HSA contribution for the calendar year. For example, if your coverage under an HSA-qualified policy does not begin until July, you can still contribute the full $2,850 (assuming you have self-only coverage) for 2007. However, you must keep your HSA-qualified coverage through at least the end of the following calendar year or you may have to pay back some of the contribution (and maybe interest and penalties).

For any year that you drop or lose your HSA-qualified coverage before the end of the year, you will not be able to make the full contribution to your HSA. You will need to pro-rate your contribution for that year. Count only those months for which you had HSA-qualified coverage on the first day of the month. For example, if you drop your HSA-qualified coverage at the end of June, you would only be able to contribute 50 percent of your allowed contribution for that year.

In the year you turn age 55, you are eligible to make the full catch-up contribution regardless of when your birthday falls during the year, if you have HSA-qualified coverage for the entire year. However, if your coverage begins on any day other than January 1, your catch-up contributions must be pro-rated for the number of months for which you have HSA-qualified coverage.

For families with married couples, the family can open one or two HSA accounts, if both spouses are eligible. However, the total contribution to the two accounts cannot exceed the maximum allowed for the year (including pro-rated amounts). If both spouses are age 55 or older, each spouse must open an account in their own name to allow them both to make catch-up contributions. As with IRAs, joint accounts are not permitted.

You may transfer funds from an IRA, but only once in your lifetime, to help fund your HSA without paying a tax penalty for early withdrawal from your IRA. However, the amount you transfer cannot exceed your annual HSA contribution for the year (does not include your allowed catch-up contribution for the year).

Buyer's Guide: Funds cannot be used for medical expenses until they are deposited into the account, so it is important to make your contributions as early in the year as you can afford to do so. If you are opening an HSA for the first time, you should open your HSA and make an initial deposit as soon as possible because only those expenses incurred on or after the date your account is opened are eligible to be paid or reimbursed from your HSA. After your account is opened and you have at least some funds on deposit, you can wait as late as April 15 to make the remaining contribution to maximize your account deposits for the previous calendar year. If you have medical expenses but not enough funds in your account, make sure to deposit to your HSA first (if you haven't already exceeded the maximum contribution for the year) and then reimburse yourself for the expenses so you get the tax savings that HSAs offer.

> *NOTE: If you make contributions to a family member's (nondependent) HSA, or transfer funds from your IRA to an HSA, consult your tax adviser before making contributions.*

Establishing HSAs

HSAs can be opened at any willing bank, credit union, or other qualified institution. The institution is the "custodian" or "trustee" of your account. By agreeing to offer HSAs, the custodian/trustee agrees to abide by banking laws, offer federal deposit insurance to protect your account, and report necessary tax information to you and the IRS.

The general process for establishing your HSA is very similar to the way you open an IRA. You do not need permission from your employer or anyone else to establish your HSA. The specific process varies from bank to bank. Generally, most trustees and custodians require that you complete an application form in writing, sign it, and return it by mail or fax. Some trustees and custodians have developed account opening processes that allow some aspects to be handled electronically.

Banks and credit unions are not required to open HSAs so don't be surprised that your local bank or credit union does not offer HSAs. Insurance companies are also approved to open your account. Many insurance companies offer HSA services through a partnership with a bank. This often makes it easy to get your account started. You always have the flexibility to transfer your funds to another institution of your choosing at a later date.

It is important that you open your HSA as soon as you enroll in an HSA-qualified plan (if not before) because your HSA can only be used to pay for or reimburse you for qualified medical expenses that you incur after your account is "established." *This is an important and subtle rule*—one that can surprise you when you enroll in an HSA-qualified plan for the first time. Typically, you enroll in the HSA-qualified plan first, then open the HSA. Many trustees and custodians allow you to complete the necessary account opening forms or other processes shortly before the date your HSA-qualified coverage becomes effective, so your account is considered "established" on your coverage effective date. As a result, any medical expenses you incur during the first few days of coverage can be paid for or reimbursed from your account.

If your employer makes contributions to your account or allows you to make contributions through payroll deduction, your employer can choose a financial institution at which to deposit the funds. This makes it easier for your employer to deposit the funds into your HSA. However, you can transfer the funds to another bank or credit union if you want your account held at a different institution.

Custodians and trustees can set administrative fees and other requirements for HSAs. These include things like minimum deposit requirements, minimum balance requirements, account set-up fees, account maintenance fees, and the like. A recent survey of HSA custodians and trustees indicated the following ranges for HSA fees:

- Account set-up fees—$0–$50 (average = $14.36).
- Monthly maintenance fees—$0–$10 (average = $2.06).
- Transaction fees—$0–$5 (average = $0.27).
- Account closing fees—$0–$30 (average = $10.17).

You should consider these costs when deciding where to open your HSA(s).

Most custodians and trustees pay interest on your account funds, just like they do for savings and checking accounts. The average interest rate paid is around 2 percent. The highest rate being paid is around 5 percent. Generally, higher interest rates are offered for larger account balances.

Your HSA custodian/trustee may also offer investment options for your HSA funds. This may be an important consideration as your account balance grows over time. Your funds can be invested in the same types of investments permitted for IRAs, including stocks, bonds, mutual funds, CDs, and the like. However, each institution can decide how many and what types of investment options it offers.

You may open and maintain more than one HSA at different financial institutions. You may deposit as much as you wish into each account as long as your total contribution to all the accounts combined does not exceed the limits for the calendar year. However, because each account custodian/trustee may charge fees, and so on., it may not be wise to open too many HSAs.

Buyer's Guide: Be sure to shop around for banks or credit unions that offer you good value for your HSA funds. Some charge high fees that may offset the growth you realize through interest payments or investments. Open your HSA before your coverage begins, or as soon as possible after it starts. Doing so will ensure that you have your account opened on the first day of your HSA-qualified insurance coverage, which for many people begins on a holiday (January 1). That will guarantee that any expenses you might incur on January 1 (or later) will be eligible for reimbursement from the account.

Using Your HSA

Once funds are deposited in your HSA, you can withdraw funds to pay for qualified medical expenses directly from the account. The types of expenses that qualify for reimbursement from an HSA include more than just what your insurance covers. In fact, HSA funds can be used to cover many items and services that insurance often does not cover, including over-the-counter medications, vision care expenses (including laser eye surgery), dental care expenses (including orthodontia), chiropractic care, and much more (see Appendix 2).

In most instances, you cannot pay for health insurance premiums with HSA funds. However, the funds can help you pay for your health insurance premiums during periods when you are between jobs. For example, you can use your funds to pay premiums for COBRA continuation coverage from a former employer. You can also use your funds to pay health insurance premiums if you are receiving federal or state unemployment compensation. In either case (COBRA or unemployment), you can pay premiums for health insurance even if it is not HSA-qualified insurance.

Looking toward retirement, HSA funds can be saved and used to pay for long-term care expenses and insurance, and Medicare out-of-pocket expenses (deductibles, co-pays, and co-insurance) and monthly premiums for Part A (inpatient hospital), Part B (physician and outpatient), Part D (prescription drugs), and Medicare Advantage plans. The only thing funds cannot be used to pay is premiums for Medicare Supplement (i.e., Medigap) insurance.

Your HSA funds can be used to pay for not only your qualified medical expenses, but also the qualified expenses incurred by your spouse and dependents. Your spouse and dependents do not need to be covered by your HSA-qualified plan.

Many banks and credit unions offer checks or debit cards that you may use to pay for expenses at the time the services are provided. These features offer easy access to your account funds, including reimbursing yourself for expenses you have already incurred. Be aware that some of these features have associated fees, especially when using a debit card to withdraw "cash" from your HSA, even if you are reimbursing yourself for a qualified medical expense.

Buyer's Guide: You have great flexibility when determining how to use your account funds. This is one of the great advantages that HSAs offer. You alone can determine whether to use your account to pay for current medical expenses or save the funds in your account to pay for expenses in retirement. However, be aware of fees associated with different ways of accessing your account funds.

How Your Health Savings Account Works

HSAs and HSA-qualified insurance work very similar to traditional insurance. Some medical providers prefer to submit a claim for the services provided to the insurance company first and bill you after the insurance company applies their discount and your policy deductible. This ensures that your claim is for a covered service, that you get the benefit of the insurance company's negotiated fee with the provider, and that your expenses are counted toward satisfying your policy deductible. Your insurance company will then likely send you an "explanation of benefits" (EOB) showing the services provided, the charges submitted, and discount(s) applied. The EOB will also let you know how much you owe the medical provider.

The medical provider will also likely send you a bill for the amount you owe. If you have a debit card or checks to access your HSA funds, you could use either form of payment the provider is willing to accept. You could also pay the provider in cash (or personal check or credit card) and reimburse yourself from your HSA later.

Your account custodian/trustee and your employer do not have any responsibility to review or approve the expenses for which you use your account funds. If your tax return is audited by the IRS, you will need to prove that your medical expenses were "qualified." You will have to pay income taxes and a tax penalty (10 percent) on the amount that was not "qualified." Once you reach age 65 (or become disabled), you no longer have to pay the 10 percent penalty, just income taxes on amounts used for nonqualified expenses.

After the end of the year, you will be sent tax forms that indicate how much you contributed to your HSA for the calendar year, how much you withdrew from the account during the year, and your ending balance on December 31. You do not need to itemize your deductions to take the deduction on your income taxes for the amount you contributed for the year. You will need to file a tax form (Form 8889) with your tax return which documents your HSA funds and tax deductions.

Buyer's Guide: When you go to your medical provider, you should let them know that you have an insurance policy with a high deductible and that you may end up paying the entire amount for the services provided. You may want to offer to pay something before you leave the provider's office, as you would do when you have to pay a co-pay under a traditional policy. Some medical providers are concerned that they will have a harder time collecting from you if you don't pay something before you leave. These concerns may make your medical providers less willing to accept your HSA-qualified insurance in the future.

If you incur medical expenses early in the year, you may not have enough funds in your account to pay or reimburse yourself for the expenses you incur. If you will not be making the maximum contribution to your account through your employer and/or by payroll deduction, you could deposit the remaining funds you are allowed to contribute into your account at any time. If you can work out a payment plan with the provider, this may give you more time to deposit funds into your account. Your employer may also be willing to loan you the money which you could pay back over time. (NOTE: Employers are not required to do this.) Over time, this may not be as much of a problem if you have unused funds that roll over to the next year.

Keep track of all your EOBs and receipts. This is the only proof you have that your expenses were "qualified medical expenses." You are responsible for using your account funds appropriately. You need to keep good records to indicate that you used your HSA funds exclusively to pay for or reimburse qualified medical expenses.

These medical expenses may not be claimed as a "medical expense" if you itemize your deductions in the same year.

You can wait to reimburse yourself from your HSA for many years into the future. There is no time limit on when you must use your HSA funds. However, if you receipts are no longer legible, you will have no proof that you incurred qualified expenses.

Beneficiaries and Estate Consequences

Upon your death, your surviving spouse automatically inherits your HSA, unless your will specifies otherwise. The account becomes their HSA. If your surviving spouse has HSA-qualified insurance, he/she may continue to contribute to the account as if it were their own. If the surviving spouse does not have a qualifying plan, he/she may not continue to contribute, but may continue to use the account as his/her own HSA for qualified medical expenses with no tax consequence.

If you are unmarried, the funds in the account are no longer treated as an HSA but part of your estate and will be subject to estate taxes. If the beneficiary is your estate, the fair market value of the account (as of the date of your death) is taxable on your final tax return. Qualified medical expenses incurred by you prior to your death may be reimbursed from the account before determining the "fair market value" of the account.

Buyer's Guide: Consult your tax adviser or financial planner if you have questions about the estate tax consequences of your account.

ADVANTAGES AND DISADVANTAGES OF HEALTH SAVINGS ACCOUNTS

Advantages	Disadvantages
• **Security** – High-deductible insurance and the HSA provide protection against high or unexpected medical bills. Most policies also cover preventive care services to help you maintain your health and avoid illness and disease.	• **Change** – You must switch to high-deductible insurance from traditional insurance. Some times this means you must change insurance carriers as well.
• **Affordability** – HSAs make health insurance more affordable by lowering your health insurance premiums. The savings can be substantial, which can help you fund your HSA.	• **Insecurity** – Switching from traditional first dollar coverage makes many people uncomfortable. High-deductible plans are relatively new to many people.
• **Flexibility** – HSA funds can pay for current medical expenses, including expenses that insurance may not cover. Funds can also be saved for future needs, such as: ♦ Health insurance or medical expenses if no longer working (unemployed or retired but not yet on Medicare). ♦ Out-of-pocket expenses and premiums when covered by Medicare. ♦ Long-term care expenses and insurance.	• **Other Coverage** – If you or a family member has other insurance coverage that is not HSA-qualified, or has an FSA or HRA through their employment, this may make you ineligible to contribute to an HSA.
• **Control** – You make all the decisions about your HSA. You can make choices that are best for you, and physicians can be more effective patient advocates, with less intrusion from insurance companies.	• **Control** – Some people prefer to have a third party (e.g., employer, insurance company) manage their health coverage for them. Employers and insurance companies are able to negotiate discounts for services and help us navigate the health care system in unique ways.

| ADVANTAGES AND DISADVANTAGES OF HEALTH SAVINGS ACCOUNTS (contd.) ||
Advantages	Disadvantages

• **Portability** – HSAs are completely portable. You can keep and take your account with you even if you:
  ♦ Change jobs or become unemployed.
  ♦ Change your medical coverage or marital status.
  ♦ Move to another state.
 	
• **Ownership** – You own the funds in your account. The funds in the account remain permanently and roll over from year to year, just like an IRA. There are no "use it or lose it" rules for HSAs.
 	
• **Tax Savings** – HSAs provide triple tax savings:
  (1) Tax deductions when you contribute.
  (2) Tax-free earnings through investment.
  (3) Tax-free withdrawals for qualified medical expenses.
	• **Emergencies** – When you have an urgent situation or emergency, it is inconvenient and sometimes impractical to consider "comparison shopping." Thankfully, most health care is provided in nonemergency situations.
	
	• **Information** – Sometimes it is difficult to get good information on health care prices and quality of services so you can comparison shop for good value in health care.
	
	• **Tax Filing** – You must file an income tax return to take advantage of all the benefits HSAs offer. Lower-income individuals and families may not realize all the savings of HSAs if they pay no income taxes.

HSA WORKSHEETS

	HSA-Qualified Plan	Current/Other Plan
Annual Premium		
Difference		
Annual Deductible		
• Medical		
• Prescriptions	(included above)	
Difference		
Annual Out-of-Pocket Limit		
Difference		
HSA Contributions		
• By your employer		**N/A**
• By you		**N/A**
• By others		**N/A**
• "Catch-up" contribution[2]		**N/A**
Total Contributions		**N/A**
Tax Savings from Personal HSA Contributions[3]		**N/A**
Sources for HSA Contributions		
• Premium savings		
• Company HSA contributions		
• HSA contributions by others		
• Tax savings		
Total Savings		
Increase in Out-of-Pocket Costs		
• Net increase in deductible		
• Net increase in out-of-pocket limit		
Total Increase		

[2] Per person age 55 or older. Maximum is $800 per person for 2007 ($900 for 2008, and $1,000 for 2009 and later years).

[3] Add contributions made by you (if not made through your job), by others, and any catch-up contribution. Multiply total amount by applicable tax rate for your income (e.g., 15 percent). This is your tax savings.

HSA Worksheets Example

	HSA-Qualified Plan	Current/Other Plan
Annual Premium	$5,600	$8,400
Difference	$2,800	
Annual Deductible		
• Medical	$5,000	$500
• Prescriptions	(included above)	$100
Difference		
Annual Out-of-Pocket Limit	$8,000	None
Difference		
HSA Contributions		
• By your employer	$1,200	**N/A**
• By you	$3,800	**N/A**
• By others	$0	**N/A**
• "Catch-up" contribution	$0	**N/A**
Total Contributions		**N/A**
Tax Savings from Personal HSA Contributions (assumes 15%)	$570	**N/A**
Sources for HSA Contributions		
• Premium savings	$2,800	
• Company HSA contributions	$1,200	
• HSA contributions by others	$0	
• Tax savings	$570	
Total Savings	$4,570	
Increase in Out-of-Pocket Costs		
• Net increase in deductible	$4,400	
• Net increase in out-of-pocket limit		
Total Increase	$4,400	

FREQUENTLY ASKED QUESTIONS

Why should I consider an HSA for me or my family?
If you or your employer are tired of sending hundreds and hundreds of dollars each month to your health insurance company, and would prefer to keep a big chunk of that money for yourself to spend on health expenses or save it for the future, then you need to look into a HSA.

Why would some one who is less healthy want an HSA?
You should also look at a health savings account if you have high medical expenses because the catastrophic protection against very high medical expenses may be superior to your current plan. There are two key reasons the less healthy should choose an HSA. The first reason is to have control over their own health care decisions and treatments, including their prescription drugs. With an HMO, the sick must face the rationing regime in place by HMOs to contain costs, which may include a frustrating waiting list to see a specialist or obtain a treatment, or prescription drug formularies that may not have the most up-to-date treatments or brand-name drugs that would make them feel the best. Furthermore, in virtually all HSA-qualified plans sold, prescription drug cost count toward your deductible.

The second reason is a financial incentive. Assuming the less healthy would rather not be in an HMO or other managed-care plan, then they would likely choose a fee-for-service plan. The standard fee-for-service plan has a $500 deductible, with a 20 percent co-pay of the next $5,000. This means the person would pay $500 for the deductible, and $1,000 for 20 percent of $5,000, before being covered 100 percent. That is $1,500 in after-tax income to be insured 100 percent for someone who is less healthy in a traditional, low-deductible, fee-for-service health insurance plan. Plus, the premium for a traditional low-deductible plan is much higher, which adds more cost.

With an HSA, the same individual could pay a much smaller premium, and in most cases, use the savings to fund a majority of the deductible in their HSA. With a $2,500 deductible with 100 percent coverage thereafter, and, say $2,000 deposited tax-free in the HSA, the less healthy individual with an HSA would have to come up with $500 to be covered 100 percent ($2,500 deductible minus $2,000

	Traditional Plan	HSA Plan
Deductible	$500	$2,500
Co-insurance above deductible	20%	0% (100% coverage)
Total patient medical expenses before plan pays 100 percent	$5,500	$2,500
Out-of-pocket limit	$1,500	$2,500
Contribution to HSA	N/A	$2,000
Amount and tax status of out-of-pocket expenses	$1,500 After-tax (not deductible unless > 7.5% income)	$2,000 Tax deductible

from the HSA equals $500 to meet the deductible). The $500 can be deposited in the account to retain the tax advantage of whatever your specific tax situation is. So the choice for a less healthy individual in a traditional health plan is: (1) pay $1,500 in after-tax funds to pay to be covered 100 percent by their insurance ($500 deductible and 20 percent of the next $5,000), or in this example, with an HSA, get a tax break on the extra $500 they would need to be covered 100 percent. The less healthy, therefore, have a financial incentive to choose an HSA.

For employee, spouse, and child coverage, does each individual open their own HSA or is there one account for all? If there is one for all on the plan, what happens to the account if the spouses divorce?
Each spouse can have their own account, and need to if you are making catch-up contributions. Either spouse can use their account for any medical expenses for any member of the family, even if they are not covered by the HSA-qualified plan. If the couple divorces, the divorce settlement will decide the fate of the funds.

If I get an HSA through my employer, how is it funded?
The first step is to find out what your employer is currently paying for your health insurance. Then find out what an HSA would cost instead. Once you have that information, you can talk to your employer and a tax adviser about ways to fund your account. It may

be cheaper for your employer to provide you with a partially or fully funded HSA compared to what he is currently paying for employee health care. Employer contributions to an HSA are excluded from employees' income. An employer can also choose to match the monthly HSA contributions made by employees. When you start a new job, find out if your new employer will contribute to your HSA each month. Employers are not obligated to contribute to your HSA, but you may also realize premium savings which can help you fund your account.

If I use the catastrophic insurance, who pays the deductible?

You pay the deductible with cash from your HSA. It generally takes about a year to build up enough money in the account to pay the annual insurance deductible. In the event you need to pay the deductible early, you can use a loan, other savings, or a credit card to make the payment first, and then repay yourself from your HSA a few months later when enough money has accumulated in the account. As long as you keep a record of the amount you first paid and when you paid yourself back, all these transactions are tax free.

If I use an out-of-network provider, will that count toward my deductible? Can I pay for these out-of-network expenses from my HSA?

Plans that cover out-of-network providers generally have a separate (higher) deductible for medical care received from out-of-network providers. These expenses do not count toward satisfying the deductible for medical care received from in-network providers. However, your HSA can be used to pay for medical care received from out-of-network providers if the care is a qualified medical expense.

Can I use my HSA for nonmedical expenses?

You can spend money out of your HSA for non-medical expenses, but you have to pay income tax and a 10 percent penalty for a non-medical withdrawal prior to age 65. At age 65, you only pay income tax on the amount of the nonmedical withdrawal.

Once I enroll in Medicare (age 65 years) can I get a Medicare HSA?

Yes, there are Medicare MSAs (similar to HSAs) available starting in 2007. As with other private plans providing Medicare coverage (also known as "Medicare Advantage" plans), the federal government pays your plan premium and makes a contribution to your account.

More information on these Medicare plans is available in the Medicare Handbook and on the Internet at www.medicare.gov.

Is there a list of over-the-counter (OTC) drugs that are always/never/sometimes covered under an HSA?

Most OTC drugs are qualified expenses under an HSA. Unfortunately, there is no definitive list available. Every day drugs are newly available OTC.

Currently, my wife and I are uninsured and generally healthy but do have some pre-existing conditions. Will an HSA help us?

HSA-qualified plans may be more affordable but medical underwriting practices may make it difficult for you to find an insurance carrier that will offer your coverage. Some states have "high-risk pools" that have HSA-qualified plans. Check your state insurance department to determine whether your state has a high-risk pool.

If the insured's expenses exceed the pre-tax contributions early in the plan year, will the insured have to pay the deductible with after-tax dollars?

No. You can deposit the funds later in the year and reimburse your expenses after the deposits are made. The deposits will qualify for the income tax deduction regardless of when they were made. Some employers will help their employees if there is a large expense early in the year. Another option is to purchase a supplemental policy such as a hospital indemnity policy that pays a certain amount if you are hospitalized and have to meet your deductible all at once. These policies can be relatively inexpensive. Ask your insurance carrier or agent where to find these types of policies in your area.

Are HSAs considered "employer-sponsored benefit plans" that are governed by ERISA if my employer contributes to my account?

The U.S. Department of Labor has ruled that HSAs are generally *not* "employer-sponsored benefit plans" governed by ERISA, even when the employer contributes to their HSAs, if:

- The employee's participation in the HSA is voluntary.
- The employer allows the employee to move his or her HSA to another custodian or trustee from where the employer deposits its contributions.

- The employer does not place limits on employees' withdrawals from their HSAs.
- The employer does not make investment decisions for employees or influence the employees' investment decisions.

How does making HSA contributions through my company save me money?

If your employer offers a section 125 plan (also known as a "cafeteria plan") that allows you to make contributions to your HSA through payroll deduction, you will save money by:

- Avoiding paying the employee share of the federal FICA tax on the amount you contribute, which results in greater tax savings than when you contribute after-tax amounts to the HSA. The employee share of federal FICA tax is 7.65 percent.
- Your tax liability and payments are reduced throughout the year when each contribution is made with each paycheck, and you do not need to wait until the end of the year to reduce your income taxes.
- Your interest or investment earnings accumulate faster if you make your contributions earlier in the year rather than waiting until the year ends.

Who can be considered by "spouse" or "dependent"? Can I use my HSA to pay for expenses of a domestic partner?

Your HSA-qualified policy should specify who is considered a "spouse" or "dependent" for purposes of your insurance coverage. In many cases, domestic partners can be considered part of the "family" for policies providing family coverage. However, the rules for using your HSA funds are more rigid and specific:

1. Your spouse must be a person of the opposite sex to whom you are legally married as permitted under applicable state law.
2. "Dependents" generally must be either:
   a. A child (son, daughter, stepchild, etc.) who lives with you more than half of the year and who is 18 years or younger for the entire calendar year (or under age 24 and a student for the entire year) or is permanently and totally disabled.

b. A "qualifying relative" (consult an attorney or your tax
   adviser for details).

If a domestic partner meets the definition of a "qualifying relative,"
you can use your HSA to pay for his or her qualified medical expenses
tax free. If the domestic partner is not a "qualifying relative," you
must pay income taxes on the amount of your HSA that you use to
pay for his or her medical expenses, and an additional 10 percent
tax penalty.

GLOSSARY OF TERMS

Catch-Up Contribution – These are additional contributions allowed for individuals age 55 or older. These contributions are allowed in addition to the annual amounts that generally match the deductible under an HSA-qualified policy. As with all contributions, these contributions must stop once an individual becomes eligible for Medicare.

Co-insurance – The percentage (e.g., 20 percent) of the cost of covered benefits you must pay. Generally, co-insurance is applied after you meet your policy deductible.

Contributions – Deposits to an HSA. Contributions must be made in cash.

Co-pay – A fixed-dollar amount (e.g., $20) you must pay directly to the medical provider at the time you receive health care services.

Custodian – The bank, credit union, or other financial institution that holds your HSA funds. In some states, the institution is considered a "trustee" of your account.

Deductible – A fixed-dollar amount (e.g., $1,500) you must pay each year before the plan pays for covered benefits.

Distributions – Amounts paid from an HSA for qualified health care services.

Embedded Deductible – The amount any one individual family member may have to meet before the policy pays for covered benefits. This amount is generally lower than an "umbrella deductible." Also known as an "individual deductible."

ERISA – A federal law (the Employee Retirement Income Security Act of 1974) that regulates the administration of employee benefit plans provided by employers.

Explanation of Benefits (EOB) – A document prepared by your insurance carrier that indicates what services were provided by a medical provider, the amount the medical provider charged for the services, the negotiated rate at which the benefits were payable under your insurance policy, and the amount you owe the provider for the services provided. The document also may show the amounts you have paid year-to-date toward meeting your deductible and/or out-of-pocket limit.

Family Coverage – For HSA purposes, any coverage that is not "self-only" coverage. "Family coverage" includes self + spouse only, self + dependent children, and self + spouse and children.

Flexible Spending Account (FSA) – A health care spending account offered through an employer to which employees make contributions through payroll deduction. The account can be used to pay for medical expenses approved by the employer. Unused funds do not roll over but revert back to the employer.

High-Deductible Health Plan (HDHP) – A health plan that meets federal requirements regarding minimum deductibles, maximum out-of-pocket expenses, covered benefits, and preventive care, and makes an individual that has coverage under this type of plan eligible to contribute to an HSA. Also known as an "HSA-qualified plan." Sometimes referred to as "catastrophic health insurance plan."

Health Reimbursement Arrangement (HRA) – A health care spending account funded by employers that may be used for medical expenses or premiums approved by the employer. Unspent funds usually can be carried over to the next year, but cannot be taken with you if you leave the company.

Health Savings Account – An account established by an individual that has "HSA-qualified" health insurance coverage for payment of out-of-pocket expenses tax free.

HSA-Qualified Plan A health plan that meets federal requirements regarding minimum deductibles, maximum out-of-pocket expenses, covered benefits, and preventive care, and makes in individual that has coverage under this type of plan eligible to contribute to an HSA. Also known as a "High-Deductible Health Plan" (HDHP).

In-Network – Care provided by health care professionals and facilities that have entered into an agreement with your insurance carrier to provide services to you and accept a negotiated fee for the services provided.

Out-of-Network – Care provided by health care professionals and facilities that have *not* entered into an agreement with your insurance carrier to provide services to you and have *not* accepted a negotiated fee for the services provided. Medical providers may charge their full amount (no discount) for these services. Your health insurance carrier may not pay these full charges. Some insurance contracts do not include out-of-network care as a covered benefit.

Out-of-Pocket Expenses – Expenses you pay for health care services your receive. Includes deductibles, co-pays, and co-insurance. Does not include insurance premiums.

Out-of-Pocket Limit (or Maximum) – A fixed-dollar amount of total out-of-pocket expenses you pay, above which your health plan pays 100 percent of covered benefits.

Qualified Medical Expense – A medical expense that is allowed to be paid tax free from an HSA, HRA, or FSA. Section 213(d) of the federal Internal Revenue Code governs what can be a qualified medical expense. IRS Publication 502 (available at www.irs.gov) provides more information about the types of expenses considered "qualified."

Trustee – The bank, credit union, or other financial institution that holds your HSA funds. In some states, the institution is considered a "custodian" of your account.

Umbrella Deductible – The total amount of out-of-pocket expenses that a family must meet before the plan pays for covered benefits. The umbrella deductible may be met by one or any combination of family members' out-of-pocket expenses, depending on the policy design.

ADDITIONAL RESOURCES

The following resources and web sites may be helpful to you in searching for HSA-qualified plans, financial institutions offering HSAs, and learning more about HSA.

U.S. Treasury Department
www.treas.gov/offices/public-affairs/hsa/
   This site is the definitive site for technical information about HSAs.

National Association of Insurance Commissioners
www.naic.org
   This site can help you quickly find your state insurance department's web site for help with insurance matters.

National Association of Health Underwriters
www.nahu.org/consumer/HSAGuide.cfm
   This it the site of the professional trade association for health insurance agents. The site includes a consumer-friendly HSA Guide.

eHealthInsurance
www.ehealthinsurance.com
   This site is a good source for people not covered by an employee health plan and who need to buy their own insurance. On this site you'll find a large selection of health plans and the ability to compare costs.

Council for Affordable Health Insurance HSA Information Center
www.cahi.org/cahi_contents/consumerinfo/hsa.asp
   This site has helpful information about HSAs. CAHI is a Washington, D.C.–based think tank.

HSA Decisions
www.healthdecisions.org/hsa
   This site is operated by America's Health Insurance Plans, the trade association for the insurance companies. This site will give you information on 1,300 health plans and tens of thousands of agents and brokers nationwide.

HSA Finder
www.hsafinder.com
   This site can help you find HSA custodians and trustees.

Other Helpful Sites

The following resources and web sites may be helpful to you in searching for information about the price and quality of health care products and services. There's no question that figuring out what your medical care costs and what health care provider offers the best quality care won't be easy. It's definitely not as easy as pricing out a Honda Accord, fully loaded. But when it comes to your health care, spend at least the same amount of time calculating the costs as you do pricing out your new ride.

HealthWise

www.healthwise.org

Healthwise develops consumer health information to help people make better informed health decisions.

Family Health Budget

www.familyhealthbudget.com

Humana Inc., in partnership with advocacy group Consumer Action, has created a free web site that includes a family health budget planner. On the site you will find a number of tools to help you choose the best health care plan and benefits. The planner takes you through a step-by-step questionnaire asking for information such as your current insurance status, how many times members of your family go to the doctor, how often prescription medicines are purchased, and how often the family visits the dentist, eye doctor, or other specialists. Once you've added the information, you get a calculation of how much you need to set aside for health expenses for the year.

WageWorks Inc.

www.wageworks.com

Wage Works is a provider of consumer-driven tax-advantaged spending accounts for health and dependent care. The site has a contribution and savings calculator for HSAs.

HealthGrades Inc.

www.healthgrades.com

HealthGrades is a health care ratings company based in Golden, Colorado, that sells reports on the cost of 55 medical procedures, based on regional averages of payments made by health plans. One report costs $7.95, but if you are facing a high deductible, it's worth the price to get detailed price information. You can also get physician reports, which include the amount that individual physicians are paid by Medicare for more than 100 types of procedures and visits. HealthGrades also offers hospital ratings of 28 procedures and diagnoses at more than 5,000 nonfederal hospitals free. If you know you'll need to be hospitalized, for $17.95 ($2.95 for subsequent reports) you can get a more detailed hospital report that looks at the price of nearly 100 procedures. Before you buy a report, check with your employer because 125 major corporations provide them free as a benefit.

Diagnostic Testing Web Sites
www.directlabs.com
www.healthcheckusa.com/tests.asp
www.medlabusa.com
www.mymedlab.com

There are several web sites that now offer consumers the opportunity to order the same diagnostic tests that they might get through traditional health care means—such as labs, hospitals, and clinics. What makes these web sites unique is that consumers do not need a prescription from their doctor to have the test. Consumers pay up front for the tests they want and receive a receipt to submit for reimbursement from their insurer, flexible spending account, or HSA.

HealingWell
www.healingwell.com

This web site is 10 years old and has more than 30,000 members. It provides access to information for nearly 40 chronic illnesses.

BlueCross and BlueShield Association "Blue Distinction"
www.bcbsa.com/bluedistinction

The Association has launched "Blue Distinction," an online-based program that includes a price transparency demonstration for medical services for 17 BlueCross and BlueShield plans around the country.

APPENDIX 1

Preventive Care Screening Services

Cancer Screening

- Breast Cancer (e.g., Mammogram)
- Cervical Cancer (e.g., Pap Smear)
- Colorectal Cancer
- Prostate Cancer (e.g., PSA Test)
- Skin Cancer
- Oral Cancer
- Ovarian Cancer
- Testicular Cancer
- Thyroid Cancer

Heart and Vascular Diseases Screening

- Abdominal Aortic Aneurysm
- Carotid Artery Stenosis
- Coronary Heart Disease
- Hemoglobinopathies
- Hypertension
- Lipid Disorders

Infectious Diseases Screening

- Bacteriuria
- Chlamydial Infection
- Gonorrhea
- Hepatitis B Virus Infection
- Hepatitis C
- Human Immunodeficiency Virus (HIV) Infection
- Syphilis
- Tuberculosis Infection

Mental Health Conditions and Substance Abuse Screening

- Dementia
- Depression
- Drug Abuse
- Problem Drinking
- Suicide Risk
- Family Violence

APPENDIX 1 (contd.)

Metabolic, Nutritional, and Endocrine Conditions Screening

- Anemia, Iron Deficiency
- Dental and Periodontal Disease
- Diabetes Mellitus
- Obesity in Adults
- Thyroid Disease

Musculoskeletal Disorders Screening

- Osteoporosis

Obstetric and Gynecologic Conditions Screening

- Bacterial Vaginosis in Pregnancy
- Gestational Diabetes Mellitus
- Home Uterine Activity Monitoring
- Neural Tube Defects
- Preeclampsia
- Rh Incompatibility
- Rubella
- Ultrasonography in Pregnancy

Pediatric Conditions Screening

- Child Developmental Delay
- Congenital Hypothyroidism
- Lead Levels in Childhood and Pregnancy
- Phenylketonuria
- Scoliosis, Adolescent Idiopathic

Vision and Hearing Disorders Screening

- Glaucoma
- Hearing Impairment in Older Adults
- Newborn Hearing

APPENDIX 2

Allowable[4] (Tax-Free) Expenditures from Your Health Savings Account

Examples of Allowable Expenditures from Your Health Savings Account

Acupuncture

Alcoholism treatment

Ambulance services

Artificial limbs and teeth

Bandages

Birth control pills (by prescription only)

Breast reconstruction surgery (mastectomy)

Childbirth, labor and delivery services

Chiropractic services

Christian Science Practitioner services

Contact lenses

Cosmetic surgery, but only if due to trauma or disease

Crutches

Dental care

Dermatology services

Diagnostic devices

Drug addiction treatment (inpatient)

Eyeglasses

---

[4] NOTE: This list is illustrative and is not meant to be an exhaustive list. There have been thousands of cases involving the many nuances of what constitutes "medical care" under the Internal Revenue Code, which governs Health Savings Accounts. A determination of whether an expense is qualified as "medical care" is based on all the relevant facts and circumstances. To be an expense for medical care, the expense has to be primarily for the diagnosis, cure mitigation, treatment, or prevention or alleviation of a physical or mental defect or illness. The determination often hangs on the word "primarily." Additional information is available from IRS Publication 502 (available through www.irs.gov). Consult your physician and tax adviser, if you have questions.

APPENDIX 2 (contd.)

Fertility treatments

Gynecology services

Hearing aids

Home care

Hospice care

Hospital services (inpatient and outpatient)

Laboratory services

Laser eye surgery (e.g., LASIK)

Long-term care (does not include custodial care)

Maternity care

Medicare deductibles, co-pays, co-insurance, premiums

Nursing services

Nursing home care

Ophthalmology services

Organ transplants (including donor's expenses)

Orthodontia

Orthopedic services, including orthopedic shoes

Osteopathic services

Over-the-counter medicines

Oxygen and equipment

Pediatric services

Personal care services for chronically ill persons

Podiatry services

Pre-natal and post-natal care

Prescription medicines

Prosthetics

PSA tests

Psychiatric care

Psychology services

Radiology services

Smoking cessation programs

APPENDIX 2 (contd.)

Splints
Surgical services
Transportation expenses for health care
Vaccines
Vision services
Vitamins (only if prescribed by a licensed practitioner)
Wheelchairs
X-Rays

Nonallowable (Not Tax-Free) Expenditures from Your Health Savings Account

Examples of Nonallowable Expenses

Advance payment for future medical expenses
Athletic club membership
Automobile insurance premiums
Babysitting (for healthy children)
Boarding school fees
Bottled water
Cosmetics and personal hygiene products
Dancing lessons
Diaper service
Domestic help
Electrolysis or hair removal
Funeral expenses
Hair transplants
Health programs at resorts, health clubs, and gyms
Household help
Illegal operations and treatments
Illegally procured drugs
Maternity clothes

APPENDIX 2 (contd.)

Nutritional supplements

Premiums for life, disability, other accident insurance

Scientology counseling

Social activities

Special foods/beverages

Swimming lessons

Teeth whitening

Travel for general health improvement

APPENDIX 3

The following comparison appeared in the *Washington Post* on October 26, 2004. The article compares how families might fare under a traditional PPO plan versus an HSA plan if they have low, medium, or high medical expenses in a given year. This article compares plans available only to federal employees for calendar year 2005 (the first year HSA plans were offered to federal employees). While this example may not be an appropriate comparison for every family, it illustrates how one could determine whether they would be better off financially under a traditional plan or an HSA.

Health Savings Accounts: Three Scenarios

This chart compares consumer costs for the Aetna HealthFund, a new health savings account (HSA) plan being offered to federal employees in the Washington area, with costs for a popular traditional health plan—a preferred provider organization (PPO). Family-coverage costs for the PPO appear in column two; family-coverage Aetna HSA costs

appear in column three. All figures and estimates are provided by Aetna. The notes in the last column are our own.

Example 1 shows estimated costs for a family with low annual medical expenses of $1,500. Example 2 shows estimated costs for a family with significant medical expenses of $20,000. Example 3 shows estimated yearly costs for a family with catastrophic medical expenses of $100,000.

The HSA calculations make several assumptions: The policyholder has made

voluntary deposits to his HSA account that may be larger than your family could afford. All medical treatments were considered eligible for coverage by the plan. Also, the family's income tax bracket is 28 percent. The calculations do not show interest earned on HSA fund deposits, expected to be around 2 percent per year. Costs for a person with a health savings account can vary, not just with individual health circumstances but with the amount of money deposited and the spending decisions made.

EXAMPLE 1: Low family medical costs of $1,500 per year	Traditional PPO Plan Deductible: $500 Coinsurance: 90/10 in network, 75/25 out of network	Aetna HSA Plan Deductible: $5,000 Coinsurance: 90/10 in network, 70/30 out of network	This scenario assumes routine care for all family members. Your HSA plan deductible may be lower. HSA coinsurance applies after deductible, up to an $8,000 out-of-pocket spending cap. PPO deductible is $100 more for in-patient hospital care.
Employee premium contribution	$3,070 ($255.79/mo.)	$2,298 ($191.53/mo.)	This is the cost of the insurance plan, usually deducted from the employee's paycheck.
Annual automatic deposit to HSA by plan	N/A	$2,500	Automatic HSA deposit is from insurer. Not all insurers or employers will contribute to policyholders' HSAs.
Voluntary HSA deposit	N/A	$1,000 ($83.33/mo.)	You may choose to deposit less or more into your HSA account than the amount shown here—up to $2,500 for the year in this example.
Tax savings on voluntary deposit at 28%	N/A	$280	Your HSA deposit is not subject to federal tax. If your tax bracket is lower or higher, your HSA tax savings will differ from estimate shown here.
Medical expenses/ deductible	$1,500/$500	$1,500/$5,000	The family's medical costs are $1,500 for the year. Note that the HSA plan's deductible is 10 times higher than the PPO's deductible.
Expenses remaining after deductible, and amount of coinsurance paid by employee (10%)	$1,000 $100	$0 $0	Because expenses total only $1,500, the family would pay no coinsurance under the HSA option.
Expenses paid out of HSA at employee discretion	N/A	$1,500	Do you really need a name-brand drug instead of a generic? That kind of decision will impact how far your HSA dollars stretch.
Actual employee-paid costs for year	$3,670	$3,018	For HSA plan, payments include premiums and contribution to HSA, minus tax savings. For PPO, payments include premiums, deductible and coinsurance.
After-tax advantage compared with PPO	N/A	$652	—
Money left in portable employee-owned HSA	$0	$2,000	This amount can be rolled over into next year's account. If the employee had funded his HSA fully, this total would be $3,500.

APPENDIX 3 (contd.)

EXAMPLE 2:

Significant family medical cost of $20,000 per year	PPO	Aetna HSA Plan	This scenario assumes the kind of costs you might expect if a family member breaks a leg. Includes ER visit, surgery, hospital stay, cast-setting, follow-up visit, some physical therapy and cast removal, as well as routine family care.
Employee premium	$3,070 ($255.79/mo.)	$2,298 ($191.53/mo.)	—
Annual automatic deposit to HSA by plan	N/A	$2,500	—
Voluntary HSA deposit	N/A	$2,500 ($208.33/mo.)	In this HSA example, the family exposed to unexpected expenses somehow knew to put $2,500 into the account. Everyone may not be so prescient.
Tax savings on voluntary deposit at 28%	N/A	$700	—
Medical Expenses/ deductible	$20,000/$600	$20,000/$5,000	PPO deductible includes $100 for hospital stay.
Expenses remaining after deductible, and amount of coinsurance paid by employee (10%)	$19,400 $1,940	$15,000 $1,500	10% coinsurance rate in both cases is for network providers only. Coinsurance will be higher for other providers.
Expenses paid out of HSA at employee discretion	N/A	$5,000	Employee paid for routine care as well as broken leg. To lower costs: use network doctors or negotiate fees before care delivery.
Actual employee-paid costs for year	$5,610	$5,598	Includes premiums, deductibles, coinsurance and out of pocket costs. In HSA example, money paid toward health care came from HSA account.
After-tax advantage compared with PPO	N/A	$12	Out-of-pocket HSA limit of $8,000 not reached. If the employee had deposited only $1,000 into his HSA, he would have realized no savings.
Money left in portable employee-owned HSA	N/A	$0	—

EXAMPLE 3:

Catastrophic family medical cost year of $100,000 per year	PPO	Aetna HSA Plan	These are the kinds of costs you might expect if a family member has open-heart surgery. Includes angiogram, surgery, multi-day hospital stay, cardiac rehab, follow-up doctor visits. Plus routine care for rest of family.
Employee premium contribution	$3,070 ($255.79/mo.)	$2,298 ($191.53/mo.)	—
Annual automatic deposit to HSA by plan	N/A	$2,500	—
Voluntary HSA deposit	N/A	$2,500 ($208.33/mo.)	Again, the assumption here is that there was full funding of HSA, something every employee may not choose to do.
Tax savings on voluntary deposit at 28%	N/A	$700	—
Medical expenses/ deductible	$100,000/$600	$100,000/$5,000	To lower costs: use network doctors or negotiate fees before care delivery. PPO deductible is $100 higher because of hospital stay.
Expenses remaining after deductible, and amount of coinsurance paid by employee (10%)	$34,000 $3,400	$30,000 $3,000	10% coinsurance rate is for network providers only. Once you pay your HSA deductible, you're liable for a maximum of $3,000 in coinsurance. The maximum PPO coinsurance is $3,400.
Expenses paid out of HSA at employee discretion	N/A	$5,000	To stretch HSA dollars: use network doctors or negotiate fees before care delivery; choose generic medications.
Actual employee paid costs for year	$7,070	$7,098	For HSA plan, payments include premiums, voluntary contribution to HSA and consurance minus tax savings. For PPO, payments include premiums, deductible and coinsurance.
After-tax advantage compared with HSA	$28	N/A	—
Money left in portable employee-owned HSA	N/A	$0	—

Notes

Chapter 1

1. "Centra Throws in the Religious Towel," press release posted on the web site of Consejo de Latinos Unidos (Council of United Latinos), www.consejohelp.org, March 27, 2007. For St. Anthony Central Hospital mission statement, see stanthonyhosp.org/index.php?s=1570.

2. Kerry Howley, "I Can't Afford to Get Sick," *Reader's Digest,* April 2006.

3. Ibid.

4. The Henry J. Kaiser Family Foundation, "Health Care Costs, A Primer, Key Information on Health Care Costs and their Impact," August 2007.

5. Peter Jennings, "Peter Jennings Reporting: Breakdown—America's Health Insurance Crisis," *Primetime Live,* December 15, 2005.

6. The Henry J. Kaiser Family Foundation, "Health Care Costs, A Primer, Key Information on Health Care Costs and their Impact," August 2007.

7. Jan Gregoire Coombs, *The Rise and Fall of HMOs: An American Health Care Revolution* (Madison, Wisconsin: University of Wisconsin Press 2005), p. 6.

8. "John Trumbull, "America's Younger Workers Losing Ground on Income," *Christian Science Monitor,* February 27, 2006, p. 1

9. Harvard Business School Report, www.hbswk.hbs.edu/industries/healthcare.

10. Peter Jennings, "Peter Jennings Reporting: Breakdown—America's Health Insurance Crisis,"*Primetime Live,* December 15, 2005.

11. Ibid.

12. Ibid.

13. Sharon Silke Carty, "GM Offers Buyouts to 126,000,"*USA Today,* March 27, 2006.

Chapter 2

1. For 42 articles about Rodney Vega and Florida Hospital, search "Rodney Vega" at www.wherethemoneygoes.com.

2. Minority Staff of the U.S. Senate Committee on Finance, "Tax-Exempt Hospitals: Discussion Draft," October 2007, p. 1.

3. "The Tax-Exempt Hospital Sector," Hearing before the House Committee on Ways and Means: Washington, D.C., 2005, p. 21.

4. "Hospital Charity Care and Tax-Exempt Status: Restoring the Commitment and Fairness," Hearing before the House Select Committee on Aging: Washington, D.C., 1990, p. 28.

5. Tiffany Rudy, Letter to George Ferguson, Consumer Operations Manager, Revenue Cycle, Centura Health.

6. Loma Linda University Medical Center, 2003 OSHPD Hospital Annual Financial Data Profile, report period January 1, 2003–December 31, 2003.

7. Loma Linda University Medical Center, 2005 OSHPD Hospital Annual Financial Data Profile, report period January 1, 2005–December 31, 2005.

Chapter 3

1. mywheaton.org/about/mission-vision-valuesasp.

2. George Askew, "A Snapshot of the Uninsured Life," op-ed, *Washington Post,* January 1, 2006.

3. Office of the Attorney General of Wisconsin, "Actions against Hospitals for Overcharging the Uninsured," News Release, November 7, 2005.

4. Cato Institute, "What Bush's Healthcare Plan Will Do," www.cato.org/pub.

5. Cato Institute, "Information and Much More," www.cato.org/pub.

6. Primetime Live, "Peter Jennings Reporting: Breakdown—America's Health Insurance Crisis," December 15, 2005.

7. OSHPD reports.

8. Consejo de Latinos Unidos (Council of United Latinos), www.consejohelp.org.

Chapter 4

1. "In Their Own Words: Bush and Kerry on the Issues," Associated Press, March 11, 2004

2. Hillary Rodham Clinton, "Now Can We Talk About Health Care?" *New York Times Magazine,* April 18, 2004, p. 26.

3. "50% Favor Government Guaranteed Health Care Coverage," *Rasmussen Reports,* September 20, 2007. Available at: www.rasmussenreports.com/public_content/politics/50_favor_government_guaranteed_health_care_coverage.

4. This anecdote was told by Senator Coats at a dinner Pat Rooney attended in Washington, D.C., in March 2006.

5. Kevin Freking, "Citizens Group Recommends Guaranteed Health Care Coverage," Associated Press, September 25, 2006.

6. Jim Phillips, "Athens County Native Coming Back for Second Try on Health Care Reform," *Athens News,* December 31, 2007, p. 7.

7. Laurie Asseo, "Administration to Release Documents of Health-Care Reform Task Force," Associated Press, December 2, 1994.

8. Mike Dorning, "Clinton Library a Closed Book," *Chicago Tribune,* November 12, 2007.

9. "Judicial Watch Files Lawsuit to Obtain Hillary Health Care Records from Clinton Presidential Library," Available at: judicialwatch.org/print/6597.

10. Hendrik Hertzberg, "Ghostbusters," *New Yorker,* October 1, 2007.

11. Morton Kondracke, "Furious '08 Debate over Health Care Could Be Good," *Roll Call,* October 25, 2007.

12. Ibid.

13. See Figure 10.2 of this book for the actual monthly premium rates for family plans in New Jersey, found on the web at www.state.nj.us/dobi/division_insurance/ihcseh/ihcratepage_sp.pdf.

14. These are January 2008 monthly premium numbers from the New York Department of Insurance's web site, and can be found here: www.ins.state.ny.us/hmorates/pdf/Westches.pdf in a document titled: "Premium Rates for Standard Individual Health Plans January 2008."

15. "Corruption, Economy, Security Are Top Issues to Most Voters; And They Still Trust Democrats More,"*Rasmussen Reports*, September 24, 2007. Available at: www.rasmussenreports.com/public_content/politics/mood_of_america/trust-on-issues/corruption-economy-society.

16. Clifford Krauss, "Canada's Private Clinics Surge as Public System Falters,"*New York Times*, February 28, 2006, p. A1.

17. Ibid.

18. Robert Blendon et al., "Confronting Competing Demands to Improve Quality: A Five-Country Hospital Survey,"*Health Affairs*, May–June 1994, pp. 119–135.

19. Clifford Krauss, "Canada's Private Clinics Surge as Public System Falters."

20. Ibid.

21. "Health Care,"*Harrisonburg Daily News-Record*, October 6, 2007. Available at: www.rocktownweekly.com/opinion_details.php?AID=12618&sub=Editorial.

22. Ibid.

23. Michael Walker, Nadeem Esmail, and Dominika Wrong, *Waiting Your Turn: Hospital Waiting Lists in Canada, Sixteenth Edition* (Vancouver, British Columbia: Fraser Institute, 2006).

24. Robert Blendon, et al., "Confronting Competing Demands to Improve Quality: A Five-Country Hospital Survey."

25. R. E. Biedermann, *The Health Care Cure!* (Tucson, AZ: Hats Off Press 2002).

26. Dr. David Gratzer, *Code Blue: Reviving Canada's Health-Care System*, ECW Press: Toronto, Canada, 1999, p. 175.

27. BBC News, "Howard and Blair Clash over NHS," March 2, 2005.

28. Ibid.

29. John Ray, "An Experience of British Health Care," posted on *Socialized Medicine* blog, June 9, 2005. Available at: socglory. blogspot.com/2005_06_01_socglory_archive.html.

30. Milton and Rose Friedman, *Free to Choose: A Personal Statement* (New York: Harcourt Brace Jovanovich, 1980), p. 115.

31. Governing.com, "The Great eHope, A Special Report on Medicaid 2006." Available at: www.governing.com/medicaid/ tech.htm.

32. Clifford J. Levy and Michael Kuo,"New York Medicaid Fraud May Reach into Billions,"*New York Times,* July 18, 2005, p. A1.

33. Ibid.

34. Gina Kolata, "Patients in Florida Lining Up for All That Medicare Covers,"*New York Times,* September 13, 2003, p. A1.

35. Ibid.

Chapter 6

1. "Medicare Prescription Drug Benefit (Part D)," www.aarp MedicareRx.com.

Chapter 7

1. U.S. Department of the Treasury, "Fact Sheet: Dramatic Growth of Health Savings Accounts," December 12, 2006. Available at: treas.gov/officies/publicaffairs/has/pdf/fact-sheet-dramatic-growth.pdf.

2. David Gratzer, "Congress Got Something Right!" *Wall Street Journal,* December 7, 2005, p. A18.

3. Ronald Bailey, "Health Insurance Crisis Again," Reason.com, October 1, 2003.

4. Kaiser Family Foundation, "Health Insurance Premiums Rise 6.1 Percent in 2007, Less Rapidly than in Recent Years But Still Faster than Wages and Inflation," Media release on their 2007 Employer Health Benefits Survey, September 11, 2007. Available at: www.kff.org/insurance/ehbs091107nr.cfm .

5. "This Won't Hurt a Bit," *Forbes,* September 17, 2007, David Whelan, On the Cover/Top Stories.

6. Jonathan P. Decker, "A Better Way to Pay for Healthcare," *Christian Science Monitor,* May 10, 2004, p. 13.

7. Laura Saunders, "Psst! Super-IRA," *Forbes,* June 16, 1997, pp. 170–172.

8. Damon Darlin, "For the Thinking Employee, No-Brainer Health Care Is Passé," *New York Times,* October 29, 2005, p. C1.

9. "Former Chairman Archer Reflects on His Role in Expanded and Unrestricted HSAs Becoming Law," *HSA Insider,* January 9, 2004, p. 1.

10. Deroy Murdock, "Democrats Use Health Accounts as Veto Bait," *Insight,* May 13, 1996. See also "Hill Briefs," *National Journal's Congress Daily,* June 22, 1992.

11. Kaiser Family Foundation, "Health Insurance Premiums Rise 6.1 Percent in 2007, Less Rapidly than in Recent Years But Still Faster than Wages and Inflation," Media release on their 2007 Employer Health Benefits Survey, September 11, 2007. Available at: www.kff.org/insurance/ehbs091107nr.cfm.

12. Jane Baird, "Health Plan Lets Employees Keep the Change," *Houston Chronicle,* July 17, 1994, *Business,* p. 1.

13. Elana Schor, "Dems Try to Do to HSAs What They Did to Social Security Plan," *The Hill,* February 8, 2006, p. 4.

14. Jerry Giesel, "Lawmaker Has No Faith In HSA-Linked Plans," *Business Insurance,* April 24, 2006, p. 4.

15. *Health Savings Accounts: January 2005–December 2005.* Available at: www.eHealthInsurance.com/content/ReportNew/2005HSA FullYearReport-05-10-06.pdf.

16. U.S. Department of Treasury, "Fact Sheet."

Chapter 8

1. Dr. Gerard Anderson. Testimony, Professor, Department of Health Policy & Management and International Health, Bloomberg School of Public Health, Johns Hopkins School of Medicine, "A Review of Hospital Billing and Collection Practices," Witness Testimony delivered to the Subcommittee on Oversight

and Investigations, June 24, 2004. Available at: allhealth.org//
briefingmaterials/GerardAndersonTestimony-20-doc.

2. Nathan S. Kaufman, Kaufman Strategic Advisors, LLC. "Peak
   Performing Hospitals" Presentation, January 2007, page 6. Com-
   plete text available at: www.kaufmansa.com/pdf/Governance
   Institute.pdf.

3. Christine Jordan Sexton,"BayCare loses BCBS Payment
   Dispute," *Tampa Bay Business Journal,* June 20, 2003, p. 1.

Chapter 9

1. Ken Carlson, "Hospital Charges Outrage Patients," *Modesto Bee,*
   October 14, 2005, p. A1.

2. "Hospitals Bristle as White House Seeks Price Disclosure," *The
   Hill,* February 16, 2006.

Chapter 10

1. Paul Zane Pilzer, *The New Health Insurance Solution* (Hoboken, NJ:
   John Wiley & Sons, 2005).

2. Christopher Conover, "Distributional Considerations in the
   Overregulation of Health Professionals, Health Facilities and
   Health Plans," *Law and Contemporary Problems,* Autumn 2006,
   pp. 181–193.

3. David Gratzer, "Simple but Effective," op-ed, *Wall Street Journal,*
   January 25, 2005.

4. Family of four, spouses in their mid-40s, two teenagers living in
   Genesse, PA, zip code 16932 found on www.eHealthInsurance.
   com, January 28, 2008.

5. Georgetown University Health Policy Institute, "High Risk
   Pools," *Health Insurance Resource Manual* (Washington, D.C.:
   Georgetown University Health Policy Institute, 2003).

Chapter 11

1. A late evening call to J. Patrick Rooney at his home by Speaker
   Hastert in March 2004. The first legislation was introduced four
   months later, in July 2004.

2. Both authors have had multiple conversations with U.S. House Republican Leadership staff and Members discussing this well-known fact that the Republican members of Congress from New Jersey and New York blocked any floor consideration of the bill that would have allowed interstate purchasing of health insurance.

3. Paul Zane Pilzer, *The New Health Insurance Solution: How to Get Cheaper, Better Coverage Without a Traditional Employer Plan* (Hoboken, New Jersey: Wiley, 2005), p. 237.

4. Editorial, "Cheaper Health Insurance," *Wall Street Journal*, July 25, 2005.

5. "72% of Americans Want Health Insurance Choice," press release issued by the Council for Affordable health Insurance, September 30, 2004, cahi.org/article.asp?id=425. Zogby International, Poll, Memorandum of September 3, 2004, re: Results from National Poll commissioned by the Council for Affordable Health Insurance

6. National Federation of Independent Business, "Health Care Choice Act" talking points, October 11, 2005. Available at: www.nfib.com/object/IO_25060?_templateId=315.

7. "Rep. Hastert Comments on Health Care Choice Act," US Fed News, June 22, 2004.

8. From a speech given by Kevin McKechnie to the author, October 23, 2007.

9. See Note 1.

Chapter 12

1. Emily Fredrix and Marcus Kabel, "Health Care Goes Retail As Clinics Pop Up in Stores," Associated Press, February 2, 2006.

2. Take Care Health Systems, "Leaders of the Convenient Care Industry Gather to Discuss Trends, Issues and Opportunities at First Retail Health Clinic Summit," media release, March 7, 2007. Available at: takecarehealth.com/corp/press_releases/press_030707_01.html.

3. CVS/Pharmacy, "CVS Teams Up with MinuteClinic to Offer Convenient Health Care Services at CVS Locations," press release, April 28, 2005.

4.   Ibid.

5.   Steve Case, "Putting the Patient First," editorial, *Seattle Post-Intelligencer,* October 21, 2005.

Chapter 13

1.   Michael Porter and Elizabeth Olmsted Teisberg, "Solving the Health Care Conundrum," Harvard Business School Publishing Virtual Seminar, posted November 15, 2004, hbswk.hbs.edu/item/4486.html/.

2.   Frank R. Lichtenberg, "Pharmaceutical Knowledge—Capital Accumulation and Longevity," in Carol Corrado, John Haltiwanger, and Daniel Sichel, eds., *Measuring Capital in the New Economy* (Chicago: University of Chicago Press, 2005), pp. 237–274. National Bureau of Economic Research Studies in Income and Wealth, v.65.

Appendix B

1.   Fla. Stat. 672.305 is patterned after U.C.C. § titled "Open Price Term" and its language tracks the Code almost identically. §2-305 states in its official comment that its intention is to reject "the uncommercial idea that an agreement that the seller may fix the price means that he may fix any price he may wish by the express qualification that the price so fixed must be fixed in good faith. Good faith includes observance of reasonable commercial standards of fair dealing in the trade.

2.   2007 U.S. Dist. LEXIS 52659.

Appendix C

1.   "In 2004, the most recent year for which data was available, hospital patients without health insurance and others who pay for medical care out of their own pockets were charged an average 2.57 times more than those with health insurance. . . . Hospitals in the United States have come under fire from patient groups and lawmakers for marking up prices for those lacking the negotiating clout of a [third party payer]" UsaToday.com, "Gap Widens Between What Insurers, Uninsured Pay," May 5, 2007.

2. *Ibid.*

3. The hospital industry calls this practice "cost shifting." Although hospitals must charge all consumers the same for identical services, they are allowed to offer discounts to HMOs and insurance companies, leaving the uninsured the only group forced to pay inflated rates. Because hospitals are not required to file "contract reimbursement information" with the government, consumers have not been able to yet uncover the full extent of this price discrimination.

4. Uwe Reinhardt, "The Pricing of U.S. Hospital Services: Chaos Behind a Veil of Secrecy," *Uwe Reinhardt, Health Affairs* Vol. 25, (1) Number 1, (January/February 2006), at 57.

5. Dr. Gerard Anderson, "From 'Soak the Rich' to 'Soak the Poor': Recent Trends in Hospital Pricing," *Health Affairs*, 26 (3) (From 'Soak the Rich' to 'Soak the Poor': Recent Trends in Hospital Pricing, May/June 2007); 26(3): at 780—789. Dr. Gerard Anderson.

6. HCRIS, Selected Departments, Self Reported cost to charge data, 12-31-05,

7. Quote of Rich Rasmussen of the Florida Hospital Association in the *Orlando Weekly*, 7/July 24, /2003.

8. U.S. Dept. of Health and Human Services, Office of the Inspector General, "Hospital Discounts Offered to Patients Who Cannot Afford to Pay Their Hospital Bills," 2 (February 2004). Available at: oig.hhs.gov/fraud/docs/alertsandbulletins/2004FA021904hospitaldiscounts.pdf.

9. Institute of Medicine, 2003 Study, Committee on the Consequences of Uninsurance.

10. *Ibid.*

11. Mike Bush, "Hospital Sued for Charging Uninsured Patients More than Insured Patients," KSDK.com, May 17, 2006.

Index

Preventive care screening
    services *(continued)*
  pediatric conditions screening,
      219
  vision and hearing disorders
      screening, 219
Prices. *See* Medical prices
Providence St. Joseph's Hospital
    (Burbank, California),
    24–25

Quick care clinics, xix, 127–130

Ramthun, Roy, 179
Rangel, Charles, 81–82
Reader's Digest poll, 3, 4
Risk pools, 109–119
  state, 115–119
Rowe, Jack, 130

Senate bill S. 2606, 88
Shadegg, John, 122, 124
Social Security tax, 46
"Solving the Health Care
    Conundrum" (Porter and
    Teisberg), 132
St. Anthony Central Hospital
    (Denver), 3, 12
St. Joseph's Regional Medical
    Center (Milwaukee), 21–22

Starbucks, 6
Stark, Pete, 82
Stronach, Belinda, 34–35

Teisberg, Elizabeth Olmsted, 132
Toombs, Orenta, 21–22

UB-04, 17, 92, 95, 97
  first request letter for, 92
UB-92, 17, 92, 95, 97
  first request letter for, 92
  sample, 96
Uninsured Americans, xvii, xix, 5,
      22–25, 144–145
University of Virginia hospitals,
      14–15
U.S. Treasury Department, 215

Vega, Rodney, 9

WageWorks Inc., 216
Walker, David W., 12–13
Wellness, innovative approach to,
      131–136
Wellpoint, 71–72
Wheaton Franciscan
      Healthcare, 22

Yale-New Haven Hospital, civil
      lawsuits filed by, 145